WAY DOWN IN THE HOLE

The Meteoric Rise, Tragic Fall and Ultimate Redemption of America's Most Promising Cop

WAY DOWN IN THE HOLE

The Meteoric Rise, Tragic Fall and Ultimate Redemption of America's Most Promising Cop

Ed Norris
with Kevin Cowherd

Apprentice House
Loyola University Maryland
Baltimore, Maryland

First Edition

Printed in the United States of America

Hardcover ISBN: 978-1-62720-144-5
Paperback ISBN: 978-1-62720-145-2
E-book ISBN: 978-1-62720-146-9

Design: Apprentice House
Cover photo by Kevin Richardson

Published by Apprentice House

Apprentice House
Loyola University Maryland
4501 N. Charles Street
Baltimore, MD 21210
410.617.5265 • 410.617.2198 (fax)
www.ApprenticeHouse.com
info@ApprenticeHouse.com

When you walk through the garden
You gotta watch your back
Well, I beg your pardon
Walk the straight and narrow track
If you walk with Jesus
He's gonna save your soul
You gotta keep the devil down in the hole.

— *Tom Waits, Way Down in the Hole*

I dedicate this book to my son Jack, whose love and mere presence in my life gave me the strength to endure it all. And to my ex-wife Kathryn, who was my rock during this witch hunt. She remains in my heart and will forever be my "ride or die chick."

FOREWORD
David Simon

Sixteen years into the rearview:

I am sitting in an Italian restaurant on Baltimore's Charles Street, picking at a salad, trying to make nice with the city's new police commissioner, a thick, fire-hydrant of a guy with a rampant New York accent. He's telling cop stories. Talking cop shit. I've traded in the stuff for years, first as a reporter and now as a television writer, and the patter of the new boss is no better or worse than many.

A case here, an anecdote there; I pair a crouton with an anchovy and lift my fork toward my face, giving a slight nod as if I actually give a damn. Because, to be honest, this lunch was scheduled as simply a polite curtain-raiser, a friendly shot-across-the-bow to let the man know that we would soon be filming another television drama in Baltimore. This one would be darker than the last. This one would critique the drug war harshly.

"Feel free," he says, when I finally get around to my purpose. "The drug war is so fucked up."

I note this with much surprise: More honesty from a Baltimore police commander than I am accustomed. On the other hand, this lunch is off the record.

"Well, I just thought it fair to let you know what will be coming if HBO picks the show up," I reiterate. "It will not be a comfortable depiction of a police department lost in drug prohibition."

He bolts his drink, shrugs: "You do what you do. And I'll do what I do."

Mission accomplished. We settle back into a reverie of cop humor, stationhouse tales and good, solid casework.

"I always liked Baltimore. I first came here on a case like, 10, 12 years ago. Great fucking case . . ."

Ah Christ. Here we go again. Some long tale of some ancient moment when this guy got to hear the handcuffs click and all was right with the world. I pretend to listen, but really, I confess that my mind is wandering. He rambles through the details of a New York murder by a Baltimore drug trafficker, a tip that the gun was down here in Maryland, the lure of the dealer to an interrogation in Manhattan and the simultaneous rush south to get a search warrant and find the weapon. I'm thinking about the desert menu. Until:

"So we hit the house with the Baltimore guys and what I remember is that every drawer we open, under the mattress, every goddamn closet, there's just all this porn. And not just regular porn, but fat girl porn. I mean really big ladies. This guy was really into big women . . ."

He laughs, remembering.

"Anyway, we found this gun in an upstairs closet."

I damn near drop my fork.

"Maurice Proctor."

He looks at me strangely.

"Maurice Proctor was your shooter. Nine hundred block of Northern Parkway. You hit the house with Roger Nolan's squad . . ."

"How did you . . .?"

"And, motherfucker, you didn't find the gun. I did. Third floor, back bedroom. In a green duffel. Under a bunch of fat girl magazines. Me and Donald Kincaid."

And so ends the anecdote of the second time I met Eddie Norris, 12 years after I watched him put down a 1988 murder – a minor footnote in a year I spent in the Baltimore homicide unit to write a book – and perhaps another eighteen months before the broadcast of

"The Wire" on HBO.

By the end of that lunch, I came to realize that whatever else the powers that be had managed to do in Baltimore, they had, for once, chosen a working cop to command its long-suffering, increasingly over-whelmed police department.

It might seem that knowing how to do police work would be an elemental skill set for anyone asked to command a major police department. It is not. There are two hierarchies in any such agency: one is the hierarchy of rank, and the other of policing, the acquired and honed ability to lock the right asshole up when a city most needs it, when the crime really matters. Seldom does anyone rising on one totem show any talent for the other.

Norris was one of the few exceptions in my memory. And for a brief period in Baltimore's modern history, he turned the slow, lumbering old freighter that is the Baltimore Police Department hard to starboard and got some people to do police work. That is neither as simple or as permanent an accomplishment as it sounds, and after accomplishing much in the first year or two, the usual political venalities and easy rhetoric began their inevitable attrition. He also made enemies. But then a good man it is routinely said, is known by his enemies.

In the end, the battle would see him walking not only from the Baltimore department, but from law enforcement, which, grievously, is his life's calling. If you know the tale – and I'm sure you will, if you have picked up this memoir – his banishment and the tarring of his reputation have more to do with fundamental questions about institutional law enforcement and political maneuver than the rote assertions of corruption. Suffice to say that an old stationhouse proverb is true in all respects: If the sonsabitches want you, they got you.

As a lark, when he was still police commissioner, we cast Eddie Norris as a working cop, a homicide detective who knew his business. That was, to us, an inside joke. But more than that, it was my nod to the fact that singularly among most of the command staff in so many departmental regimes, this man actually knew why good police work matters. And why bad police work matters, too. And when Norris was struggling, we made sure to keep his character in our fictional world. He was made to give up so much; knowing the whole story, we could not ask him to give up more.

Here's the whole of his tale.

David Simon
Baltimore, Md.
November 27, 2016

INTRODUCTION
Keeping the Rats Out

People always ask me what the worst moment was. That one's easy. The worst moment was like something from a Fellini movie.

The time: September of 2004. The place: the U.S. Federal Penitentiary, Atlanta, a shadowy Gothic-looking structure with gun turrets looming over high stone walls that emitted a strange greenish glow.

Months earlier, I had stood in front of a Baltimore courtroom packed with family, friends and national media and listened in stunned disbelief as a judge sentenced me to six months in prison on trumped-up charges of corruption and tax evasion.

Now, after serving time in Florida and Mississippi, I'd been transferred to Atlanta, one of the most notorious lock-ups in the country.

It was my first night in the "Big House" and the guards had just escorted me through a corridor ringed by howling inmates to a sweltering cell. My two new cellies were straight out of Central Casting: hulking, sullen and inked from head to toe with garish testimonials to the thug life. Neither seemed thrilled to be sharing his quarters with another wretched guest of the government.

Gazing around, I noticed there were only two bunks. Guess who was sleeping on the floor? I sighed and threw down my newly-issued pillow and blanket.

As I spread out on the hard concrete, one of my cheerful new roomies handed me a tube of rolled-up newspapers wrapped in tape. He pointed at the cell's battleship-gray steel door.

"Hold that roll under the door with your feet," he said. "It'll keep the rats out."

Rats?!

Really?!

With that, he turned around and fired up a meth pipe. Soon he and his charming companion were beaming upward into another world, the dope leaving them giggling and muttering gibberish to each other.

Watching this surreal scene, I began to laugh uncontrollably.

It was the shrill, frenzied laughter of someone on the edge of a crack-up.

Look at me! I thought. *I'm wearing orange prison pants that are way too small and a T-shirt the size of a Bedouin's tent. They didn't even give me sneakers that match! Meanwhile, my welcoming committee over there is getting blasted on meth and I'm crumpled on the floor like some kind of skid row Orkin Man, trying to keep the rats out!*

A year ago, I was the superintendent of the Maryland State Police! Before that I was the police commissioner of Baltimore! How the fuck did they ever get away with this?!

I stifled a sob. Sleep didn't come for hours as the absurdity of my situation plunged me deeper and deeper into despair.

Prison?!?

Me?

In the same place where they locked up Al Capone?

The same place the Cuban "Mariel boatlift" detainees burned in the late 80's riots?

How could any of this be real?!

All my life, I'd thought of myself as one of the good guys. You could say I was born to be a cop. My father had been a cop. So had my grandfather. So had four uncles.

As a boy growing up in Brooklyn, N.Y., I thought of the police as super-heroes. Instead of colorful capes and tights and masks, they wore crisp uniform shirts with brass buttons and blue woolen jackets, shiny badges on their chests and no-nonsense Smith & Wesson revolvers on their hips. They were fearless and taciturn and had each other's backs no matter what. Everyone in the neighborhood looked up to them.

Little wonder that at age 20, I went into the family business and joined the New York Police Department, determined to do my part in the endless war against the bad guys. There was certainly no shortage of them. Mid-town Manhattan, my first assignment, was a toxic stew of stick-up boys, drug dealers, pimps, hookers, pickpockets, car thieves and con men preying on the wide-eyed tourists and down-and-out drifters that poured off the buses daily at the Port Authority.

For a rookie cop who craved action, who relished breaking up a good old-fashioned poolroom brawl or rolling around the sidewalk with a twitchy junkie flashing a knife, it was intoxicating.

Once, working plain-clothes on 42nd Street, I saw this guy smack a girl across the face. I was wearing a red-white-and-blue satin USA jacket, the gold Olympic rings gleaming in the late-day sunshine.

The guy saw me staring at him and smirked.

"What are *you* going to do about it, Captain America?" he said. "You want to be a hero?"

Yep, I sure did.

I hit this fool so hard that when my partner Dan Mullin joined the fracas, the three of us went crashing through the doors of a Popeye's before I could get out the handcuffs.

Captain America?

Hell, I was starting to feel like him!

From the beginning, I was on the fast track in the NYPD, shooting up the ranks in anti-crime, narcotics, the detective bureau. I headed the warrant division and we doubled the yearly number of fugitives caught from 6,000 to 12,000. I was put in charge of the department's first Cold Case Squad, which won national acclaim and was the subject of a best-selling book and NPR special.

In the eyes of the brass, I was now a genuine superstar. And at the tender age of 36, I was named deputy commissioner of operations, the youngest in the department's history.

My star kept rising. When I took over as commissioner of the Baltimore Police Department in 2000, the city's murder rate was seven times the national average. Over 300 homicides had been recorded each year for the past decade.

Morale in the department was horrible. Corruption was pervasive. Modern policing equipment was largely non-existent.

But with the eager blessing of the city's charismatic new mayor, Martin O'Malley – the newspaper called us "Batman and Robin" – I set out to change all that. And we did. Crime went down almost immediately, dropping 29 percent the first two years. The murder rate plummeted from 305 to 262 the first year, to 253 the year after that.

And when I jumped out of a police car at a busy drug corner to wrestle a heroin dealer to the ground – "Unit One in pursuit!" squawked over the radio – it only heightened the mythology already building around me.

The new commish did what?

Ran down a corner boy and put the cuffs on him?

No one had ever heard of such a thing.

It was clear that crime in Baltimore was undergoing a seismic shift for the better. The bad guys were on the run. The streets felt safer. I was a rock star. I ate in the city's best restaurants and drank in the finest bars. Men elbowed each other aside to buy me another round. Women wanted to be near me.

I had a recurring role on "The Wire," HBO's hit police drama, playing a street detective from New York named – wait for it – Ed Norris. Even when I became burned out and disillusioned and took the top job with the Maryland State Police in 2002, I remained hugely popular in Baltimore.

Veteran cops, city council members and ordinary citizens would say I was the best police commissioner the city had ever had.

The business school at the University of Virginia would teach a graduate class about how my leadership skills transformed the police department.

I felt bigger than Cal Ripken Jr.

Then it all came crashing down.

It started with stories in the *Baltimore Sun* about an off-the-books expense account while I was still the city's police commissioner. This was followed by the steady drip-drip-drip of ominous rumors about an investigation by the U.S. Attorney's office.

At first I was unconcerned. The account involved no taxpayer money. Zero.

But the feds wanted their pound of flesh. Their claws were in me. And they had no intention of letting go.

Even after an independent audit showed almost all the money was spent on departmental business, even after I paid back $20,000 in personal expenses for which the receipts had been lost, federal prosecutors brought a sham indictment that included lurid allegations of gifts spent on women at Victoria's Secret and extra-marital affairs.

Now the case contained the whiff of sex.

And we all know what that can do in today's over-heated media climate.

The feds went into over-drive looking for dirt on my love life. The press beat me like a piñata. It was all so sickeningly unfair. And I had to sit back and take it.

Let me say this up front: I was a damned good police commissioner in those days. But I was no angel. I strayed in my marriage. I worked hard and partied hard. And some of that partying was with women I had no business being with.

But this is the truth: I never stole even one thin dime from that fund. Never used it to pay for gifts for anyone except my staff, such as flowers for my secretaries and holsters for my bodyguards. Bottom line? I never abused that fund in any way, shape or form.

Of course, I pleaded not guilty to the charges.

"It's all bullshit," I told my lawyers. "Let's go to trial."

I wanted to take on the bastards.

But you go up against the federal government at your peril. Those guys don't like to lose. They have armies of lawyers and an endless supply of cash to throw at you.

So it was that a few months later, I lay in a dank cell in the Atlanta penitentiary, half-crazed with fear and anxiety, listening to the giddy ravings of a couple of dopers as I pressed my shaking feet against the bars and prayed for the rodent hordes to stay away.

So this is my story.

It's the story of a good cop's life, his exemplary 23-year career and the dark forces that eventually took him down.

It's a cautionary tale about government over-reach and naked prosecutorial ambition that can seemingly target any public figure at any time for any reason.

And maybe my story can also serve as a primer of sorts for how to rebuild a life after you're stamped with the permanent tag of "convicted felon," a situation familiar to far too many men and women in this country.

In the words of the great Tom Waits, I was way down in the hole. So far down you could have whacked me over the head with a shovel and buried me with a few more scoops of dirt.

This is the story of how I got so low.

And the story of how I dug myself out.

1

From Brooklyn to the Land of Lacoste

My father, Ed Norris, became a New York City policeman when he was 33 years old and I was seven. Before that he had been a butcher. Even then I knew how dangerous a cop's life could be. Cutting and packaging meat in a cozy store seemed far safer and less stressful than patrolling the treacherous streets of the Big Apple, where more than a few of the citizens tended to greet the presence of a blue uniform by reaching for a weapon.

"Why would you leave the other job?" I remember asking my dad. "Why would you do *this*?"

"Somebody has to," he replied.

It sounds like a line from an old Western, something the square-jawed hero says as he hoists his shotgun and goes off to face the gang of gimlet-eyed gunslingers terrorizing the sleepy cattle town. But those words stuck with me forever.

It didn't help my anxiety levels – or those of my mother, Catherine, and my special-needs younger brother, Robert – that my father worked in the 77th Precinct in Brooklyn's Bedford-Stuyvesant neighborhood, one of the most dangerous parts of the city. And it *sure* didn't help when, after he'd been on the job just four years, the Black Liberation Army began assassinating police officers.

The BLA was a radical, underground organization in the early 1970's that had vowed to take up arms "for the liberation and self-determination of black people in the U.S." In time, it would be blamed for the murders of some 13 police officers, including the high-profile New York ambush slayings of Officers Joseph Piagentini and Waverly Jones in May of 1971, and the executions of officers Rocco Laurie and Gregory Foster in January of 1972.

From the beginning, it was clear that the cops were severely outgunned by the BLA. The BLA's murderous followers were armed with rifles and machine guns while the police carried .38 specials, six-shot revolvers that were no match for heavier firepower.

To even the odds, off-duty officers began backing up on-duty cops. I remember my father's friends coming over to our house in Flatlands with their hunting rifles and shotguns, whatever they had, and loading them with ammunition. I remember my father emptying a box of bullets and filling his pockets with them.

Then these off-duty cops, dressed in street clothes and driving their personal cars, would go back to the 77th precinct. There they'd monitor their precinct radios and shadow the on-duty cops when they responded to even the most innocuous calls: disorderly male, suspicious package – anything that could lure an unsuspecting officer into a BLA ambush.

I remember being terrified of what could happen to my father and his friends. But I was proud of them, too.

This is pretty cool, that these guys would do this for each other, I remember thinking. And seeing this "Brotherhood of Blue" come to life in my living room every night stirred in me the first inklings that someday maybe I could be a cop, too.

I learned early in life that my father was never truly off-duty, either. He was a hard-working guy who had grown up extremely poor. His mother raised six children by herself after his father died – from alcoholism, we think. What we *know* is that the family would get evicted from their apartments all the time for non-payment of rent

– my dad talked often about sitting on the curb with the furniture as a kid after another hard-hearted landlord had tossed them out.

Maybe that explains why my dad couldn't stand idly by and watch people be mistreated – whether he was in uniform or not.

One day when I was 12 – just after we had moved to Flatlands, a neighborhood near the south shore of Brooklyn – he was driving me home from a doctor's appointment when we heard a woman's cries for help.

My father threw the car in park. Without a word, he leaped out and began running in the direction of the screams. It turned out a woman had just been mugged. A couple of moments later, he returned, huffing and puffing, and gave the grateful woman back her purse.

I had been frightened when my father took off after the bad guys. He was all by himself, after all, and this was long before the era of cell phones. When he finally came back to the car and filled me in on what happened, I didn't feel much better.

The foot chase had been brief – he had run down the muggers, two teenagers, and drawn his gun on them.

Suddenly, one had whirled and thrown the woman's purse at him. Then the two muggers had vaulted a fence and escaped.

At a time when police officers were being killed at a rate of about 10 per year, my father's actions struck me as incredibly brave, but incredibly risky, too. But as I was to learn over and over again, there was little about being a cop that didn't involve risk.

By the time I was in high school, I was learning first-hand about how dangerous the streets could be – and not just for the police. Brooklyn Tech was one of the top schools in the city, specializing in science, math and engineering. But it was in Fort Greene, a rough neighborhood, and the white kids who attended it were often the targets for muggings, assaults and robberies.

On my first day of school there, an older guy walked up to me with a bunch of his friends. Just like that – *BAM!* – he hauled off and slapped me in the face. It began a long pattern of intimidation that many of my friends and I would be subjected to for the next four years. It also solidified my life-long hatred of bullies.

One day I was so tired of being victimized that I took the subway all the way to Sheepshead Bay, the last stop for the D train. It was a fisherman's haven in those days, with a number of fishing supply stores scattered about.

I bought a big knife and carried it every single day for the rest of my high school career. I never stabbed anyone. But I pulled it out a couple times to let guys know I wasn't fucking around when they started their usual menacing bullshit.

I joined the football team my sophomore year. We didn't have a home field, so we practiced on a crappy city park field some distance away, underneath the Brooklyn-Queens Expressway.

To get there, we had to walk through Fort Greene Park and the nearby housing projects, where they would routinely welcome us with bottles, bricks and rocks tossed from the roofs of the buildings. We weren't the brightest kids around, but we soon figured out it was a good idea to leave our helmets on during these walks.

We even had a sniper use us for target practice one afternoon in the projects. He was on one of the roofs, firing at us with a rifle. He didn't hit anyone and the police soon arrested him, which was a cause for celebration. But even when we started two-a-days, the harassment never stopped. After we'd change into our uniforms on the field and leave our clothes on the sidelines, the neighborhood kids would go through our pockets and steal our money while we were doing drills or scrimmaging.

Every once in a while, though, there would be small moral victories that would buoy our sense of justice and fair play.

One day, a couple of my teammates were walking ahead of the rest of us on our way home from practice. As the two rounded the corner, they were set upon by a pair of older guys who tried to rob them.

When the rest of us came upon the scene, we quickly unstrapped our helmets from our military duffle bags and proceeded to beat the crap out of the two muggers. Someone called the police and a few transit cops ran up from the nearby subway station.

This would prove to be my very first take on the powers of police discretion. Because by the time the cops got there, the bad guys were bloodied and bruised and splayed out on the sidewalk. The cops could have probably busted us for assault. But they knew the two local scumbags who had tried to rob us and quickly sized up what had happened.

"Get out of here," one cop said with a wave of his hand.

How about that? Common sense had prevailed! The police realized there was no point locking up a bunch of kids who had essentially been crime victims a few minutes earlier.

Maybe all of this made us tougher than a lot of other football teams. In any event, we were good – very good. We were 6-2-1 my senior year and lost in the playoffs to Bayside High, which ended up winning the city championship.

At least four of my teammates went on to play at Division I schools, and a bunch of others got scholarships and aid to go to D-II and D-III schools, too. As for me, an undersized outside linebacker with more heart than talent, I would go off to D-III University of Rochester, where I'd be converted into a safety.

Rochester, on the southern shore of Lake Ontario in western New York State, was booming when I arrived on campus in the summer of 1978. Multi-national corporations such as Kodak, Xerox and Bausch & Lomb were going great guns and pouring gobs of money into the school.

The university was considered a "rich kids" haven, filled with moneyed undergrads who couldn't get into Harvard, Yale, Williams, etc. I was there because it was a great science school and I had aced my physics exams. I had also actually begun to dream about becoming a doctor.

But for a poor kid from Brooklyn just getting by on a package of loans, scholarships, federal grants and on-campus work opportunities, the U of Rochester was a total cultural shock.

Let's start with how I looked back then.

Remember, this was the summer of '78. What was in the movies? Right, the monster blockbuster "Saturday Night Fever." And like a lot of other Brooklyn kids, I fancied myself another Tony Manero, the John Travolta character who worked in a paint store and lived for the weekends so he and his buddies could dance all night in glittering discos.

Blow-back haircut, paisley shirts, leather jackets, white suits – oh, yeah, that was me. And now I was going to this fancy-ass school with all these preppy kids who were definitely *not* dressed like me. It was the first time I'd ever seen L.L. Bean duck boots. Not to mention pink Lacoste shirts worn with the collars popped.

It was the kind of place where kids were going to Aspen and Switzerland over Christmas break.

When I came back to school after my first year, a girl asked me: "So . . . where did you summer?"

Where did I what?

Summer?

I had no idea what she was talking about. I'd never heard the term before.

"Well," she said, "I went to Italy."

Ohhhh, I said. Well, I sold shoes at a mall in Brooklyn.

That's how I *summered*.

But even if I didn't totally assimilate at Rochester, I thrived. I loved college. I was promptly recruited by the two jock fraternities and joined Theta Delta Chi. This was a football/lacrosse fraternity, and I quickly found myself surrounded by smart, ultra-competitive people.

The football was great, too. The team went 5-4 my first year. As a freshman, I didn't start, but traveled to away games as part of the kickoff team. No one on the roster, least of all me, was under any delusions that we were headed for the NFL. And if I ever did entertain such a notion, events on the field would quickly bring me back down to earth.

Once, when we were playing the University of Buffalo on a freezing, rainy day at ancient War Memorial Stadium, the former home of the Buffalo Bills, the coaches put me in to defend on a two-point conversion try. UB had a receiver who was also a world-class sprinter, so everyone knew they would throw the ball.

Sure enough, UB threw the ball. And my jersey was practically on fire when Mr. World-Class Speed blew past me for the score with whatever remnants of the tiny, chilled crowd still remained. But football kept me in shape. And it was the perfect sport for a kid who liked to hit – sometimes a bit too much.

That off-season, one of my on-campus jobs was as a security guard. Many of the football players had similar jobs – we'd accompany armed security guards on patrol. One night, as this older security guard and I made our rounds, we saw a kid breaking into a car.

The kid spotted us and took off.

"I'll get him," I said.

The older security guard rolled his eyes.

"Yeah, sure," he said sarcastically. "You'll get him."

But why *wouldn't* I get him? I was a defensive back on the football team. I was also pretty fast for a white guy. And I was in great shape.

Anyway, I ran this would-be thief down easily and tackled him. We were rolling around on the sidewalk when it looked to me like he was going for something in his waistband.

A knife? A gun?

I didn't know for sure. And I wasn't about to ask.

So I hit him – WHAM! – with a left hook. The guy went limp. Seconds later, his eyes just blew up. From the swelling, I knew he was hurt.

The kid was locked up, but that wasn't the end of the story – at least not for me.

Instead, I was brought up on charges by the student-faculty disciplinary council, who thought I had used excessive force during the incident. Now they were threatening to kick me out of school.

At a hearing in front of the council a couple of weeks later, the guy I had hit was brought in as a witness. He still had blood in his eye, which wasn't exactly helpful for my defense. I repeated the story of what had happened from the time we saw the kid breaking into the car.

"But why did you *hit* him?" a council member demanded.

"I thought he was going for a weapon," I said. "I saw him reaching for his waistband."

Now they all seemed incredulous.

"Why would you think he's going for a *weapon?*" they asked.

"Well," I said, "where I come from, *everyone* carries a weapon. At least a knife."

Now they seemed even more incredulous.

"Where did you grow up?" they asked.

"Brooklyn," I said.

"*Ohhhh,*" they all said in unison, nodding as if a great revelation had suddenly dawned on them.

In the end, they decided not to kick the poor kid from Brooklyn out of school. Instead, they just rewrote the security training guide, probably something to the effect: Try not to batter the local car thieves and cause retinal damage if humanly possible.

But by that summer, it was clear that the kid from Brooklyn was literally too damn poor to continue attending ritzy U of Rochester.

My parents couldn't afford to help me with tuition or room and board, and my aid package was falling short. But I desperately wanted to return to school. So I decided to work as an exterminator, save my money and go back to Rochester at some point.

That winter, on a whim, I took the train up to school and visited my frat buddies. I had so much fun I decided to stick around for a while, which didn't exactly sit well with my parents.

Then, at the school's Winter Carnival, I got into a brawl with this big, drunk townie who was hassling my buddy's girlfriend.

After the townie and I exchanged a few pleasantries – it ended with him calling me a "fucking stupid football player" – I popped him hard enough that they had to call an ambulance. My friends all grabbed me and told me to run before the cops came, since I'd already been in trouble at the school.

When the assistant football coach, John Vitone, got wind of all this, he sat me down and said: "You want to fight? OK, you can fight." It turned out his friend, the sheriff of Monroe County, had a boxing club. I had boxed in Police Athletic League centers in New York when I was 16 and 17, and I took to it again with renewed interest – if only to stay out of trouble.

Suddenly, it seemed as though things were looking up again.

Coach Vitone, who was a mentor to me, helped me get a little more money from the school. I stayed there for the spring semester, rejoined the football team and came back in the summer for two-a-day workouts to start the new season.

Which is when everything blew up in my face again.

One day before practice, I was summoned to the dean's office. The conversation started on a promising note as he read from my transcript.

"You're a dean's list student, a varsity athlete and a fraternity member," he began. "You're such an asset to this campus."

Listening to this, I puffed out my chest.

Danm right! I thought, as if a cartoon bubble had suddenly appeared over my head. *This is gonna be great! I see a bagful of money coming! More financial aid! Maybe some kind of big grant or scholarship add-on!*

Instead, it turned out to be, uh, exactly none of those things.

"You know," the dean went on, "you should really look into a state university. Because I don't see how you're going to make this work financially."

I was stunned as I left his office. In possibly the most low-key and polite way ever, I had just been thrown out of college.

Great, I thought. *How's that for hitting the trifecta? No college. No job. And my parents are rip-shit pissed at me. Going home should be loads of fun.*

Arriving back in Brooklyn in late August, I was notified that the New York Police Department was installing a new class of recruits. At the urging of my father, I had taken the written exam – and aced it – back in high school. My dad had always considered a police job to be a great back-up plan for me.

But when the last class of recruits had been installed, I was only 19 and the hiring age was 20. Now, though, there was nothing preventing me from going into the police academy and beginning my new career.

Except . . . I wasn't thrilled with the prospect at all.

Sure, my dream of being a doctor had died a quick death. And, yes, the idea of being a cop had been in the back of my mind since childhood.

But more recently, my plan had been to finish college and become an FBI agent. Yet when I had looked into all the federal law enforcement agencies – FBI, Secret Service, CIA, etc. – they all seemed to want lawyers and accountants and experts on foreign languages. Or they wanted men and women with a college degree and three years of military experience.

So on Sept. 2, 1980, with very little fanfare and not exactly brimming with enthusiasm, I reported to the police academy on East 20th St. in Manhattan.

It would turn out to be the best move I ever made.

Unless you consider that, 22 years later, it would lead to my personal destruction.

2

"The Last Great American Heroes"

At the risk of understatement, it's fair to say I came to the police academy with a *major* attitude problem.

"This job sucks," became my mantra.

I said it dozens of times a day. I said it out loud. And I said it to whoever would listen.

I was 20 years old, thought I knew everything and was supremely bitter about having to leave college. Plus from the moment I started at the academy, it seemed that the instructors were intent on busting my balls, either for the sheer thrill of it or because it afforded a break from the tedium of their miserable, ho-hum lives.

Now, not only were they telling me I had to shave every day, I had to shave "close," which no one seemed able to fully describe or quantify.

And the ball-busting didn't stop there. Our uniform consisted of navy blue pants, light blue shirt, clip-on black tie and black shoes, which looked about as fashionable as it sounds. I'd shine my shoes to a high gloss, only to have an instructor stare at them as if I'd just chased weasels through a swamp.

"Those shoes look like shit," he'd say. "I'm writing you up."

I understood it was all part of the game. It was what they did in an effort to instill discipline in the new cops and make them part of a team.

But I wasn't in any mood for it. Just a few weeks earlier, I'd been a college hotshot, an All-American frat boy – at least in my own mind – with unlimited potential. Now I wasn't sure what I was.

This is stupid, I told myself over and over again those first few weeks at the academy. *I hate this place.*

But ever so slowly, my perspective began to change.

For one thing, I became good friends with a core group of smart guys in our class who'd had successful jobs, but for various reasons now wanted to be cops. And because I was in such great shape from football two-a-days at Rochester, I enjoyed all the physical aspects of my new life.

In many ways, academy training was like going to college. You worked out every day, ran, boxed, learned self-defense, how to use a nightstick and how to handcuff people. You took college level classes in political science, social science and law.

Except . . . you also visited extremely weird places.

Like the morgue.

Policemen see death on a regular basis, of course. So to ensure that a rookie cop wouldn't react to the sight of his or her first corpse by panicking or passing out in the street, new recruits were acclimated to stiffs amid the cheerful ambience of the mortuary and autopsy rooms at famed Bellevue Hospital.

I thought I'd have no problems handling the morgue.

Years earlier, when I was 15 and on one of my long commutes to Brooklyn Tech, I had seen the gruesome results of a mob hit. Changing buses one day, I saw a bunch of cops surrounding a roped-off car, where a crowd had quickly gathered.

In the front seat of the sedan was the body of a man who'd been shot in the head. He was the first dead person I had ever seen outside a funeral home, and the sight had not greatly disturbed me.

But apparently it hadn't prepared me for the assault to the senses that was the Bellevue morgue, either.

I was OK when we toured the mortuary and they began opening stainless-steel drawers on which dead people were arrayed in various poses.

But the autopsy room came as a total shock.

Under brilliant white lights, against a backdrop of more dazzling whiteness reflecting off the walls, were a row of bodies, all in various states of dismemberment.

One man's chest was being cracked open. Another man's skull was being sawed off. Yet another body was being sewn back together with a giant needle. Livers were being extracted and brains were being measured on scales like so many slabs of meat at the supermarket.

And at each of these tables, streams of blood were flowing down big built-in metal grooves leading to collection buckets on the floor.

I thought I was going to pass out.

I had to get out of there. So I bolted for the door. And it took me quite a few minutes to regain my composure. (After the training session, we all went out for pizza, which I found to be funny. You're seeing all this blood and all these organs, intestines and tissue everywhere – and then you go out for a large sausage and pepperoni pie? I guess we were becoming inured to the sight of gore already. Either that or we were all sick puppies.)

Within weeks of entering the academy, though, the former Mr. Bad Attitude was all-in on the cop life.

I remember being on a date with an old high school flame – we were headed to the movies – when, in the middle of Flatlands Avenue, I saw two guys beating the hell out of another guy with baseball bats.

I was still in the academy, but we had already gotten our guns and shields. So I was armed and had a badge.

Damn, I thought, *I can't ignore this! I'm a police officer now. My days of driving past things like this are over.*

So I stopped my car and got out, drawing my weapon. Just then a police car with a couple of older cops pulled up. To this day I don't know if someone called them or they happened by on patrol.

But the three of us broke up the assault, and we all went back to the precinct house with the bad guys. ("Sorry, no movie tonight," I had to tell my date. "Take the car home.")

"OK, kid, here's your collar," the two older cops told me back at the station house.

Wait, they were giving *me* the collar?

I had never made an arrest before! I had no idea what to do.

So I called my father, whose first reaction was: "Oh, geez, what the hell did you do?" But he met me at the precinct, helped me with the initial processing and accompanied me to Central Booking for further processing of the two perps.

By this point, the two older cops were long gone, thrilled to have avoided the burdensome paperwork and next-day court appearance that comes with being the arresting officer. The two, I would learn, had a reputation for being lazy cops. It was my first up-close-and-personal look at that particular sub-section of the force – although not, unfortunately, my last.

Six months after entering the academy, I was part of a class of 500 rookies who became full-fledged police officers during graduation ceremonies at Brooklyn College. My family threw a big party for me afterward and friends and cousins showered me with gifts that included things like a shoulder holster, which provided a new dose of reality.

It made me realize I'd be carrying a gun every day for the rest of my working life. Nevertheless, I felt very proud of getting through the academy and excited about starting my new career.

Here I was officially a New York City police officer and I had yet to turn 21. Less than a year earlier, my biggest concern on the weekends was: which keg party should I go to tonight and what girls would be there?

Now, in less than 48 hours, Eddie Norris would be carrying a gun and badge and patrolling Times Square, tasked with the awesome responsibility of keeping the masses safe from the unsavory army of lowlifes who preyed there day in and day out.

So it was that on the evening of Jan. 27, 1981, I reported to the Midtown North precinct for my very first shift, 5 p.m. to 1 a.m.

Some 40 rookie cops from three precincts – Midtown North, Midtown South and the 17th – joined me at that roll call. We were turned out by a lieutenant named Lou Anemone.

Anemone cut an impressive figure. He had a rep as a cop who could walk the walk. He had worked everywhere, all the toughest precincts in the city, including Harlem at the height of the BLA cop-killings.

He was trim, dark-haired and only in his early 30's, but looked totally squared away in his uniform, with a rack of medals on his chest so shiny they could cause retinal damage.

"You guys are the last great American heroes!" he thundered, proceeding to give us a terrific motivational talk about what it meant to be a police officer and how much good we were doing for society.

I want to be like that guy, I thought, as I was driven to my post on 42nd St., between 7th and 8th Avenues.

That first night as a full-fledged cop, I felt proud, excited and awestruck at being in Times Square in uniform and carrying a gun, with people looking at me for help. You become a magnet for people with problems. In that teeming acre of concrete, with thousands of people passing my post by the hour, I was a reassuring presence for the wide-eyed tourists making their first visit to the Big Apple, and a source of consternation for all the bad guys bent on ruining that visit.

Nothing terribly crazy happened on that first shift. At one point I was sent to provide back-up at a nearby demonstration. This being New York, of course, a demonstration was not at all unusual – New Yorkers will demonstrate over getting a bad pastrami sandwich if you let them.

The only other noteworthy thing that happened was that I responded to a radio dispatcher's 10-13 call, the signal code that means "officer needs assistance."

I took off sprinting to the location of the call, which was a couple of blocks away. But when I arrived breathless and red-faced, there were already a bunch of police cars there, lights flashing, and the other cops were looking at me like: *Kid, what the hell are you doing here?*

It would prove to be an unfounded call. As I was to learn, "10-13" calls come in all night from the dispatchers. If you hear a cop scream-ing "10-13!" over the radio, you know that's different. That's *serious.* But store owners call these in all night long if, for instance, they want you to toss a sleeping homeless guy from their establishment or break up a fight.

Even the crooks themselves will call in a "10-13" to create a diver-sion and have the police respond to one part of town while they're pulling off a crime in another part.

Being in Times Square, an area saturated with cops, I probably shouldn't have responded to that "10-13" in the first place. I was a little embarrassed that I did. But the veteran cops already on the scene didn't make me feel like a jerk. They just counseled me on why my response was unnecessary.

My first days on the job were with a training officer, and they continued to be exciting, even if the work had its mundane aspects.

Basically, your night consisted of moving along the drunks who were causing disturbances and the shitheads who were trying to intim-idate people and disrupt businesses. Often, these lowlifes would go into one of the numerous pizza and gyro places, take food and refuse to pay. Or they'd threaten to come back and kill the owner if he did anything about it.

Needless to say, these business owners loved having cops patron-izing their joints. They'd feed us and take care of us. In turn, we'd respond quickly whenever there was some skell who needed to be grabbed by the back of the neck and tossed out.

In the summer of '81, I was transferred to Midtown South, which is exactly where I wanted to go. They had a big sign in the station house proclaiming: "Busiest precinct in the world." And from the volume of crime being handled there every day, that was no exaggeration.

By now I had seen plenty of dead people. I'd seen people shot to death, stabbed to death and run over by a subway train. I'd seen people who had keeled over from heart attacks. So when I was assigned to watch over a DOA at the Hotel Carter, it seemed like pretty cut-and-dried duty.

The Carter was an aging, 24-story hotel just off Times Square with a reputation as a hangout for thieves, hookers and all sorts of other underworld denizens. (In the early 2000's, it would achieve the unenviable distinction of being ranked the dirtiest hotel in America. TripAdvisor warned its clients of the Carter's bedbug infestation and generally "unsafe" conditions, the main one apparently being that you could get murdered there in a heartbeat.)

The dead person in this case was a black male in his early 30's. He'd been shot right between the eyes. When I got to his room, he was stark naked and laying half-off the bed, blood leaking from the hole in his head.

Now that all the crime scene technicians had left, my job was to watch over the stiff until the medical examiner came to collect him. I knew this could take all day. So to kill time, I'd brought along a paperback book aptly entitled "No One Here Gets Out Alive," the biography of the Doors charismatic lead singer, Jim Morrison.

For an hour, I stood and leaned against the door in this tiny room, trying to get comfortable. Finally I thought: *Fuck this. No one's coming to get this guy for hours.* With that, I slid into bed next to the corpse and continued happily reading for the rest of the afternoon.

The irony of the whole scene wasn't lost on me.

Here was a young cop who, just a year earlier, thought he was going to pass out in the morgue. Yet now he was comfortable enough with death to be reading in a bed next to a naked murder victim with blood dribbling from his forehead.

As I was to learn quickly, there were times on the job when you could go from the ridiculous to the sublime in the course of a single shift.

Not long after baby-sitting the stiff at the Hotel Carter, my partner Dan Mullin and I were asked to "clean up the block" on 41st St. near the Nederlander Theatre.

This was because the great singer and actress Lena Horne was appearing there in a one-woman Broadway show called "The Lady and Her Music." And the area around the theatre was dark and desolate at night, with all manner of pickpockets, thieves, panhandlers, junkies and hookers ready to waylay anyone stupid enough to cut through on their way to the Port Authority bus terminal.

"Clean up the block" was a police euphemism for "Get these scumbags out of here any way you have to."

At first, Dan and I tried to kindly ask the more shady citizens of 41st St. to relocate their "businesses" elsewhere. But if that didn't work, we were forced to give them an "attitude adjustment" and convince them they weren't coming back to the block any time in the near future.

Pretty soon, with all the riff-raff gone, the area around the Nederlander looked much more inviting. The theater people and patrons were grateful for our efforts. And, as it turned out, they weren't the only ones.

One night, as I was stood outside the theatre in a driving rainstorm not long after the show let out, a cab pulled up to the curb. In jumped Lena Horne. Seconds later, she was followed by another musical legend, Harry Belafonte, the "King of Calypso" and crooner of the "Banana Boat Song" himself.

The cab took off and went about 10 yards before the cabbie abruptly slammed on the brakes. Out jumped Belafonte into the pouring rain. Walking over to me, he shook my hand and said: "Thank you for all you do."

Inside the cab, I could see Lena Horne smiling and waving, too. Then Belafonte jumped back in and the cab took off again, leaving a young cop dazzled by the classy gesture he had just witnessed from two show business icons.

Yet the old line about race car drivers, soldiers and cops – that their work involves hours of boredom punctuated by moments of sheer terror – definitely proved to be true. Especially when I was involved in my first shootout.

I'd been on the job two years and was working plainclothes with my partner Dan Mullin in the Midtown South Anti-Crime unit. It was a blistering hot July 3 and we were driving a fake medallion cab around the city.

No, check that, *I* was driving the fake cab, because Dan was from Long Island and couldn't stand driving in heavy traffic. On this day, Midtown was even more of a traffic-choked nightmare than usual, with everyone scrambling to get to Penn Station and out of town for the holiday weekend.

We had just gotten in the cab when we heard a male cop's frantic voice over the radio: "10-13! 10-13! Shots fired!"

This one was for real. Some two hundred yards in front of us, a man and woman had just robbed a furrier and jumped into a getaway car, which was now stuck in traffic. Detectives having lunch at a nearby Irish pub had heard the call and confronted the robbers, who had shot at them through the car's window.

One of the detectives had been hit in the neck. Now the scene was chaos, with hundreds of people screaming and running in panic, and police converging on the car.

We jumped out of our cab and ran to the getaway car with guns drawn. The police were returning fire, but I couldn't get off a shot because there was a cop between me and the car. Suddenly, I saw the male suspect, who was in the passenger seat, get hit and slump over. We could immediately see he was dead – brain matter was oozing from the wound.

I ran around to the driver's side, stuck my gun in the woman's ear and dragged her out of the car.

"GET YOUR HANDS OFF ME, MOTHERFUCKER!" she

kept screaming. "CANT YOU SEE I'M SHOT?!"

She sure was. She had a couple of .38-caliber slugs in her, but she was still mean as a snake, cursing me the whole time. (Later, I would be told that the detective who was shot was rushed to Bellevue and would survive. But the getaway driver with the cheerful manner and charming vocabulary would end up paralyzed for life.)

As for me, after the first shooting incident of my police career, I sat on the curb in stunned silence for several minutes, numb but also happy to be alive. My hands weren't shaking. I hadn't felt frightened. But replaying it all in my head felt like I was watching myself in a movie.

Interspersed between the routine parts of the job and the adrenalized moments when your life could hang in the balance, there were also moments of dark humor. Some were so delicious as to be unforgettable.

On patrol in uniform one night, Dan and I spotted a suspicious-looking car with New Jersey license plates parked in an alley at the end of a block.

Shining our flashlights inside, we were treated – if that's the word – to the sight of a teenager behind the wheel getting a blowjob from a woman in the passenger seat. Two other boys, who looked to be high school age, were in the back seat.

We ordered all four out of the car. The hooker, whom we immediately recognized as a local, seemed unperturbed. But the three kids were practically hyperventilating, no doubt contemplating the cosmic shit-storm that was about to descend on them for soliciting a prostitute.

Not only were they now entertaining visions of being carted off to jail and sexually violated by all manner of hardened criminals looking for fresh meat, but it was a sure bet mommy and daddy back in Jersey weren't going to be thrilled with junior's new hobby of patronizing streetwalkers, either.

Yet the fact was, Dan and I had no intention of making a prostitution arrest. That was just not something that a uniform cop would do.

If you came back to the station house with a hooker in handcuffs, your bosses would be furious. For one thing, now you'd be off the street for the night filling out paperwork. Plus you'd have to go to court with the hooker the next day. And finally your supervisors would assume you made the arrest just to get some easy overtime. That's why prostitution arrests were mainly left to the Public Morals Division.

But if Dan and I weren't going to bust anyone here, at least we were going to get a few laughs out of the whole thing.

"Look," I said to the hooker, "we'll make you a deal. Either you're gonna get locked up, or you're gonna show them and I'll let you go."

The kids looked puzzled. The hooker smoothed her slinky red dress. Then she patted her towering blonde wig, which looked like something out of the Dolly Parton Collection, and laughed nervously.

"C'mon, I don't have time for this!" I barked. "Show them or you're going to jail! Your choice!"

With a shrug, the hooker pulled up her dress, pulled down her panties – and out fell the biggest cock you've ever seen outside an NBA locker room.

Two of the kids looked like they were about to puke. The third started to laugh.

"What's so funny?" I demanded, shining my flashlight in his face.

"It's just . . . I didn't get a turn with her," he said, still giggling.

He sounded eternally grateful for that, too. I always wondered if the kid made it back to Jersey alive, or whether his buddies dumped his battered body somewhere in the Meadowlands to preserve their mortifying secret.

Dan and I chuckled as the kids took off in their car and the street-walker tottered away unsteadily on six-inch heels, off to find another lonely and horny john in the city that never sleeps.

Watching her disappear into the night, I had something of an epiphany.

God, I thought, *I'm really starting to love this job.*

3

"Better Get a Good Mouthpiece"

In December of 1984, at the age of 24, I was promoted to sergeant and assigned to the 13th Precinct in the affluent Gramercy Park area of Manhattan.

Looking back on it now, I was *way* too young to be a sergeant. But I had aced the test and had just passed my three-year anniversary on the force, making me eligible for the position.

Right away, I made all the classic mistakes of a newbie suddenly thrust in a leadership role. You try to be everybody's buddy. You're a great guy until the first day you turn somebody down for a day off. Suddenly – *Boom!* – you're a scumbag.

You want to get close to the guys you're working with, figuring it will make you a better supervisor. So you drink with them. You hang out with them. You want to be their friend. But the fact is, you have to be their boss, not their buddy. And the stark realization of this will quickly slap you in the face.

At the Thanksgiving Day parade the following year, I spent hours looking for two senior patrolmen who had been assigned to a post near Macy's department store. I was there to sign their memo books – we called it "giving them a scratch" – to make sure they were on the job and doing what they were supposed to do.

Except . . . guess what? These two knuckleheads were nowhere to be found.

I couldn't get them on the radio, either. Now I was getting madder and madder. They were obviously goofing off somewhere. By the time they showed up at the end of their tour with some lame excuse, I was steaming.

So I wrote them up – reported them on a command discipline form. Now it was up to the captain to decide their punishment. But because they were older guys with 30-some years on the job, the captain didn't punish them at all.

Instead, they were given a slap on the wrist – which made *me* look like a total jerk. That day I made a mental note to myself: you need to take care of this stuff on your own. In the future, if this sort of thing happened, I'd find ways to punish the dipshits myself.

Maybe I'd assign them to watch over so many dead bodies they'd think they were in a war zone. Or I'd take them out of a radio car and make them walk a beat again. Or every time another precinct needed extra officers for some particularly crappy assignment, I'd send these two lazy bastards. If it wasn't against union rules, I'd have 'em clean up horseshit after a parade.

My days as a sergeant also marked the first time I got in trouble for using excessive force.

This was after I'd been transferred to the 6th Precinct in the West Village. One day, I was working a Spanish-American pride festival when I spotted a big muscular guy, shirtless and crazy-looking. He was storming up and down the block, muttering to himself, snatching food from the vendors and scaring the hell out of everybody.

I tried to grab him by the arm and talk to him, but this did not go well. He pushed me into a store window. I bounced off the glass, grabbed my radio and called for an ambulance to pick up an emotionally-disturbed person. I also called in a "10-85," which basically means a cop needs assistance, although not as urgently as a "10-13."

My struggle with the deranged man continued. He was fighting me and sweaty as hell, and it was hard to get a grip on him. Finally, when he charged at another officer who had just arrived on the scene,

I took out my nightstick and whacked him across the neck.

He fell like a tree, toppling face down on the sidewalk, leaking blood everywhere. We managed to handcuff him and get him into the ambulance strapped to a gurney, but he still resisted us all the way, biting, spitting and head-butting.

Soon enough, we'd learn he had either escaped or been discharged from Creedmoor, the notorious psychiatric hospital in Queens. And right away, people started coming out of the woodwork, eager to testify that I had been too brutal with the man.

None of this was particularly surprising. Greenwich Village was maybe the most left-wing neighborhood in New York City, and many of the residents made no secret of their antipathy toward the police.

Also, it was not unusual to be hit with an excessive force charge if you were an aggressive police officer intent on doing your job well.

People wanted to believe that cops were so well-trained they could subdue a raving 220-pound man by grabbing his pinkie and doing some kind of sick ju-jitsu move to drop him to his knees. This was a complete fantasy.

Hell, no one – not even the Navy SEALS – is *that* well-trained.

The fact was, this unhinged man was intent on hurting another person. And he *would* have if I hadn't hit him with my nightstick as I did.

Nevertheless, I was ordered to appear before the Civilian Complaint Review Board, where I told my story and was promptly exonerated, to my tremendous relief.

My next assignment was a stint in Brooklyn South narcotics, supervising buy-and-busts in the streets, parks and nightclubs.

Narcotics was wildly exciting to me. It was dangerous, unpredictable work, but important, too. It was also unlike anything I had ever done before. We wore disguises, listened in on wire taps, hung out in discos all night long to observe dozens of furtive – and not-so-furtive – drug transactions taking place.

One case in particular would stick with me for years. We had been buying heroin and cocaine from this one particular group of dealers for many months. In fact, we'd infiltrated the ring so successfully – hanging with them, joking with them, drinking with them – that the dealers came to regard us as fast friends and not simply as business associates.

On the last day of the operation, when it came time to take everyone down, we fanned out in teams and hit the various locations of the dealers simultaneously. This way they couldn't warn one another when an arrest was made.

I went with an officer named Brian McCarthy to the house of one dealer, who was in his early 20's and still living with his parents. Brian had been buying dope off the man for months, and he greeted us with a big smile.

For all the man knew, Brian was there looking to buy some more stuff and I was one of Brian's partners, which seemed perfectly reasonable.

When we arrived, the dealer's mother was in the kitchen making pasta for dinner. We talked to him in the living room. After a hasty greeting, Brian quietly informed him that we were police officers.

The guy was incredulous. He managed a nervous grin.

What?! You guys are cops? No way!

But within seconds, it dawned on him that his life was about to go completely off the rails.

You never know what a drug dealer will do in moments like this. Some try to bolt. Some try to fight you. Some whip out a gun or a knife.

To make sure he didn't try anything stupid, I grabbed him by the arm. My gun was already pointing at him in my coat pocket.

"Listen," I said in a low voice, "if you do anything stupid, I'll kill you right in front of your mother. Think about that."

The kid turned pale. The grin was gone.

"How about you tell your mom you're leaving for a few minutes?" I went on.

The guy looked at me. Then he looked at Brian. Now the light seemed to go out of his eyes and his shoulders sagged. Finally he nodded.

"All right, ma, I'll see you!" he yelled into the kitchen. "I'm going out for a while."

We took him outside and cuffed him and brought him to the station house. All across this part of Brooklyn, the same scene was being repeated over and over: dazed-looking drug dealers were being hauled off to jail by their former "buddies," many of the dope peddlers still convinced this was some kind of gigantic crazy prank being played on them.

This was the first time that the so-called "war on drugs" really hit home with me.

This is serious, I remember thinking. *These guys are in their early 20's. And they're going to jail for a long time, maybe decades. They'll be middle-aged men when they get out.*

Over time, I would come to believe the war on drugs was folly, a huge waste of time and money. The flow of drugs is impossible to stop. And did we learn nothing from the Prohibition era?

Didn't we learn that if people want to get drunk, they're going to find a way to get drunk? And if they want to get high, they'll get high? We can't legislate morality, it's that simple. And even though we've tried for hundreds of years, it's insane to think we'll ever be successful.

But on this chilly fall night in Brooklyn, it somehow seemed as if we were doing God's work, ridding the streets of dangerous people and fulfilling our vow to keep the peace.

After narcotics, my next stop was the 7th Precinct detective squad on Manhattan's Lower East Side. Here the work was even more interesting, in my opinion – and more meaningful, too. I lived for the days when I got to break the news to a grieving widow or mother that we'd arrested the lowlife who'd killed her husband or son.

Then, when I least expected it, another bombshell hit.

Right after I took the test to become a lieutenant – and finished no. 5 on the list – Michigan Congressman John Conyers, then the chairman of the House Subcommittee on Criminal Justice, opened a 17-month inquiry on racism and police brutality in New York and other large cities.

And the NYPD, because it has no balls, caved in immediately to the publicity-seeking politician.

Instead of standing up for its officers and saying no, fuck you, we've investigated these cases ourselves and there's no pattern of brutality, the NYPD re-opened 50 old excessive-force cases.

And guess whose case was included?

Bingo.

Just like that, the bogus charge that I had brutalized a disturbed man in the Village went from "unsubstantiated and exonerated" to: "You're going to trial, kid. You and the rest of these rogue cops. Better get yourself a good mouthpiece."

Which is exactly what I did.

Faced with criminal prosecution and the chance I might lose my job altogether, I was forced to hire an expensive lawyer, instead of the hacks the department routinely provided gratis. My trial, a formal, nerve-wracking affair, was held at police headquarters.

Thankfully, the unhinged man I'd arrested was never found by the time the case went to court. And the witnesses summoned by the prosecution gave so many conflicting versions of what had happened that the judge became exasperated at one point and shouted: "Would you please make up your mind on *one* story?!"

Still, the tension was high until the very end, when I was again cleared of any wrong-doing.

The only bit of levity I remember came when I bragged to my lawyer, Rosemary Carroll, that I had just aced the NYPD's lieutenant's test.

"Hey, I'm no. 5 on the list!" I told her. "And something like 3,000 sergeants took the test. What do you think of that?"

Rosemary, a tough Irish attorney married to a Jewish judge,

quickly shot me down.

"Yeah, that's really good," she said. "For a Jew, you're about average. For an Irishman, you're a fucking genius."

Me? A genius? Hot damn!

I wondered if that could be noted on my official transcript.

4

The Assassination of Meir Kahane

My promotion to lieutenant in November of 1989 was bitter-sweet. The good news: I was now in charge of the 7th Precinct detective squad. The bad news: I was still in the 7th Precinct.

The 7th, right by the Williamsburg Bridge on the Lower East Side of Manhattan, was a real shithole back then. It was infested with heroin and every other drug, and sometimes it seemed as if the streets were owned by vacant-eyed zombies and lowlifes at all hours of the day and night.

The precinct house was on the aptly-named Pitt Street. You couldn't make this up.

This is the kind of neighborhood it was: on Halloween, another detective and I were headed out to dinner when we heard a series of gunshots: *pop! pop! pop! pop!* We heard over the radio that the uniforms were chasing a suspect in the shooting. We joined the pursuit and the guy was quickly caught.

It turned out that somebody had been throwing eggs at him. So this genius had picked up a brand-new Heckler & Koch 9-mm pistol and decided to murder the egg-thrower. He attempted this by firing wildly into the street, not exactly caring whether he might cut down an innocent bystander – or maybe 10 of them – in the process.

Needless to say, when I was offered the command of another detective squad, this one at the 17th Precinct, I leapt at the opportunity.

The 17th was in mid-town Manhattan and considered one of the two or three nicest precincts in the city.

Some of the wealthiest people in the country had homes in the neighborhood, including Henry Kissinger, Katherine Hepburn, fashion designer Bill Blass, cabaret singer Bobby Short and Mets' first baseman Keith Hernandez.

I was barely 30 years old. Compared to the 7th, it was like I'd died and gone to heaven. Everywhere you looked there were terrific restaurants, beautiful women and interesting people doing the most interesting things.

On the other hand, I didn't exactly have a chance to ease into the job.

No, after my very first day as the commanding officer of the 17th squad, just as I sat down to dinner in my Staten Island condo, the phone rang. Calling was Eileen Brennan, the woman I was replacing as head of the 17th's detectives.

"Eddie," she said, "we have a shooting."

What? I thought. *A shooting? Nobody gets shot in that neighborhood!*

Which was mostly true. Maybe there were one or two murders a year on average. And those were often, ahem, "business-related," like when mob boss John Gotti had fellow Mafiosi Paul Castellano whacked in front of Sparks Steak House a few years earlier.

"A guy's dead in a hotel," Eileen continued. "It's a rabbi. Meir something or other . . ."

"Meir Kahane?" I asked.

"Yeah, that's him," she said.

Holy shit! Oh, I knew all about Meir Kahane.

Kahane, 58, was the founder of the ultra-conservative Jewish Defense League. He was a fiery orator who had called for the expulsion of all Arabs from Israel and the mass emigration of U.S. Jews to their biblical homeland, presumably to save them from a "second

Holocaust."

He called Arabs "jackals," pushed for laws that would bar Arabs and Jews from having sex and organized "defense squads" to patrol Jewish neighborhoods and beat the shit out of anyone deemed a possible threat.

Hmmm, I thought, *who would want to kill a sweetheart like that?*

After hanging up with Eileen, I packed a duffle bag with a couple of days' worth of clothes and drove straight to the crime scene at the Marriott East Side hotel.

What had happened was this: some 90 minutes earlier, Kahane had finished another of his rabidly anti-Arab speeches to a fervent group of his followers in one of the hotel conference rooms.

He had left the podium and was shaking hands, posing for pictures and signing copies of his book, when a man named El Sayyid Nosair walked up behind him.

Nosair, Egyptian by birth but now an American citizen, was wearing a yarmulke and posing as a Sephardic Jew. Suddenly, he produced a .357 magnum and squeezed off two shots that struck Kahane in the neck.

Amid the screams and confusion that followed, Nosair had tried to flee.

"It's Allah's will!" he reportedly shouted.

When an elderly follower of Kahane's had tried to stop him, Nosair had shot the man in the leg before bolting out the hotel's front door.

Once outside, as we would learn later, he had expected to jump in a get-away cab driven by one of his confederates, a hulking, red-headed Egyptian named Mahmoud Abouhalima.

But the cab had been prevented from parking in front of the hotel by police who were in charge of security on traffic-choked Lexington Avenue. Confused and panic-stricken now, Nosair had jumped in another cab by mistake, then leaped out when the driver slammed on the brakes.

Fleeing the scene, Nosair had come across a uniformed U.S. Postal police officer named Carlos Acosta. Spotting Nosair's gun, Acosta had drawn his own weapon. Nosair had shot first, the bullet grazing Acosta's bulletproof vest. Acosta staggered, but was able to return fire, hitting Nosair in the neck.

Nosair toppled to the sidewalk, blood pouring from his wound. Thus ended the dramatic chase, in a wail of ambulance sirens as the assassin was rushed to Bellevue Hospital. Ironically, he would arrive shortly after another ambulance screamed up to the ER entrance, this one carrying the lifeless body of Kahane.

Nosair, though, would survive.

When we went through his pockets, we found a wallet and papers listing prominent Jewish politicians in the New York area. It looked for all the world like a hit list. I then sent detectives to the address we had from his driver's license, which was an apartment in Jersey City, N.J.

By the time the detectives got there, it was around 1 in the morning. Yet after just a few knocks, the door was answered by a tall, strapping Egyptian with bright red hair. Another Egyptian man – identified as Mohammed Salameh – was also there.

Neither appeared to have been sleeping. And neither seemed particularly surprised at finding police on their doorstep at that hour.

In short order, both men admitted to knowing Nosair, but said he did not live there anymore. Both also said they were cab drivers. And both disclosed that they'd been in the vicinity of the Marriott hotel at the time of the Kahane shooting.

So what we had – for all intents and purposes – were the getaway car drivers. Since the NYPD had no jurisdiction in New Jersey, we got them to "voluntarily" come back to the 17th Precinct for questioning. And as soon as they crossed the Hudson River, they were arrested.

Not long after, my detectives managed to find out where Nosair had been living, which was in a rental house in Cliffside Park, N.J., just across the George Washington Bridge. We obtained a warrant, searched the house and came up with a veritable treasure trove of information.

What were brought back to me were two file cabinets full of all kinds of documents, most written in Arabic. There were obvious bomb-making manuals. There were maps and 8x10 photos of city landmarks such as Police Headquarters, St. Patrick's Cathedral, the Brooklyn Bridge, the World Trade Center and FBI headquarters.

In a black-and-white marble composition book, there were notes in Arabic and drawings of a city street with little symbols of cars blocking intersections. (I thought the drawings might have something to do with an armored car stickup Nosair and his associates were planning. But they would later turn out to be related to a plot to kill Egyptian president Hosni Mubarak on his visit to New York.)

Finally, there were also classified U.S. documents as well as training manuals from the Army Special Warfare Center and School at Fort Bragg, the huge military base in North Carolina.

It was all eye-popping stuff. My head was spinning as I wrestled with the myriad implications of what we'd found.

The next morning, I headed down to headquarters at One Police Plaza for a big briefing with the department's chief of detectives, Joseph Borelli.

Borelli was a man who favored cardigan sweaters and curved smoking pipes right out of a Sherlock Holmes movie. The whole effect made him seem avuncular and low-key. He was a nice enough guy. But some thought he was still living off his rep as the head of the task force that had tracked down the notorious "Son of Sam" serial killer, David Berkowitz, in the summer of 1977.

Arrayed around the table in the big conference room were various police commanders, FBI agents and Joint Terrorism Task Force agents.

As the lieutenant in charge of the case, I filled everyone in on what we had on Nosair and the Kahane killing so far.

When I was done, Borelli said: "Eddie, can you tell me this guy acted alone?"

"Of course not," I said.

I told him about the two suspects, Abouhalima and Salameh, who were under arrest, charged with being the getaway drivers. The shooter, obviously, was also under arrest. And now we had reams of drawings, photos, maps and classified U.S. documents taken from the shooter's house.

"I have *something* here," I told Borelli. "I don't exactly know what it is. But it's big."

It quickly became apparent that the chief of detectives did not share my viewpoint.

"Oh, you shut up!" he barked. "You handle the murder OK?" He pointed at the FBI agents across the table. "*They* handle the conspiracies."

I was stunned. My Irish temper flared as I sat down.

"This is bullshit!" I whispered to my captain, Mike Gardner. "What are we gonna do?"

Gardner shrugged and pointed to Borelli.

"You want to tell him again?" he asked.

No, definitely not.

As angry as I was, Joe Borelli was a three-star chief and I was a young lieutenant. And the police department was still a paramilitary organization. The chief tells you to shut up, you shut up.

I was steaming, but I wasn't stupid. No way was I going to get in a shouting match with a well-respected superior and risk derailing my career completely.

So it was that later that morning, at a packed press conference, Borelli would insist that Kahane's murder was the result of a "lone deranged gunman."

"He didn't seem to be part of a conspiracy or a terrorist organization," the chief of detectives would add for emphasis.

Unfortunately, there were more shocking developments in store for me and my detectives after the chief met the media.

While I was out to lunch that day, the feds came into our squad room and removed the file cabinets containing the damning evidence seized from Nosair's house. We would never learn where the files ended up, either.

This was followed by another jaw-dropping event: Abouhalima and Salameh were released from custody, on the grounds there was not enough evidence to hold them.

Again, I was livid.

Ordinarily in policing, if you have enough probable cause to lock someone up, they're locked up and *stay* locked up. And you let the district attorney and judge sort out the details of the case.

Maybe later on it turns out you don't have enough probable cause to hold the suspect or suspects. But there was no question that the quick release of the two Egyptians in such a high-profile case was highly unusual, to say the least.

Over the years, historians combing the Nosair case have advanced a number of theories for Joe Borelli's reluctance to dig deeper into the circumstances surrounding the Kahane murder.

In "Two Seconds Under the World," a book about the developments that led to the first World Trade Center bombing in 1993, *Newsday* reporters Jim Dwyer, David Kocieniewski, Diedre Murphy and Peg Tyre wrote: "There hadn't been any political assassinations in New York in more than a decade and Borelli didn't want one on his watch."

And in the exhaustively-researched 2002 book "The Cell: Inside the 9/11 Plot and Why the FBI and CIA Failed to Stop It," one of the authors, John Miller, wrote: ". . . (Borelli) was a loyal general, not a revolutionary, and the prevailing theory in the NYPD was 'Don't make waves.' . . .So in the Nosair case, when Chief Borelli turned a blind eye to the obvious, he was only remaining true to the culture of the NYPD.

"The thinking was, Don't take a high-profile homicide case that could be stamped 'Solved' and turn it into an unsolved conspiracy. To do so would create a lot of extra work."

Whatever the reason for Borelli's stance, it would leave me irate and disillusioned for years.

Our investigation into Kahane's death continued, but I was soon transferred to the Department of Investigation, the watchdog agency that roots out corruption among police, city employees and elected officials. This was considered a prestigious assignment and a big step up the career ladder.

In my heart, though, I would always believe El Sayyid Nosair and his accomplices were part of a vast and dangerous conspiracy bent on doing irreparable harm to this country – and that the NYPD missed a golden opportunity to stop them.

Unfortunately, subsequent events would prove me right.

On a cold February afternoon in 1993, I was in my DOI office in lower Manhattan when I heard what sounded like an explosion.

At first, we thought nothing of it. We thought it was a subway transformer exploding, which happened from time to time.

But within minutes, I got a call from Inspector Don Morse of the detective bureau.

"Eddie, we gotta talk," he said. "They just bombed the World Trade Center."

History would record that six people were killed and over 1,000 injured when the 1,200-pound bomb, planted in a Ryder truck in a parking garage beneath the North Tower, exploded.

Six suspects would ultimately be convicted of the plot. The mastermind, a Kuwaiti named Ramzi Yousef, would be found to have spent time in an al-Qaeda training camp in Afghanistan. The bombing, he would claim, was done in retaliation for the suffering the Palestinian people had endured at the hands of U.S.-backed Israel.

But the names of two of the convicted terrorists would haunt me for a long, long time.

Mohammad Salameh would be identified as the man who rented the Ryder truck. And Mahmoud Abouhalima, the big red-headed

Egyptian, would be seen by witnesses with Salameh at a storage facility in Jersey City where the explosives were allegedly prepared.

To this day, the idea that I was sitting on three major suspects and important information in 1990 that might have prevented future attacks on this country – and that no one acted on it – makes me sick.

"Many officials," the authors of "The Cell" wrote, "Norris among them, have since claimed that the (Nosair) files provided a virtual road map to future terrorist acts, including the 1993 World Trade Center bombing. Along with the military documents, the bomb manuals, and the diagrams and photos of New York landmarks, the Nosair papers contained a manifesto exhorting his associates to topple the 'tall buildings of which Americans are so proud.'"

In a later aside, "The Cell" co-author John Miller added:

"Nosair turned out to be the pioneer of a new kind of terrorism, the first to act out the malicious ideology of a rogue strain of Islam that would eventually seek to eviscerate the American way of life. More than a symbol, he would prove to be, even as he sat behind bars, an instigator and source of inspiration for other like-minded militants. In fact, in any attempt to understand the events of Sept. 11, 2001, it makes sense to begin with El Sayyid Nosair.

"That's where the law enforcement aspect of the Sept. 11 story began, and where American law enforcement agencies first revealed themselves to be institutionally ill-equipped for the war this new enemy had brought to U.S. shores."

All I can say to that is: Amen.

5

"MC-BEE! MC-BEE!"

New York in the early 1990's was dangerous and dirty, a chilling portrait of a once-proud metropolis in steep decline.

Crime was out of control. Under the administration of genial, dapper and largely-ineffective mayor David Dinkins, the number of murders, assaults, robberies, burglaries and car thefts had skyrocketed.

Racial tensions, especially between the Jewish and black communities, were at a boiling point. Predators and crazies seemed to rule the streets. Aggressive panhandlers were everywhere. So-called "Squeegee Kids" descended on cars at busy intersections, ran a dirty sponge over windshields and demanded money for this "service." Drunks and junkies urinated on the sidewalks, seemingly without consequence.

It was so bad the *New York Post* tabloid ran a front page headline in huge type imploring the mayor: 'DAVE, DO SOMETHING." And Time magazine piled on in superb fashion, running a cover story a few months later entitled: "The Rotting of the Big Apple."

In 1993, new mayor Rudolph W. Guiliani was swept into office on the promise of change. A former hard-nosed federal prosecutor, Guiliani vowed to get tough on crime and quickly hired a career law enforcement heavyweight named Bill Bratton as his new police commissioner.

Bratton, who had headed the New York City Transit Police and the Boston Police Department before taking over the NYPD, was very popular with the rank and file. Bratton "got" what policing was all about. And he knew how to motivate people.

In his earlier stint with the transit cops, he had ditched their bland light blue uniform shirts and outfitted them with sharp-looking dark shirts and commando sweaters. He'd also replaced their old side-arms with 9 mm revolvers, a significant upgrade in firepower. The troops loved their new look – it put some swagger in their step.

Meanwhile, those of us in the regular PD were envious. We were still wearing old-fashioned uniforms with light blue shirts that screamed: condo maintenance man. We looked like we were there to fix your air-conditioner.

Now, as commissioner of the NYPD, Bratton began energetically assembling his new team. John Miller, a high-profile TV newsman whom I'd known for years, became Bratton's deputy commissioner of public information. And Jack Maple, who would become a great friend and like a brother to me, was named deputy commissioner of crime control strategies.

Maple and I had actually met way back in 1981, when I was a patrolman in Manhattan and ran down to a subway platform to break up a fight. One of the combatants, it turned out, was Maple, who was on plainclothes duty as a transit cop and trying to make an arrest.

He had a big, bushy beard back then and was wearing a Playboy sweater and pink Converse sneakers. I mistook him for the bad guy – or a weirdly-dressed skell at the very least. In fact, I was just about to crack him over the head with my nightstick when he looked up and shouted "No, I'm on the job!" Meaning he was a cop, too.

As the commander of DOI now, I was one of the promising young lieutenants in the NYPD, and Bratton's new team soon reached out to me.

First, Miller called me to a clandestine meeting in the back of a black car. He was gathering intelligence on the commissioner's new command staff and produced a book with the profiles of every chief in the NYPD, asking my opinion of each.

A short while later, at a black-tie New Year's Eve party at Miller's apartment, I renewed my acquaintance with Maple and congratulated him on his new position. And within weeks, I was working for him as the commander of the police commissioner's investigative unit, charged with looking into all types of extremely sensitive cases that concerned the new boss.

Some of these were Internal Affairs cases: in one, we looked into a captain rumored to be spending his working days with his girlfriend at her apartment. Others were potentially more deadly, such as the time the picture of an informant of ours somehow ended up on the front page of *The New York Times*.

After a panicked call from a superior, a detective named Jimmy Nuciforo and I made a hurried trip to Harlem, found the informant on a street corner, threw him in the car and took him to a hotel for his own protection.

Working for Jack Maple was an experience unlike any other.

The man was the proverbial "piece of work." He was the quint-essential New Yorker, a tough-talking Queens guy who rose through the ranks as a street cop. Whip-smart and a savant on all matters of crime and policing, he was funny, ribald, exacting – and a ton of fun to be around.

Oh, there were times I wanted to poke his eyes out with pencils, because he tested you constantly. But he made you work harder in shitty conditions than you ever thought you could.

His wardrobe had certainly changed over the years, too, which was a source of tremendous amusement to the rest of the department. A short, stout man – his nickname was "Fatso" – he now dressed like a dandy, favoring finely-tailored suits, bow ties, Homburg hats and spectator shoes, polished to a high gloss.

But even if he looked like a character straight out of "Guys and Dolls," Jack Maple was determined to shake up the NYPD.

In his estimation, it had grown stagnant and woefully inadequate at fulfilling its central mission, which was to fight crime and catch crooks.

To operate effectively, he felt, every police department needed to concentrate on four principals:

1. Accurate timely intelligence.
2. Rapid deployment.
3. Effective tactics.
4. Relentless follow-up and assessment.

So he mapped out each precinct and pinpointed where crimes had occurred, giving each precinct commander a better overall picture of what the crime situation was in his district. Incredibly, this was the first time in NYPD history that patterns of crime were being tracked in real time. Maple also instituted weekly meetings at which he and the department's top brass grilled these commanders – and not gently – on what the hell they were doing to bring crime down.

The meetings were called Comstat, named for the ancient computer used to collate and store crime statistics back then.

Another of his first moves was to make me the head of a unit charged with tracking down fugitives, then a huge problem for the NYPD.

As Maple would write of that time in his book, "The Crime Fighter": "In the previous two years alone, at least 12,000 people who had been positively identified as the perpetrators of violent crimes in New York City hadn't been arrested for those crimes.

"These crimes weren't page one material, so the suspects, instead of being hunted down and thrown in the pokey, had suffered no further inconvenience than that their names were entered into index cards and filed in drawers marked WANTED."

Nothing fried Maple more than to ask a commander about someone who was wanted for murder, or for a series of violent robberies, and be told: "We can't find the guy. He's in the wind, commissioner."

So Maple sent me, Nuciforo, a terrific detective named Sonny Archer and a few others to Brooklyn's dangerous 75th Precinct, where some 300 bad guys were wanted for violent crimes.

"Don't show your faces again," he told us, "until you catch 100 people."

Our mission, in effect, was to quickly round up as many of the fugitives as we could so Jack could embarrass the lazy commanders who'd thrown up their hands at the problem.

I wanted to embarrass them, too.

"Look, these bad guys didn't go to South America for plastic surgery," I'd tell my men. "They're not Carlos the Jackal. They're around here somewhere. And we'll get them."

Every morning at 4:30, we'd literally get dressed in the darkened streets. We'd pull up in a van and put on our black pants, black bullet-proof vests and black gun-belts. It was a serious ninja look. Well, only if ninjas wore baseball caps.

Sonny Archer would then produce a package of manila envelopes crammed with info – including photos and last known addresses – of a dozen wanted suspects. Then we'd hit a neighborhood or two and go look for them.

There was a whole art to finding people who were wanted. Sonny was a terrific tracker and we used some creative methods to ferret out these fugitives. We had a ton of disguises and posed as UPS delivery men, Job Corps workers, housing project maintenance men, anything that allowed us to get close to the criminals we were looking for.

On one occasion, when we were having a particularly hard time tracking a man wanted for murder, Sonny somehow got the name of the man's girlfriend and her work phone number. Once we found out where she worked, we had one our detectives, posing as a delivery man for a local florist, surprise her with a dozen roses.

A card attached to the roses said they were from "Anonymous." She immediately thought they were from her boyfriend. We waited for her to get off work and followed her home. And we quickly confirmed that her boyfriend lived at the same address, which just as quickly led to his arrest.

We arrested another fugitive, wanted for multiple murders, when he showed up for his mother's funeral. Hey, even crooks turn out for family events. So we had undercover detectives sprinkled throughout the funeral home, signing the visitors' book and chatting with the other mourners until the murderer appeared and was arrested.

We even managed to apprehend a fugitive by literally annoying him into handcuffs.

This was a dangerous stick-up guy named McBee, believed to be armed with a Mac-10 assault pistol. Once we discovered where he lived, we showed up at his apartment door one day at the crack of dawn.

First we listened for noise. Sure enough, we could hear kids' voices and the sound of a TV, as well as the occasional voices of a man and woman. But when we knocked, no one answered. Instead, the apartment suddenly grew quiet.

We didn't have a court warrant for this guy, just a "want" card. That meant he'd been identified as a suspect in a crime and was wanted. Technically, then, we couldn't arrest him until he stepped out of the apartment. And he apparently wasn't coming out voluntarily.

To "persuade" him to come out, we launched into our own little version of a psy-ops campaign, with the intention of getting on the guy's nerves.

Remember the classic tactic the FBI used on the Branch Davidians during the Waco siege in Texas in the early 1990's? How they blasted loud, annoying music (Nancy Sinatra's "These Boots Are Made for Walking" was a favorite) and sounds of sheep being slaughtered to coerce David Koresh and his loony followers into giving up?

Looking back on it now, I think what we did next to McBee was even worse.

Sonny Archer kept knocking.

I took a quarter out of my pocket and starting tapping on the door.

And Jimmy Nuciforo added a different percussion to the mix, rapping on the door with his detective's ring.

Soon we added a new and even more obnoxious element: singing. And not *good* singing, either.

"MC-BEE!" we cried in an other-worldly falsetto. "MC-BEEEEE! MC-BEEEEEE!"

After a few hours, the girlfriend cracked. Wordlessly, she left the apartment with the children.

Still, we kept it up: the knocking, the rapping, the tapping, the shrill crooning of "MC-BEEE!" that echoed off the apartment's steel door and down the hallway.

It took another hour, but finally the door opened and thoroughly worn-looking McBee gave himself up.

All our hard work in this new job, all our persistence, began paying dividends from the very beginning.

By the end of the first week chasing fugitives, Sonny, Jimmy and I had already managed to arrest 14 of them. Maple was thrilled. Soon he would have us chasing missing bad guys in other parts of the city, too.

"Gee," he needled chief of detectives Joe Borelli, according to "The Crime Fighter," "my Naugahyde squad caught 14 crooks in a week working out of their cars in the Seven-Five. Imagine if we had sent some real cops to do the job."

This he would punctuate with a loud cackle. Hey, if the boss was happy, I was happy. And the boss was practically blissed-out.

I was working 12- and 14-hour days, getting no sleep, existing on coffee and adrenaline. But I felt good. I knew we were doing important work. I knew that my mentor, Jack Maple, was changing the very culture of the NYPD, bringing effective new methods, computerization and accountability to crime-fighting that was making the city safer.

And I had a front-row seat to watch the whole glorious mission unfold.

6

The Cold Case Squad

As hectic as the job was by the fall of 1994, there was also a familiar rhythm to it that was comforting.

In the morning, I'd be out with my little faux-Ninja squad, doing investigations, tracking fugitives and locking them up. In the afternoon, I'd put on a suit, go down to headquarters and handle administrative duties for the rest of the day.

But that all changed in October with my promotion to captain, a move that would turbo-charge my ascent up the ranks.

In order to become a captain, a candidate had to pass the Civil Service exam. But once you hit captain, the sky was the limit for your career. Every rank attained after that was a discretionary appointment made at the pleasure of the police commissioner. And there were many higher ranks that an ambitious and hard-working young captain could aspire to.

Still, now that I was a captain, it was hard to justify my continuing in my present role. Captains commanded precincts. They commanded 200 to 400 people, uniform and civilian, and generally had enormous responsibility. So because I had shown I was good at investigations and fugitive hunting, the logical landing place for me was the Warrant Division.

This was a big squad. There were some 500 investigators in the Warrant Division, which investigated old arrest warrants that precinct detectives hadn't cleared. There was one central office in Manhattan and satellite offices in each borough.

But when I sat down with one of my lieutenants, Vertel Martin, to examine how the division worked, I was appalled.

For one thing, we discovered the Warrant Division was basically working Monday to Friday, 9 a.m. – 5 p.m. This is a wonderful schedule if you work in a bank or run a souvenir shop in a sleepy seaside village. But not if your job is catching crooks in the big city.

You didn't have to be Columbo to figure out that the bad guys probably wouldn't be home if you were calling on them at, say, noon. If they weren't out robbing or assaulting someone, they were probably having a nice quiet lunch somewhere.

But getting the division to accept new ways of doing things wasn't easy.

It's hard to tell people: "For X amount of years, you've been working Monday to Friday with weekends off, getting home at 7 in the evening like a regular person. Well, now you're gonna wake up at 3 in the morning. And we're gonna hit our first door by 5 a.m. at the latest."

Oh, God, some of my men wanted to burn my house down when they heard about their new schedules! They *hated* me!

But we had a lot of success from the outset. We went from catching 6,000 fugitives a year to catching 12,000 and getting all this attention and publicity from the media.

And all those grumpy lieutenants who were really unhappy with me when I took over? Now they were thrilled! Because now they were piling up tons of overtime and making money. Now we were considered an elite unit, a place where other cops desperately wanted to work.

The culture had changed so much that at the end of that first year, for Christmas, all the lieutenants chipped in and bought me this beautiful – and expensive – humidor for my cigars.

"Captain," one said when they presented me with the gift, "when you got here, we wanted to slash your tires. But you got us from fishing for crappies in the Chattahoochee River to fishing for marlin. Thank you."

Bill Bratton, the new commissioner, was understandably delighted with the results the squad was getting, too. And he was delighted with all the national attention, too.

He wanted to make a statement that this was a new day for the NYPD, and that all the old, ineffective ways of doing business were being thrown out the window. So he selected a few standout captains throughout the department, most of them young, for promotion.

No longer would promotions go to the guy with the grayest hair, as they had for decades. Before, the thinking among the rank-and-file was: *Whether I bust my ass or not, the reward is the same.*

But now Bratton was signaling that promotion-by-geriatrics was a thing of the past. *If you perform*, he was saying, *I don't care how old you are. You can be rewarded here.*

This proved to be a brilliant motivational move. And so it was that 11 months after attaining the rank of captain, I was promoted to Deputy Inspector at the age of 35.

I was assigned to the detective bureau in Queens South as the deputy inspector in charge of all detectives, where I languished for a while pushing papers and doing administrative stuff. It was boring and frustrating. Every time I tried to go out in the field and pull homicides, I was told to come back to the office.

Finally I went to Jack Maple with a simple plea.

"Give me *something*," I asked. "Give me a precinct *somewhere*. Let me get back to police work. I'm totally wasting my abilities."

Jack could hear the urgency in my voice.

"OK," he said, "what could you do?"

"What if we had a unit," I proposed, "to investigate old murders?"

The fact was, there were so many murders in New York at the time that the police were simply overwhelmed.

Detectives were assigned to investigate murders on a rotating catch system. It worked like this: Detective Jones catches one, two days later Detective Smith catches one, then Detective Adams catches one. And then we're back to Detective Jones, because it's a week or two later, and now he's got another homicide. Except he still hasn't solved the first one.

But now he has a fresh homicide and maybe it's a bigger news story. Maybe it's high-profile because the tabloids are heating it up pretty good, putting pressure on the brass to get this thing solved. So now Detective Jones puts the first homicide to the side and starts working on the second one, and then he catches a third one and . . . well, you get the picture.

So it goes on and on like this. And somehow the first murder ends up in a drawer, with very little attention paid to it. And then Detective Jones gets promoted to sergeant, he goes somewhere else, and no one ever looks at that old homicide.

Now multiply that across a huge department, where thousands of murders are piling up. At the time, New York had an average of 1,500-2,000 murders every year. If even 200 murder cases a year are shunted to the side, in five years you have 1,000 murders that have not been worked on – and therefore not solved. And that was probably a conservative figure.

So I proposed to Jack: "How about I start working on those old murders?' And he liked the idea."

So we started pulling cases. And I started working with Louie Anemone, who was now the chief of the department, selling him and Jack on how much our work would benefit the city.

My premise was: people don't commit a murder and go drive a truck or work a straight job after that. They're in the drug business, or they're enforcers, or they're just general criminal scumbags. And they're going to continue to commit crimes until you stop them.

So if they've committed a murder, chances are they're still robbing people, or shooting people, or doing other terrible things. So if we started to catch these guys, crime would definitely go down.

That was the real selling point for Jack and Louie – aside from the obvious, that any murderer should be caught.

Jack asked me how a unit looking into old murders would be structured. I told him I'd have a mix of homicide investigators and fugitive detectives, because half of a murder investigation is finding the suspect.

Maple, bless his heart, agreed to my plan.

I was quietly yanked out of the Queens South detective bureau and given my pick of whoever I wanted to make up this new unit. I quickly chose Sonny Archer and Jimmy Nuciforo among a select – and diverse – group that had worked with me in narcotics.

"Not every detective is a superstar," I told author Stacy Horn for her 2005 book "The Restless Sleep: Inside New York City's Cold Case Squad." "It's true in every business or corporation; it's the same at IBM or Mrs. Field's Cookies, and the police department is no different.

"In the Detective Squad you've got one or two guys who are real warriors, one or two lunkheads who shouldn't be there, and the rest are guys who do what they're told to do. You assign them a case and they'll do a decent job. But that's *all* they're going to do for you. They're not going to knock themselves out."

Of course, we wanted the warriors. I went out and got as many as I could. And this, then, was the beginning of the NYPD's first Cold Case and Apprehension Squad.

We were not exactly given palatial digs for the monumental task that lay before us.

Bratton and Maple did not want it to look as if my squad and I were getting special privileges. So we had to find out own office to work out of. We found a place in Brooklyn that looked more like a storage room, filled with dust, cobwebs and broken furniture.

We had to clean it up ourselves, furnish it ourselves, have desks delivered and phones installed.

Then we went to work. We started pulling cases. And of course, the resistance we got right off the bat from other chiefs and detectives was ridiculous.

The chief of detectives, a tall, silver-haired 39-year veteran named Charles Reuther, wanted there to be special criteria for which cases we could investigate. Like you could only take a case if the detective who had worked on it was retired or dead.

No one wanted to be embarrassed for doing – or condoning – sloppy work in the past.

"They're going to go in and try to find something we didn't do," one anonymous detective fumed about us to the *Daily News*.

Being allowed to look only into certain cases frustrated all of us. But when the unit was moved under the authority of Lou Anemone instead of Reuther, that problem disappeared.

Eddie Norris, Anemone told the *Daily News*, would have "the authority of the chief of department to go in and pull cases rather than running into problems in the detective bureau, creating a lot of animosity."

Freed of the constraints created by inter-departmental bickering, the Cold Case Squad started kicking ass.

Within six weeks, we solved 27 murders. It was a stunning number. And these weren't what were called "fake arrests," where the murderer was already in prison, or dead, and you had simply figured out who he was.

No, these were guys put in handcuffs for the first time for the crime they had committed. These were "real" arrests for "real" open murder cases. Our success attracted quite a bit of media attention, first in New York and then nationally when NPR's Melissa Block featured the Cold Case squad on her "All Things Considered" show.

Though it all, there was tremendous pressure on me. The top brass had given me this squad, and they continued to want results.

So I pushed my guys hard. I pushed them *really* hard. I think I'm a decent guy. But I can be a bit of an asshole. I'm aware of that. I'd push my guys to the point of embarrassing them. After all, the whole reason we were there was because there had undoubtedly been some sloppy or lazy detective work done in the past. And I didn't want my guys to be that way.

I definitely didn't want them just hanging around the office killing time. They were supposed to be out looking for criminals. So if I saw someone reading, say, the *Daily News* sports pages at his desk, I'd start reading over his shoulder.

"Oh, is that him?" I'd ask innocently.

"What do you mean?" the detective would say, looking up.

"Is that the suspect there?" I'd say, pointing to a photo. "God, it looks like he's wearing a Yankees' uniform! Who the fuck is that? Are we looking for him? Now get the fuck out of here! Go catch somebody!"

Jonathan Cumbo, I remember, was a good detective going through a particularly long dry spell of solving cases. He was also a friend of mine of many years. Which of course made him a prime target for the Deputy Inspector to torture unmercifully.

"Jonathan," I'd say loudly, in front of the others, "let me ask you this: are you ever gonna catch anybody again? I just want to know. I'm not mad at you. I just need to know. 'Cause if you're not gonna catch anybody . . ."

He got the message. He was a good cop and a good human being. But that's how I would push my guys every day. I was already unpopular – people in the office were circulating 8x10 photo-shopped images of me with horns coming out of my head. And now I was making the problem worse.

Within months, as we became more and more successful – and more and more well-known – the general public began calling and writing for our help.

Some of the entreaties were heart-wrenching. This one's son was killed – could we look into the case? This one's mother had been murdered – no leads, please help. We began investigating other violent crimes, such as rapes, as well.

Now we had officially become known, in a strange parlance of cop lingo and FM radio jargon, as "that squad that does requests."

During it all, my career was rocketing on an upper trajectory I could never have envisioned.

As far as my bosses were concerned, I was the Golden Boy, destined for greater and greater things. A woman from RKO, the film production and distribution company, called to say they were interested in doing a TV series on the squad.

"Would you consider being a consultant for the show?" she asked. "With a contract that would pay, oh, $40,000 the first year?"

"Uh, yeah," I answered, my eyes practically bulging out of my head, "I think that might work."

It sounded like a pretty great part-time job. And it wasn't exactly like wielding a pick in a coal mine.

Rubbing elbows with TV stars, grazing at the catered on-set buffet, occasionally waving dismissively at an actor and sniffing: "No, that's *not* how you pull a gun out of a holster!" – how hard could it be?

Yes, life was setting up particularly well for young Deputy Inspector Eddie Norris.

Then, without any warning, it all began to crater.

7

Dead Man Walking

In the spring of 1996, a reordering of the NYPD hierarchy occurred with all the subtlety of a Third World palace coup.

My buddy, John Miller, had been the first to go, fired earlier as deputy commissioner of public information. He was crushed, the move seeming all the more ominous because he was never really told why he was terminated.

Then a few months after we got the Cold Case squad up and running, Bill Bratton, who had famously vowed to "take the city back block by block," resigned as police commissioner after only 27 months on the job.

It was generally agreed that Bratton had been pushed out by mayor Rudy Giuliani. There was no shortage of theories as to why. The most popular held that Giuliani resented all the attention Bratton was getting for lowering the city's crime rate.

Just two months earlier, Bratton had appeared on the cover of *Time* magazine, under the headline: "Finally, We're Winning the War Against Crime. Here's Why." The good mayor's photo, on the other hand, was nowhere to be found.

There was also talk that Giuliani felt Bratton was moving too fast in his quest to modernize and reform the NYPD. Whatever the reason, Jack Maple, my mentor and protector, loyally followed Bratton out the door.

Uh-oh, I thought when I heard Maple was leaving. *I'm doomed. This is not good at all.*

All of a sudden, I had no political protection at all in the department. And nobody needed protection more than I did.

The fact was that all these plum assignments I'd received – working in the commissioner's office, working for Jack Maple, heading up the Warrant Division and the Cold Case Squad – had created a lot of embarrassment for a lot of people.

I had made a ton of enemies. So many people in the department were convinced my goal in life was to make them look bad – and nothing could have been further from the truth.

We weren't trying to embarrass people. We were trying to solve crimes. We were trying to lock up bad guys, plain and simple.

And yet this hyper-sensitivity to being embarrassed pisses me off to this day, because it's so pervasive in policing in America.

Let me get this straight: we would rather let a murderer go free than have somebody in the department be embarrassed? Really? How does that even register with people? Because I can't justify that in my own mind.

OK, Detective Jones in the 44th Precinct may look bad on one particular case. First of all, who's going to know? So he didn't catch the bad guy for whatever reason. Maybe he was over-worked. Maybe he was incompetent, maybe he wasn't. Maybe he was a great detective with too much on his plate.

What's the difference? Isn't the goal to catch bad people?

But that was definitely the message that was tacitly conveyed throughout the department, especially when I ran the Cold Case Squad: don't fucking embarrass anyone.

Nobody wanted to rock the boat. And I never abided by that philosophy – ever.

So now, with Bratton and Maple gone, I became a pariah.

"They're gonna come kill me next," I told my inner circle on the Cold Case Squad. "That black Cadillac is gonna pull up and I'm gonna get that ride. But you guys should go. Pick a place in the department where you want to go. I'll try to help you get there."

Most of the guys, however, remained intensely loyal to me.

"No, I came with you and I'll go with you anywhere," said detective Rick Burnham, a sentiment expressed by others. "I don't care if it's foot patrol in the Bronx."

My enemies, though, were cackling gleefully at the thought of me twisting in the wind. They were sure I was about to get my comeuppance.

During a routine visit to the 13th floor of police headquarters not long after Maple announced he was leaving, I ran into chief of detectives Charlie Reuther.

"Ha! Dead Man Walking" he chortled. Which was exactly how I felt at that point.

Reuther wasn't the only one writing me off. Even before Bratton and Maple were gone, other chiefs had told me directly: "Eddie, your career's over when they leave. You know that, right?"

So now, with Maple gone, I was basically radioactive. No one wanted to be seen with me. Or heard talking to me. Or linked to me in any way.

It was during this time that Mayor Giuliani appointed Howard Safir as the new police commissioner. All I knew about Safir is that he had been the Fire Commissioner of New York before taking over the top job with the police, and that he'd done some kind of comedy bit on David Letterman's show.

But Safir, a tall man with baleful eyes and a formidable presence, turned out to have an extensive background in law enforcement. Before taking the top job with the Fire Department, he'd had a stellar career with the DEA and the U.S. Marshall's Service, where he was Chief of the Witness Security Division.

Soon, he would also prove to be one of my biggest benefactors.

On May 11, 1996, I married the love of my life, Kathryn. She worked at Faconnable, a high-end French clothing store, where I'd met her while shopping for shirts for Jack Maple. (Maple at the time was like a nutty professor-type. He was divorced and too busy for mundane stuff like clothes-shopping. So he'd give me wads of cash and send me off with gruff instructions to take care of it for him.)

When Kathryn and I returned from our honeymoon in Bermuda, a couple of my detectives picked us up at the airport. They arrived bearing news.

"The commissioner wants to see you in his office," one told me.

"Oh, yeah?" I said. "What's this about?"

"It's about you," was the answer.

My heart sank. Even in the best of times, you never wanted to hear that you were the subject of a sit-down with the commissioner. And these were hardly the best of times, not with so many of the department higher-ups licking their chops and thinking: *Payback time for Eddie Norris! Can't wait to see it!*

As it happened, Safir had also requested the presence at this meeting of the chiefs of detectives from the various boroughs. Lou Anemone was there, too. But he was the only friend in a roomful of hostile faces glowering at me when I sat down.

Quickly, it became apparent that the meeting was about the Cold Case Squad and my role in heading it. And just as quickly, it became evident that, aside from Louie, the other chiefs wanted it disbanded.

Safir asked me why I formed the squad, and I told him. But Reuther attacked me immediately. He basically called me a fraud and said the Cold Case Squad was stealing cases and doing a horseshit job all around.

All the other chiefs, except Louie, soon happily joined in ripping me.

"He's embarrassing us," one said.

"He's taking easy cases," said another.

He's doing this, he's doing that – the accusations flew one after another. None of them were true.

But the long knives were out, and I felt cornered. Then an eerie sort of calm settled over me.

They're going to kill me anyway, I thought, *so fuck it. I'm going to speak plainly and defend myself.*

Now things got even more heated.

I began quizzing the other chiefs, asking them what they knew of how we worked, insisting that the success of our squad was based on sound detective work, perseverance and the ability to spend more time with the cases – not on any special privileges or crime-fighting tools unavailable to the rest of the department.

"We use the same computers you use," I said. "Like the CARS computer that every squad has."

All around the room, there were puzzled expressions.

"What the fuck is the CARS computer?" one chief demanded.

I explained the acronym stood for Computer Assisted Robbery System, which basically compiled lists of criminal suspects for investigation.

"You're a chief of detectives and you don't know what the CARS computer is?" I asked, zeroing in on the poor dunce. "Shouldn't *you* be the one who's embarrassed, and not me?"

I mentioned a couple of other acronyms and the chiefs looked at me as if I were speaking Mandarin Chinese.

But I was on dangerous ground here. I was arguing with men who out-ranked me by five levels. Anemone was the only one defending me.

Suddenly, some 15 minutes into the meeting, Safir raised one of his huge hands – believe me, you would not want this guy giving you a prostate exam – and slammed it on his desk.

"I got it," he said firmly. "I understand the issue."

And he walked out of the room. End of meeting.

When Anemone and I got on the elevator to leave, I said: "Dude, I'm dead. Just do me a favor and put me in a precinct somewhere. I'll go anywhere. I'll go back to a uniform. Just get me away from these guys. They're gonna make my life miserable."

"All right," Louie said. "We'll figure something out."

A week later, though, I was summoned before the commissioner once more. I was in my dress blues and clearly nervous when I was ushered into his office. But Safir put me at ease right away.

"Eddie," he said, "tell me what's wrong with the department."

Huh?

Yet this time I was hesitant about telling the truth. I was already in enough trouble. Ripping the department didn't strike me as a wise move. *Instead of being yourself,* I thought, *be smart. Try NOT to be yourself for once.*

"Sir," I answered, "this is a great agency. I don't know what we could do to improve it. We have a lot of smart people here."

Safir shot me a withering look.

"Cut the bullshit," he growled. "Don't waste my time. What's wrong with this place?"

"You really want to know?" I said.

Apparently, he did. So for the next 30 minutes, virtually without a break, I ticked off all the things that pissed me off about the department: people not working the proper hours, people being lazy, people being rewarded who should never be rewarded, the twisted idea that it was better for a murderer to go free than to embarrass a detective who didn't do his job, etc.

On and on I went. Safir listened intently until I was through.

"OK," he said finally, "how would you fix things?"

I told him all the things I would do.

"The key to reducing crime is not a uniform presence," I told him. "The key to reducing crime is investigation. You go out and you drag these motherfuckers from their beds at 4 in the morning and put them in handcuffs. You do it in big numbers and crime goes down. It's not rocket science. It's fairly simple. But we're not doing that.

"Say you've got a guy who's doing burglaries or robberies or whatever," I continued. "He does so many in a week. Pick a number. Pick 10. If you get him today as opposed to six months from now – or,

God forbid, *never* – you've prevented all those crimes from occurring in the future. Do that in big enough numbers, think about how many people you've saved in the city."

The commissioner ended the meeting shortly after. Soon I began to hear from Louie Anemone and others that Safir had something in mind for me.

Hmmm, I thought, *maybe I'll get a nice job somewhere after all. Maybe I'm even on the road to inspector at age 36!*

Ten days later, Safir again summoned me to a meeting. As was his style, he got right to the point.

"I want you to be deputy commissioner of operations," he said.

I was floored. Was he serious? He was offering me Jack Maple's old job?

"I . . . I'm not Jack Maple," I managed to stammer.

Are you crazy? I wanted to scream. *You're asking me to replace one of my best friends, the guy who's helped revolutionize law enforcement agencies all over the world with his Comstat system and his bold new ideas! It's like you're asking me to step in after Muhammad Ali or something!*

"I don't want you to be Jack Maple," Safir said. "I want you to be Eddie Norris. That's all I want. I want you to walk around here and . . . no, I want you to STOMP around here! You walk in this office without knocking anytime you want.

"I want people to know you're my guy, and you can look at anything you want, any aspect of the department. You have complete authority. *My* authority."

I was almost too stunned to talk.

Two weeks earlier, my career had been on life support. No Bratton or Jack Maple around, no one to watch my back, the rest of the chiefs ready to whack me the minute they could.

And now this was happening. Whatever *this* was.

It was one of the most surreal moments of my life. I don't think I ever actually said I would take the job. Again, the police department is a paramilitary organization. You don't ask. You just do.

The fact was, I had a new job – whether I liked it or not.

"Who . . . who do I report to?" I said at last.

On his desk, Safir had the NYPD organizational chart that represented over 50,000 employees – four times more than the FBI – operating on a budget of over $2 billion. He pointed to the top of the chart.

"Here's me," he said. He pointed to a space directly below. "And here's you."

Next he drew a straight line from Commissioner to Deputy Commissioner of Operations. I was right at the top of the hierarchy. The only people higher than me were the Chief of the Department and the First Deputy Commissioner.

What happened next was almost equally unreal.

Safir stepped away from his desk, an ornate 122-year-old piece of furniture once used by Teddy Roosevelt. (Roosevelt had been the president of the board of the New York Police Commissioners before becoming the country's 26th president.) The two of us walked out of his beautiful office and across the carpeted floor to his conference room, with its stunning view of Manhattan.

Waiting for us there was the command staff of the department. There were some 20 people in the room: eight deputy commissioners including the ones in charge of public information, community affairs and budget, plus all these bureau chiefs, including some of the ones who hated me.

Everyone was staring at me. I had presented reports in front of many of them in the past. Now, I guess they thought I was about to give another report – maybe on fugitive hunting or something – that they would immediately deem more bullshit.

Instead, Safir cleared his throat.

"I guess you're all wondering why Eddie's here," he began. "I just named him commissioner of operations. I want him to look at all your shops. He has complete authority. He speaks for me and begins immediately."

With that, Safir banged one of his meaty paws on the table, turned to the First Deputy Commissioner and said: "OK, what do you have for me?"

And that was it.

Now it was on to the business of the day.

I was still astonished. Lou Anemone pulled up a chair for me. I sat and looked around at the equally-dumbfounded faces staring back at me, including Charlie Reuther's.

You could read the panic sweeping through the room: *Holy shit! This is the guy we were threatening! And now we work for him!*

In her book "The Restless Sleep," author Stacy Horn labeled that moment "Dead Chiefs Sitting." And that was about right. Reuther was soon ousted as chief of detectives and took a job heading up the less prestigious Criminal Justice Bureau. Others would soon follow him out the door, grumbling about their mistreatment and no doubt cursing me along the way.

Meanwhile, the Cold Case Squad would thrive now that their old boss, former Dead Man Walking Eddie Norris, was the new Deputy Commissioner of Operations. Whatever manpower they needed, whatever equipment they needed, whatever bureaucratic bullshit they needed to quietly disappear, it was theirs in the blink of an eye.

(The squad would get even more publicity when the CBS TV series "Cold Case" debuted in 2003, even though it was about a fictionalized unit in the Philadelphia Police Department. My new promotion, though, now precluded me from having any role with the show.)

As for me, I essentially took over Jack Maple's role. I was now in charge of creating and implementing crime-fighting strategies for the department. I worked in Jack's old office, sat in his chair, took over his staff.

Now it was me briefing Mayor Rudy Giuliani every Thursday and coming to him with suggestions on how to better the department and make it more efficient. At one point, I put together a big proposal asking him to hire 1,373 new officers that were desperately needed in some of the city's worst neighborhoods.

All the older guys in the office made fun of me.

"Ha, you're gonna ask the mayor for 1,300 new cops?" they'd say. "Good luck with that one. He's gonna fucking *scream* at you."

But when I made my big, formal presentation to the mayor at City Hall, with Howard Safir looking on and beaming like a proud uncle, Giuliani was silent for a moment, his face impassive.

"Tell you what," he said at last. "Let's make it an even 1,500 new cops."

Score one for the new guy. I don't think I stopped smiling all day.

Another part of my duties was to run Jack's beloved Comstat meetings twice a week. These were often tense three-hour sessions in which the command staff and uniform guys with the rank of captain or above were grilled about crime in their precincts and their methods for attacking it.

My staff and I prepped for these meetings for hours. We looked at major crime patterns all over the city, what strategies were working, which ones weren't, and where the ball was being dropped in certain cases.

There is no other way to say it: the weak-link commanders were thoroughly beaten up in these meetings.

Some would lose their jobs if they consistently under-performed. But my feeling was: if you had a store that was constantly losing money, how long would you keep the store manager? Eventually, you'd have to make a change, wouldn't you?

The same principal applied with the NYPD. Only here it was critically *more* important to have strong leaders, because people's lives were at stake. And for too long, weak commanders who wouldn't make changes had been countenanced in the NYPD. Often this was because they had been on the job for ages. But often it was also because no one wanted to – here comes that word again – *embarrass* anyone.

In any event, all our hard work in the next few years started to pay dividends.

The crime rate in New York went down, and all the attendant media attention led to requests for me to lecture at police departments all over the U.S., and in France and Germany as well.

Life was good for Eddie Norris again. I was working my tail off, but having fun, too. The city was a safer place, my bosses loved me and in June of 1999, I became a new dad when my son, Jack, was born.

Then one day in November, the phone rang in my Manhattan apartment.

The mayor-elect of Baltimore was on the line.

And he wasn't calling to chat about the weather.

8

Welcome to Charm City

It's safe to say that our conversation did not get off to a rousing start.

"I'm Martin O'Malley and I'm going to be the mayor of Baltimore," the voice on the other end said. "I'd like to talk to you about a job."

I replied in my usual gentle, understated way.

"Who the fuck *is* this?" I said. "I don't have time for this shit."

Was somebody from my office pranking me? God knows those assholes were capable of it.

"No, really, I *am* O'Malley," the voice said. "I just won the election."

As I would soon learn, both statements were true. The voters of Baltimore had just elected as their leader the young, charismatic former prosecutor who wore muscle T-shirts, played guitar and fronted an Irish rock band.

In a majority black city, Martin O'Malley, a white city councilman, had pulled off an improbable victory, soundly defeating two African-American opponents by vowing to reduce Baltimore's staggering levels of crime with what was being labeled a "zero tolerance" form of policing.

(Also called the "broken windows" approach, it basically involved cracking down on minor offenses in the hope that would also lead to a reduction of major crimes, something we'd done, in one way or another, in New York for years.)

Dimly, I recalled that O'Malley had been part of a fact-finding delegation that had visited NYPD headquarter years earlier, looking for ways to make Baltimore safer. He and the others had even sat in on our Comstat meetings. And they had come away impressed with how our policing methods and computerized, performance-based system had dramatically lowered violent crime levels in the largest city in America.

Apparently, Baltimore's mayor-elect had also reached out to Jack Maple for advice on filling the top law enforcement slots in his new administration. Since leaving the NYPD, Maple was doing consulting work for big-city police departments with his partner, John Linder. And both men had recommended me highly.

Now, O'Malley was asking me to come down to Baltimore to meet him and see if I would be a good fit in his new administration.

The truth was, I was immediately intrigued.

For one thing, it was my 20th year on the job with the NYPD, which meant I could soon retire, collect my full pension and start a new career. I was still young, only 39. And as the Deputy Commissioner of Operations, with a big role in New York's extraordinary crime turn-around, I knew it was just a matter of time before a slew of job offers started rolling in.

There were also other quality-of-life issues to consider.

Manhattan was an incredibly expensive place to live. My son, Jack, was an infant and both my wife and I were working. Together, we were making decent money. But this being New York, we were basically just getting by.

I'm a native New Yorker, but it's a tough place to live unless you're very wealthy. If you're making seven figures, sure, you can have a nice town house and send the kids to private school and have a comfortable life. Otherwise, good luck affording all the charms the city has to offer.

Finally, there was this: I missed being in uniform. I missed running the streets and locking up bad guys. Maybe I'd be able to do some of that again in Baltimore. It was definitely worth exploring.

The following Monday, I went to see Howard Safir and told him all about O'Malley's job offer – even though nothing concrete had been discussed.

"You deserve it," the commissioner said. "I'm happy for you."

Yet he also had a concerned look on his face.

"You know," he said after a pause, "Baltimore's a very dangerous place."

"Commissioner," I said, "I did the most dangerous work we have here, which was chasing down fugitives for years. I was in the projects every morning of my career, it seemed."

Safir shook his head.

"I don't mean *that* kind of dangerous," he said. "I mean politically dangerous. Just be careful."

At the time, I didn't really know what he meant. Now I do. Safir had always been a savvy guy. And his conversations with Baltimore's previous police commissioner, Thomas Frazier, had convinced him that there was a poisonous racial dynamic at play within the police department, the City Council and ordinary citizens that could made policing in Baltimore exceedingly difficult.

But I was blithely ignorant of all that when I took the train to Baltimore two days later and met O'Malley in the bar at the Hyatt Regency Inner Harbor.

He was accompanied by Michael Enright, who would become the city's First Deputy Mayor. O'Malley was charming as could be. He told me how impressed he was with what I had done in New York. And he picked my brain about various crime-fighting strategies, wanting to know if I thought they'd work in Baltimore.

He shared his vision for the city and said he felt the police department was broken and in desperate need of fixing.

Finally, we got down to it: he wanted me to interview for the police commissioner's job, although he said there would be other candidates coming in to interview as well.

On my return trip to New York, I was really excited. A chance to be a big-city police commissioner didn't exactly come around every day. Eventually, I thought, it might even lead to my getting the top job in New York – my ultimate dream.

Kate was thrilled for me, but apprehensive, too, about moving to Baltimore. She was originally from California and had moved to New York a few years earlier knowing no one. Now we had just started a family – and I might be asking her to move again?

But the prospect of me essentially having two different incomes, and us living in a far more affordable part of the country, meant she wouldn't have to work and could stay home with Jack. I took to selling that point hard.

"We can actually live like Americans," I told her, "instead of just New Yorkers."

The interview the following weekend back in Baltimore proved to be intense. The interview panel consisted of three people: Bishop Robinson, the former police commissioner and Secretary of the Maryland Department of Public Safety and Corrections; Sean Malone, who would go on to be the police department's chief legal counsel; and attorney Michael Brown.

Now the questions about crime reduction were more pointed and technical. No one sugar-coated how difficult the job would be. For the past 10 years, more than 300 homicides had been recorded annually. Three hundred and five people had been killed in 1999 and over 1,000 of Baltimore's citizens had been shot.

I talked about my philosophy for making a city safer and talked about the tactics that had worked in New York. I stressed the need to have a sizeable police presence in places like East Baltimore and West Baltimore, where the crime numbers were off the charts. But Robinson also asked me my thoughts on policing the Inner Harbor, just to see if I understood that you still had to protect the thousands of tourists who descended there annually.

When it was over, I knew the interview had gone well. Not to brag, but I knew the subject matter better than just about anyone. After all, I had learned how to reduce crime at the foot of the master, Jack Maple. That, to me, was like getting your black belt from Bruce Lee.

Also, I'd been able watch Bill Bratton and Howard Safir run the best police department in the country for years, which meant I'd been exposed to the best leaders and most innovative ideas in law enforcement.

So I knew my stuff. In fact, I'd later find out I was the highest-scoring candidate interviewed.

It didn't matter.

I still didn't get the job.

The next time I sat down with Martin, he laid it out for me in no uncertain terms.

"We just can't have a white mayor and a white police commissioner in this city," he said. It would be too politically combustible, he went on, in a town where African-Americans made up close to 70 percent of the population.

Instead, O'Malley wanted me to take the no. 2 job in the department: Deputy Commissioner, Operations.

Well, thanks, I thought. *But I think I deserve the top spot. And the word is that Seattle, Denver and Los Angeles will all be looking for a new commissioner. And all three are terrific places to live.*

"I already have the operations job in the biggest department in America," I told Martin. "Why would I take the job here?"

But Martin O'Malley wasn't one to give up easily. He had faced long odds in winning the mayor's race and defied the skeptics at every turn. Even *The Washington Post* had seemed flabbergasted when he won the city's hotly-contested Democratic primary, headlining the next day's story with this beauty: "White Man Gets Mayoral Nomination in Baltimore."

No, Martin wasn't about to just shake my hand and say: "OK,

Eddie, thanks for coming down. Have a nice life."

Instead he said: "Let's take a ride."

Moments later, we climbed into the back of an SUV and he took me on a tour of the city. It was late now, going on midnight, as we cruised the darkened streets, Martin making a point of showing me some of the worst neighborhoods.

It was an eye-opening ride, to say the least.

Even at that hour, there were young children out everywhere, toddlers some of them, some with no coats, some with no shoes, despite the cold weather. There was obvious drug-dealing taking place on many blocks and empty crack vials littering the sidewalks and gutters.

At one point, off in the distance, we heard the unmistakable crackle of gunfire.

Jesus, I thought, *what kind of place is this?*

I had worked in some of the roughest parts of New York. But nothing had prepared me for the bleakness that was a place like West Baltimore on a chilly winter night.

"Look," Martin said as we rode along, "I get it. You *should* have a crack at a top job somewhere. But given your talents, where else could you make a bigger impact? This city has the biggest need. I doubt Seattle is as dangerous as this."

Oh, Martin knew how to press your buttons, all right. It was a good argument and it appealed to my sense of duty and my desire to help people, which had only grown stronger from the first day I pulled on a blue uniform.

On the train ride back to Manhattan, I called Kathryn. It wasn't a long conversation.

Taking the No. 2 job in Baltimore, I reasoned, wouldn't really be a step back career-wise. I'd be making decent money ($125,000) and collecting my pension, too. We could actually buy a house now and have a good life in a nice part of the country.

Kathryn was on board. She was willing to take a chance on me – and another new city.

After that, I called Michael Enright. Martin had used a number of football analogies in his sales pitch to me. He'd talked a lot about team-building and needing a quarterback. Whenever he did, though, I'd correct him.

"Hell, you're the mayor," I'd say. "*You're* the quarterback. I'd be the fullback."

Now when I got Enright on the line, I said: "OK, you got yourself a fullback."

It was a momentous decision, probably the biggest of my life. Now I just had to believe it was the right one.

Over the next few weeks, though, I did not exactly wind down my career with the NYPD thumbing through fishing magazines with my feet on the desk.

No, in the waning days of December 1999, the police department – as well as the entire city – was obsessed with what was being called the "Y2K Nightmare."

With the date fast approaching when the calendar would turn from Dec. 31, 1999 to January 1, 2000, it was feared that the world's computers would not be programmed to automatically register a year that began with "20" instead of "19."

Many direly maintained that computer networks would simply shut down, causing catastrophic problems with utility power grids, hospitals, airports, banks, etc.

A number of doomsayers even predicted the end of civilization as we know it. People began withdrawing all their money from ATM's and hoarding food, going into full survivalist mode.

Every day, the NYPD command staff would meet to talk about what terror attacks would come with the Y2K bug, what planes would fall from the sky, what trains and subways would shut down in darkened tunnels or careen off the tracks in smoldering wrecks, what looting hordes would prowl the streets when the lights went out.

We welded manhole covers shut, put snipers with binoculars on rooftops to scan for suspicious activity, installed surveillance cameras everywhere. I had a tremendous responsibility overseeing many of the preparations and was working non-stop.

And then, as the clock struck midnight on New Year's Eve . . . nothing happened.

Well, very little happened, anyway. A few minor technological glitches caused a few machines to shut down, but that was about it.

Civilization did not end. The city was not engulfed in flames. Marauding bands of thugs and killers stayed home. The country woke up the next day with the usual collective big-party hangover, and life went on.

Ten days later I was in Baltimore, eager to begin my new career and the Herculean task of bringing order to what the mayor was calling "the most violent, the most addicted and the most abandoned city in America."

Oh, it sounded like a veritable garden spot, all right.

Tell us how you really feel, Mayor, I thought.

But as I'd soon discover, Martin's bleak description was fitting.

9

The Bloom Comes Off the Rose

After just a few days in Baltimore, I had a serious case of buyer's remorse.

Life was lonely, for one thing. My family was still in Manhattan and I was living alone at the Hyatt downtown, attempting to acclimate myself to this strange new city. I was also working long hours at police headquarters trying to get up to speed with how the department ran.

I had already met the new commissioner, Ronald L. Daniel – Martin O'Malley had sent him up to New York to meet me – and I liked him. Now I was spending a lot of time evaluating the command staff, hoping to determine who the warriors were as opposed to the empty suits, the mopes who were afraid to make decisions, who were just keeping their heads down, putting in their time and hoping for another bullshit promotion.

But the negative vibes I was getting were almost palpable.

It didn't take long to realize that O'Malley was spot-on: the entire department was broken and woefully unprepared for modern-day crime-fighting.

To his credit, Martin had implemented a version of ComStat, the computerized crime-tracking system developed by Jack Maple. But the ComStat meetings here were a far cry from the probing, take-no-prisoners sessions in New York, where precinct commanders and others were interrogated relentlessly and held directly accountable for the crime patterns on their watch.

In Baltimore, only the chief of detectives could ask questions of the detectives. Similarly, only the chief of patrol could grill – and I use that term loosely – patrol officers. The truth was, very little grilling was taking place.

These ComStat meetings featured little more than softball questions lobbed from commanders to staff members, who had clearly been prepped on the subject matter beforehand.

Unlike the heated meetings in New York, here everyone seemed to know the answers to every question. It was absolutely fascinating! No one was ever stumped at all!

Of course, I quickly found out that it was all total bullshit.

During my second Baltimore ComStat meeting, for example, I asked a question about a robbery pattern being discussed.

"What about this guy who's sticking up all the convenience stores?" I said. "What's the status of his case?"

"Well, it's closed," said a detective.

"Oh, good," I replied. "Then the pattern's down. When's the guy's court date?"

"Oh, he hasn't been apprehended," the detective answered. "We haven't arrested him yet."

What?!

Could I have possibly heard that right?

"What do you mean you haven't arrested him?" I demanded.

"Well, I just closed the case," the detective went on. "Meaning he's been identified."

Now the Jack Maple in me came out, the sarcastic, scornful tone my mentor often took when listening to some nervous captain, flop-sweat glistening on his forehead, stammering a mealy-mouth explanation of why he'd failed to do his job properly.

"Ohhhh, OK, I get it now," I said. "So you have his *picture*. So you're going to put his *picture* in a shoebox with the *pictures* of the other crooks, so he'll be in shoebox jail? Is that what we're gonna do with this guy?"

Everyone in the room cracked up. Well, *almost* everyone. I could see the commanders looking uneasily at each other. They weren't real happy with me. Nevertheless, they got the message: the case isn't closed until the arrest is made. No one would forget that going forward.

There was also a relaxed, we'll-get-to-it-when-we-get-to-it attitude permeating the Baltimore PD that I found unsettling.

One day early in my tenure, I was in my office around noon when the police radio squawked: "Man with a machinegun in Patterson Park . . ."

I had only been in town a couple of weeks and had no idea where Patterson Park was. Nevertheless, I jumped up, grabbed my hat – I dressed in full uniform again – and ran down to the patrol side of headquarters.

There I found the chief of patrol and his staff members sitting in their office, calmly eating lunch.

"There's a guy with a machine gun in Patterson Park!" I said. "Let's go!"

No one made a move to get up.

"Yeah, we know," someone said.

I looked at them incredulously. And I said it again, this time louder and more slowly: "THERE'S A GUY . . . IN ONE OF OUR PARKS . . . WITH A MACHINE GUN! DOES THIS HAPPEN EVERY DAY AROUND HERE? ISNT THIS KIND OF A BIG DEAL? LET'S GO!"

Clearly, they were bent on finishing their lunch.

I guess they were thinking: *Well, the precinct closest to the park will take that gun call.* Which was true, of course. But, my God, this was the chief of patrol not making a move to respond! When he was only a few miles away, too!

I was horrified. As I would say over and over during my time in Baltimore, I believe in leading from the front, not from headquarters.

What kind of example was this top commander setting for his troops?

As it turned out, the man in the park didn't have a machine gun after all – he had a rifle. But it didn't matter at all to my way of thinking.

Let's go over it again: there was a guy with a long gun in a public park.

At noon.

On a busy weekday.

This wasn't just some scumbag with a gun at three in the morning on the corner of Monroe and Fayette streets. This was a potential disaster in the making in a park. That chief of patrol and his men, I concluded, had different priorities than I did.

Very different.

Underlying this reluctance to get off their asses was an attitude that seemed prevalent throughout headquarters: *Hey, the police work is done by policemen. We work at headquarters – we're administrative guys.*

I vowed that way of thinking was going to change. I let my people know I wanted to see them in the street, which was one of the reasons I went on patrol every day.

In the days and weeks ahead, it seemed that everywhere I looked in the department, there was a major problem.

Once, I asked to see what kind of wiretap and active cases we had going.

"We have no wiretaps, sir," was the reply.

Ohhh-kay. Baltimore has the biggest drug problem in America – and we're not tapping any phones?

What about surveillance vans? I asked. And video cameras to monitor drug trafficking corridors?

"We don't have any, sir."

OK, I said, what about helicopters? *Please* tell me we have helicopters . . .

"No helicopters, sir," was the answer.

What I learned was that there had been a tragic accident involving the police chopper, known as Foxtrot, a year earlier. It had spiraled out of the sky due to a mechanical failure and crashed into the B&O Railroad Museum downtown.

The flight officer at the controls had been killed. The aerial observer with him had been seriously injured.

Yet instead of trying to find out what had caused the accident – and how to prevent another in the future – they had scrapped the whole program!

Now, one of the biggest police departments in the whole country was without an aviation unit. How could that possibly be?

Photo arrays were another area in which the Baltimore PD seemed positively medieval. When you have a criminal suspect to be identified by a victim, you put the suspect's photo in an array with five other photos showing people of similar appearance. In policing, this is known as a "six-pack."

But this was not the procedure being followed in Baltimore. Here, they were showing crime victims paper photos out of shoeboxes and photo albums, the kind you'd buy at Wahlgreens. And the photos were of every variety – color, black-and-white, Polaroids – in all different shapes and sizes.

In terms of how backward this was, it was like doctors still using leeches to treat infections.

Holy shit! I thought. *This place is totally dysfunctional!*

What else was wrong? There were 250 people wanted for murder or attempted murder in Baltimore, and exactly three officers looking for them in the warrant division. Meanwhile, we had 90 officers helping run the Police Athletic League, which was nationally known and extremely popular with both the cops and the citizens.

Understand, I was a big supporter of the PAL centers. Hey, I had been a PAL kid myself growing up. The PAL center was where I had learned to box. But in a city faced with the fifth- highest homicide rate in the country and a heroin epidemic that had produced some 60,000 addicts, devoting 90 cops to essentially baby-sitting kids all day and shooting baskets with them was a twisted priority, in my view.

"Congratulations," I said to the PAL people. "You have the best PAL program in the country because the streets are so dangerous, you have to lock the kids inside."

So I promptly closed some PAL centers. And people were not happy with me. But I saw PAL as a social services agency, not a police agency.

I had heard that the previous commissioner, Thomas Frazier, a California transplant, had said he felt police were essentially social workers with guns. But I didn't agree with that philosophy. In fact, I hated it. So I used the freed-up manpower from the PAL program to start the department's first dedicated warrant squad.

In addition to some of the archaic and misguided ways in which the Baltimore police operated, there was also a culture of vengeance within the department that was unnerving

This was a score-settling place worthy of a mob family. When I got here, people loyal to the previous police administration were being summarily fired before the new commanders had even settled into their desks and put up photos of their kids.

In New York, I had always been loyal to the commissioner's chair – the *position* of commissioner, if not the actual person who held it. But here, people deemed loyal to the previous administration were canned immediately, no matter how talented and dedicated they were.

The forced resignation of Colonel Margaret ("Maggie") Patten showed me just how vicious these department coups could be.

Patten, 52, was a 26-year veteran of the force and a tireless advocate for the victims of domestic violence in the community. Extremely effective and popular within the ranks, she had nevertheless been asked to leave by incoming commissioner Ron Daniel.

The night after she got whacked, I was on patrol. When I pulled into the police parking lot around 11, my headlights caught the administrative deputy commissioner and a sergeant jumping up and down and yelling like crazy men.

What the hell? I wondered.

It turned out that they had just ripped down the metal sign for Maggie Patten's parking spot, and were now gleefully stomping on it in celebration.

As the expression goes, sometimes there are no words. I just shook my head, walked into the building and headed to my office.

Where in God's name am I? I wondered. I couldn't picture any executive in the NYPD *ever* doing what I had just witnessed. No, commanders there didn't get to the top by being nice guys all the time. But most were pretty dignified. I couldn't imagine any of them ripping down parking signs and jumping on them like school kids.

But no matter how lonely I was in Baltimore, or how depressing the new job seemed at times, the fact was: I wasn't going anywhere else.

I couldn't go home to New York – my old job had already been filled. And since I was the deputy commissioner of ops in Baltimore and not the commissioner, I couldn't really change a lot about the culture of the department without the approval of my boss.

For the time being anyway, I was going to have to make the best of it. And I would do what I came here to do, which was to help make the citizens of America's 19th largest city safer.

It sure as hell wouldn't be easy, though, as I was reminded on one of my very first days on the job.

"Show me around the city," I had asked a member of my security detail. "And I don't want to see the Inner Harbor or the stadiums. I want to see the bad areas. That's the reason I'm here. So show me the toughest places in town."

We went for a ride in a marked car, with me in the passenger seat. It was a bright sunny day and I was in full uniform, wearing my hat, when we pulled up to a busy corner in East Baltimore.

I looked to my right and saw a cluster of men in their 30's and 40's gathered on the sidewalk. Clearly there was a drug deal going down. Or as we say in court: "From my experience as a police officer, Your

Honor, it looked like a hand-to-hand drug sale."

Now, part of what you do every day as a cop in a drug neighborhood is this: you pull up to a corner, give the dealers a look, and they run. Or at least they move on.

They give you some respect. But on this particular day, one of the dealers apparently wasn't playing that game. Instead, I looked at him, he looked at me – and then he went back to transacting business!

Did I mention all this was taking place in broad daylight?

And I was in a *marked* police car?

Wearing a uniform and hat with enough gold braid to make me look like a Mexican general?

But this dealer was totally unfazed. He looked so comfortable, you'd think him and his buddies were trading baseball cards. Or exchanging Tupperware.

I flung the door open and flew out of the car. Now everyone on the corner started to run in different directions. But I caught the guy who'd been staring at me, who was apparently the slowest dealer of the group, maybe the slowest in Baltimore.

As I tackled him and we fell to the ground, he started frantically stuffing something into his mouth. I grabbed him by the throat, reached into his mouth, and yanked out some heroin gel capsules.

After I cuffed him, I got right in his face.

"Dude," I said, "what the fuck? You don't give me any respect? I'm in full uniform, I got gold all over me and you don't run? You stand there and make me look like an asshole?"

Now the guy wore a sheepish look.

"Well," he said, "a lot of times the *poh-leece* ride by and don't do anything. So I thought you were just going to ride by."

The guy was telling the truth. I *knew* he was telling the truth. And it was a sobering moment for me.

Wow, I thought, *Baltimore has really raised the white flag when it comes to drugs and crime. The city has totally surrendered. Can I really hope to change the culture of this place? Or is it too far gone at this point for anyone to make a difference?*

In any event, word of the new deputy commissioner of operations running down a "corner boy" and arresting him spread rapidly across the city.

When I got back to the office, a reporter from the *Baltimore Sun* called, asking for details. And the next day there was an article in the newspaper chronicling the heroics of the city's new no. 2 cop

It was framed as a bit of a man-bites-dog story: top police honcho deigns to actually leave his patrol car and dirty his uniform wrestling with a dope dealer! Who had ever heard of such a thing!

Soon my take-down of the dealer was all over TV, too. Oh, well. At least I had made a good first impression with my fellow police officers and a fair number of Baltimoreans.

I'd need every bit of that good will just a few months later, when the politics of saving America's most dangerous city would devour yet another good and decent man.

10

"You Sit Like a Racist"

In the weeks that followed, a good deal of my gloom lifted as I adopted a new philosophy. It was almost laser-like, if not Zen-like, in its focus: I would concentrate only on matters I could control within the police department, which was the crime side, the operational side.

The drug war, I thought, was unwinnable. It was ridiculous and a waste of everyone's time and money and blood. But I knew how to reduce crime quickly. It was no big secret. We had done it in New York and we could do it here. And the key, once again, would be fugitive enforcement.

First I decided to concentrate on catching the predatory core of criminals wreaking havoc on Baltimore. You're not going to rid the street corners of drugs anytime soon in America. But we could do something about the thugs wanted for crimes.

It was the easiest, most effective way to make an impact. When people already have warrants on them, they've already been indicted for a crime. So you don't have to develop a case. All you have to do is find out where they sleep. That's it.

To help track down the 250 fugitives we had wanted for murder or attempted murder, I met first with the U.S. Marshal's Service. That's what they do for a living. Sure, they protect courthouses and judges. But what they're really known for, going back to the days of the Old West, is chasing fugitives. That's their history. That's their biggest source of pride.

They gave us tremendous cooperation and lent us a lot of deputy marshals. The collaboration was so successful that I decided to hit up the FBI and Secret Service, as well as the surrounding counties, to help us track down bad guys, too.

In addition to that, I knew we had to beef up the ComStat system, too. The rehearsed questions and the even more scripted answers at our weekly meetings were getting us nowhere.

ComStat was not supposed to be theater. It wasn't designed to be a feel-good pageant, so that everyone in the room left thinking: "Yeah, we really grilled them today, boss!" It was devised to be a real management tool to figure out what was causing crime in the districts.

Also, it gave commanders a chance to – for lack of a better word – audition their employees. It was a great exercise for an ambitious police officer to show what he or she was made of, too. In what other line of work do you get a chance to stand up in front of the CEO every week to show how smart you are?

Or how stupid.

Yes, it's a powerful tool that can work either way. But if you're good, you *want* to stand up in front of the boss. *Let me show him what I think* should be your mindset. *'Cause I know these other mopes in the room are just faking it.*

But this brutally honest back and forth was lacking at our ComStat meetings.

The crime assessments rang false. It was as if you were showing someone a major league baseball game for the first time, except the pitcher's only throwing it 60 miles an hour right down the middle of the plate and every batter is knocking it out of the park.

That's not how the game's really played! But our earliest ComStat meetings in Baltimore were equally artificial. They were a Potemkin village of what the real thing should look like.

Commanders weren't prepared. The questions weren't probative. Supervisors would prepare to be questioned on one subject and one subject alone, such as robberies, when I wanted them to address *every-thing* under their command: burglaries, shootings, prostitutes on the corner, you name it.

The four basic tenets of ComStat – accurate and timely intelligence, rapid deployment, effective tactics and relentless follow-up and assessment – that's what I was trying to teach.

Understand, I had nothing but compassion for precinct commanders, because they were responsible for everything. They got shit from the community, they got shit from their officers, they got shit from me.

But sometimes I just wanted to scream at the incompetence shown during these meetings.

I would bring in the head of the auto larceny task force, for example. And the conversation would go something like this:

Me: "What's the most frequently-stolen vehicle in Baltimore?"

Him: "I don't know."

Me: "Well, where are they taking them?"

Him: "I don't know."

Me: "Are they stealing them for parts? Are they shipping them out of the country? Where are they stealing them from?"

Him: "I . . . I don't know."

Now he's stammering and sweating and thoroughly humiliated.

OK, I'd think. *Now I'm going to teach you how to do this...*

"You start to plot where your cars are stolen and where they're recovered," I'd explain. "You can't hide cars like dead bodies, unless you're cutting them up and shipping them out in containers. In that case, where are the chop shops?

"And use the computers! You have all these reports of cars stolen by vehicle type and time of day. Put them in the computer! You know where it was recovered. Put it in the computer! Let's say 50 cars have been found in the same location within a few miles' radius. There's probably a road between where they were taken and where they were found. Set up there!"

Oh, God, I would get so frustrated in my early days on my new job! As it happened, I wasn't the only one being driven to wit's end.

Ron Daniel, the new commissioner, was having a tough time, too, only for an entirely different reason. Martin, in his zeal to get the police department up to speed and make good on his campaign promise to slash the crime rate, was micro-managing Ron to death.

In our daily conversations, I could see Ron getting more and more beaten down.

"I *cannot* get my work done," he'd say of Martin. "The man is driving me crazy."

Ron said that Martin would call him all day, every day, wanting to know about this new shooting or that new case that a city councilman was bugging him about. It was as if the new mayor had suddenly decided he wanted to be the new police chief, too.

"I don't know how much more I can take," Ron would say mournfully. "I don't know if I'm going to stay."

"You *can't* quit!" I would yell. "I just moved here! I'm not working for somebody else!"

At the time, I didn't think I had a chance in hell of replacing Ron as the new commissioner if he stepped down. I hadn't been here long, but I'd already gotten a quick taste of the racial racketeering that was going on in Baltimore.

No one on the City Council, or in the African-American community organizations or the churches, would want me in that post.

A white guy from New York City with a thick accent replacing a popular black commissioner who'd been a 27-year fixture in the department?

Uh-uh. Not going to happen.

No, my fear was that if Ron left, I'd be out of a job. The new commissioner would want to name his own second in command. And Eddie Norris, having just moved his pretty wife and infant son from his hometown, would be hung out to dry.

Yet after only 57 days on the job, Ron Daniel finally had enough of Martin's antics and abruptly resigned in March of 2000.

"Ron Daniel and I both share a commitment to make Baltimore a safer place," Martin announced in a masterful job of soft-soaping the news to the press. "But we have come to the conclusion that our differences in how to get the job done make it impossible for us to collaborate in achieving that common goal."

Daniel's resignation sent shock waves through both the city and the police department.

City hall sources told the *Baltimore Sun* that, in addition to have Martin on his butt constantly, Daniel simply couldn't work with Jack Maple and John Linder, who were still doing crime consulting for the city at Martin's behest.

In a damning report by the Maple/Linder team released that month, the city was found to have "a police culture characterized by cynicism and distrust"; "unreliable and poorly-designed data systems"; "little, if any, discussion about crime trends in command meetings or during roll calls"; "an extraordinary number" of complaints about police conduct and awful morale among officers because of the department's "tarnished reputation."

Yet, the *Sun* reported: "When the Maple/Linder group offered 87 suggestions for how to reduce crime in Baltimore, Daniel rejected half."

Other sources, according to the *Sun*, blamed both O'Malley's impatience and "Daniel's history of bucking authority" for the break-up, suggesting it had been a toxic mix from the beginning.

Whatever the reason for Ron's departure, my phone rang later that day, with Martin summoning me to City Hall. When I got there, the media was already camped outside, the whiff of another big story creating the usual frenzy.

Martin told me I was now in charge of the department – the acting commissioner, at least for the time being. He said he still didn't think the city would go for a white police chief. Yet he talked about wanting me to stay on no matter who was eventually named commissioner.

But I was having none of it.

Even though I thought the mayor's reading of Baltimore's racial landscape was undoubtedly correct, I had nothing to lose at this point. If they were going to start interviewing for the top job, white man or no white man, I at least wanted to be considered.

"Look," I said, "I agreed to work for Ron Daniel. I didn't agree to work for just 'some guy.' I was fine working for him. But I'm not going to work for a total stranger now that you're going to plop someone over me for racial reasons.

"I'm a qualified candidate," I continued. "In fact, I was your *most* qualified candidate, according to what I heard. I deserve a shot at this job now. If not, I'm going to go."

Martin, to his ever-lasting credit, finally agreed to go to bat for me as the next police commissioner.

We both knew it would be a damn tough sell. A hard-working, well-liked black chief stepping down – no, *forced out*, the critics would say – with a white assistant commissioner conveniently waiting in the wings to take his place, would set off a political firestorm.

Martin was already getting hammered by many in the black community for his "zero tolerance" policing, decried as brutal and racist. Thankfully, Ron Daniel didn't lash out at Martin when he resigned, leaving as professionally and courteously as he had comported himself throughout his career. But there was a huge outcry in the black community over his perceived mistreatment.

With City Hall in full crisis mode, Martin began working the City Council hard on my behalf. He used up a lot of favors, burned a lot of political capital. With the help of Jack Maple and John Linder, I quickly came up with a plan, a codified document, of how I planned to reduce crime in the city.

It did not exactly have a catchy name.

"The Plan to Dramatically Reduce Crime in Baltimore," as we called it, was originally drawn up on cocktail napkins in a hotel bar as Jack, John and I huddled feverishly night after night. It involved everything from fugitive enforcement to beefing up our technology with wire-tap capabilities and cellular phone tracking to bringing back helicopters and acquiring surveillance vans.

I also wanted pay raises for the department as a morale booster. We were paying our police laughable wages, way less than the county agencies and the State Police were paying their employees. As a result, we were losing our best people; experienced investigators and trained snipers were leaving year after year.

Now, armed with a bound copy of "The Plan," we set off to sell the idea of me as the next police commissioner to the good people of Baltimore.

It was an absolutely draining task.

For weeks we appeared at town hall meetings in auditoriums at various schools throughout the city. At each event, I would get up before the question-and-answer segment and go over the details of how we proposed to bring order to the city. These were often heated, chaotic sessions that lasted for hours, with Martin and I seated on the stage as citizens took the microphones one by one, to grill us.

Some questions were legitimate and probing; others, prefaced by long, angry screeds, were more agitprop than anything else.

We took a good deal of abuse, as we knew we would, with some of the same professional agitators showing up at each event to inflame the crowd, insisting that the plot all along was to get Ron Daniel fired so a white guy could take over as Baltimore's top cop.

At one raucous meeting, someone yelled at me: "You were involved in the Amadou Diallo shooting!"

"No, I was not," I said.

Firmly, I explained I had nothing to do with the infamous case of the 23-year-old immigrant from Guinea who was shot 41 times by four plainclothes officers in the Bronx a year earlier, an incident which set off a firestorm of controversy nationwide over alleged police brutality and racial profiling.

"You look like a racist!" a black woman shouted.

Another black woman nearby turned on the person who had just shouted and barked: "What do you mean he looks like a racist?! Shut your mouth!"

"Well," the first woman grumbled, "he *sits* like a racist!"

We lobbied in front of the City Council, too, and in front of the state delegation in Annapolis. I was working all day, attending these meetings in the evenings and somehow existing on three hours of sleep a night.

But I was a true believer in what we were doing. And I knew the fate of the city hung in the balance.

"There's a crisis going on here," I said on a local radio talk show. "The mayor won the election with a 'zero tolerance' program. That tells me a lot of people are tired of having people standing in their neighborhood selling drugs openly."

Addressing the concerns of the African-American community, I made it clear we weren't just going to start locking up people who were littering or urinating in alleys. We were going to use targeted enforcement to attack the bad guys who were creating specific problems in city neighborhoods.

Right now, I said, the lack of leadership in the department was destroying the morale of the 3,188 sworn officers, which in turn was endangering the lives of Baltimore residents.

For weeks, we pressed on in our campaign to convince lawmakers and citizens alike that I was the best man for the job. Martin launched a full-blown letter-writing campaign, sending out some 28,000 pieces of mail to residents.

But I was also getting angry and frustrated with this Kafkaesque process of begging people to let me save lives.

"You know," I said to Martin, during one of my lowest moments, "I have a better chance of being an astronaut than I do of becoming the police chief here."

At a meeting with the state delegation in Annapolis, one of the African-American lawmakers took me aside for a few words.

"We know you're the most qualified candidate," he said. "But we were expecting a different, um, hue."

I became so angry, the top of my head nearly exploded.

"Really?" I said. "If the guy who can save more black lives in the city is white, you don't want me? Because I'm not black?"

Finally, though, the arduous campaign came to an end and all our hard work paid off.

On the night of May 8, 2000, I was unanimously confirmed by the City Council to be the new police commissioner. And nearly three weeks later, with Kathryn and 10-month-old Jack at my side, I was sworn in during a public ceremony at the War Memorial Building, after which I was given a standing ovation.

"It was a long process and a difficult time for the Police Department and this city," I told the crowd. "I will certainly show you that you made the right decision."

Remembering my astronaut line, Martin gave me the gift of a model rocket as an inside joke. It would be something I would keep for years.

After that it was time to roll up our sleeves and make good on our promises.

In a majority black city, a white mayor and a white police chief were now leading the fight to pull Baltimore out of the long death spiral it had been in for over a decade.

Our grand "Plan to Reduce Crime" was about to be tested in the dangerous drug-infested streets in a big way.

God help us all if it didn't work.

11

Batman and Robin Bring Hope

"The Plan" might have been the dullest-sounding policy paper on earth, but the mandate from City Hall was to implement it at breakneck speed. The pressure to do something about the violent crime ruining life in so many of Baltimore's poorest neighborhoods was constant and overwhelming.

"Eddie had a high level of energy," my chief of staff, John Stendrini, told a reporter, "because things had to be done quickly."

One of my first moves was to petition the local business community to create the Baltimore Police Foundation, which would help us buy much-needed equipment we couldn't purchase under the city's tight budget.

A big priority was finding a way to run the department from the field in the event of a terrorist incident. This was a year before the horrendous Sept. 11 terrorist attacks that would shake the country to its core. But terrorism had been on my mind for a long time, certainly since the days of the Meir Kahane assassination and the revelations of El Sayyid Nosair's ties to a shadowy network of Middle Eastern and Islamist radicals.

America's enemies, I knew, were constantly studying our nation's security systems and probing for weak spots to exploit. To operate the department remotely in case of a direct attack on the city and our headquarters, we used Police Foundation money to buy a big, million-dollar RV, which we painted black and named our Mobile Command Vehicle.

At the time, it was the most technologically-loaded vehicle in the country. From it, we could run every facet of the department. We would go on to use the vehicle for many different functions, such as monitoring big events – like the annual Fourth of July celebrations – at the Inner Harbor and responding to hostage situations.

I also brought back something that was decidedly low- tech: the espantoon, the traditional Baltimore nightstick so beloved by most of the force. Thomas Frazier, my predecessor, had felt the age-old practice of cops twirling the heavy nightstick was intimidating to citizens.

So he'd replaced the espantoons with something called Koga sticks, longer and lighter batons which could be used in conjunction with the martial arts to subdue the bad guys. But espantoons had been used by Baltimore cops since the turn of the century, and many had seen Frazier's move as the further eroding of the traditions of a once-proud police department.

During this time, I'd have lunches with the city's movers and shakers, such as Baltimore Orioles' owner Peter G. Angelos and bakery mogul/developer John Paterakis Sr., to wrangle money for such necessities as K-9 dogs, bulletproof vests and saddles for our mounted patrols.

I was hitting up everybody I could think of, doing my song and dance about items we needed to make the city safer.

Martin and I went to Washington D.C. and talked to Eric Holder, then the U.S. Deputy Attorney General, about getting funding from the Community Oriented Policing Services (COPS) program to hire more police and provide raises for existing officers.

Hard-charging doesn't begin to explain the mindset I brought to the job in those first months. Going after bad guys on the run, targeting high crime areas, beefing up our ComStat system, fund-raising for better, more modern equipment, improving the morale of the department with raises – all of it began to have a noticeable effect on

Baltimore's crime statistics.

At a news conference at the Inner Harbor, I pulled a page from Joe Namath's Super Bowl III scrapbook and guaranteed we'd drive the homicide rate under 300 for the first time in a decade. (It was 305 the year I took over.)

Reporters rolled their eyes and laughed. Members of my command staff had a similar reaction.

This is Baltimore, they thought. *He doesn't know. It's never going to work.*

I never mentioned an explicit number as our goal. The truth was, I was never comfortable thinking of the city's homicide epidemic in numeric terms.

To me, these homicide victims weren't just brown folders that went in a file cabinet. These were real people, many of whom had been cut down in the prime of their lives and had left behind grieving families that would be forever shattered. If you framed all this simply in terms of numbers, it de-humanized the killings even further.

Martin O'Malley heard about my prediction of a sub-300 year for homicides and liked it – mainly, I think, because my soaring confidence gave him a shot of confidence, too.

"If you just believe in me and let me do my job," I would promise him, "crime is going to go down."

Martin was totally on board with my Namath-like bluster to the press.

A friend of mine had just returned from a trip to Ireland, and had brought me a bottle of *poitín*, or Irish moonshine. Martin and I agreed that if we finished the year with fewer than 300 homicides by New Year's Eve, we would celebrate with a belt of the poitín. He squirreled the bottle away at City Hall for safe-keeping.

As that first year rolled on, we continued to make progress. But there were plenty of rough patches, too.

That May, I fired four high-ranking commanders. Two were African-American and two were white. But when the *Baltimore Sun* trumpeted the story in the next day's newspaper, the photos of the black officers appeared on the front page, while the white officers were pictured on the jump page inside.

Guess who was promptly – and predictably – called a racist?

But the story behind the firings – it couldn't have been more bizarre, more thoroughly Baltimore – was this: a lieutenant had been taking his departmental car home at night while not authorized to do so. And someone eventually ratted him out.

But instead of simply investigating the officer and disciplining him, Deputy Police Commissioner Barry Powell and Col. James L. Hawkins, the two black officers, took it upon themselves to take a spare set of car keys and drive to the lieutenant's house in Carroll County.

Instead of simply observing the car in the driveway and taking pictures of it – which should have rightfully been a job for a detective from Internal Affairs – they used their spare keys to steal the car. Then they drove it back to Baltimore, abandoned it on Northern Parkway and placed a call to 911 – using the worst fake voice in history – to report the location of the car.

The entire charade was done because the two men wanted either the lieutenant or his commanding officer, a good cop named John Bergbower, fired. Except the faux, stuttering voice on the 911 recording was quickly recognized as Hawkins,' and the plot unraveled just as fast when Powell was alleged to have known about the caper.

When I heard what had happened, I summoned Powell and Hawkins to my office and laced into them.

"What the fuck?" I yelled. "How many bodies a day do we have dropping in this town? And this is what we're concerned about?"

To me, a shake-up was clearly needed. To the howls of the City Council, I got rid of both of officers, along with two white officers who were also contributing to the culture of vengeance in a department where, as *Sun* columnist Gregory Kane noted: "scores get settled with old enemies and favors are handed out to friends."

Unfortunately, the embarrassing incident cost the department dearly. Bergbower, 49, and the head of our important Regional Warrant Apprehension Task Force, soon resigned over the flap, yet another victim of the sharp-elbowed vindictiveness rife within the agency.

I tried to persuade him to stay on. But he was too hurt and disgusted over the histrionics of Powell and Hawkins to change his mind.

Another officer eventually forced out was an African-American lieutenant named John M. Mack, a 17-year veteran of the department who was discovered providing muscle for a bunch of pimps. He was essentially running a floating whorehouse, an operation that would set up shop in empty bars and clubs to provide patrons with booze, drugs and prostitutes.

This, of course, was the worst kind of corruption imaginable: actively cooperating in a criminal endeavor. Martin O'Malley and I had both promised to clean up the department; it was one of our core missions. But when the City Council got wind that I had fired the pimp-friendly cop, they summoned me to a meeting and pressured me to bring him back.

I was astonished and angry that they would question my judgment and waste my time over such an egregious case of police misconduct. My sarcasm, which had been simmering throughout the meeting, finally bubbled to the surface.

"You know, you're right," I told the council members. "On second thought, I *will* hire Lt. Mack back."

Now you could see the wary looks on their faces: *You will?*

"I just need to know who wants him in their district," I continued.

Now I went around the room, pointing at individual members.

"Do you want him, Councilman?" I said. "How about you? I'll put him in your district tomorrow. What about you over there?"

No one responded, of course. Suddenly, all the members were looking down at their shoes or developing a renewed fascination for the paperwork in front of them.

With that, I reached for my hat and motioned to my command staff.

"We're leaving," I said. And that's exactly what we did.

On the walk back to my office, one of my staff members marveled at how I'd been able to back down the once-angry council members.

"When I get home," he said, "I'm gonna drink a big glass of testosterone."

Sure, he was kidding. But the fact was, an industrial-strength shot of that stuff was often what you needed in this job to fight for what was right.

We did the same thing to root out corruption in the internal affairs unit – and ran into stumbling blocks there, too.

When an officer named Brian L. Sewell was caught up in a drug sting and indicted on charges of criminal perjury and misconduct, a secret internal affairs office in Dundalk was burglarized and trashed three months later, and the evidence in his case was taken.,

This totally freaked me out. It showed the level of corruption in the department and the utter lack of concern among the participants about being discovered. The message was clear: *We're not afraid of anybody. We're not afraid of you, Commissioner. And we're sure as hell not afraid of internal affairs.*

Sure enough, the case was soon dropped by the state's attorney Patricia Jessamy, causing Martin to go ballistic and me to wonder, once again, at the culture of lawlessness all around me.

Combine all this with the crime wave we were facing, and the sheer brutality playing out on the streets, and the challenges that year were enormous.

Nevertheless, in December of 2000, we were holding our breath as the number of homicides held at around 260. A terrible month with 40-some killings, we knew, could still push that number over 300.

Not only would it make my boasts ring hollow, we would take a significant PR hit in our effort to convince the citizens that Baltimore was now a safer place.

But as the New Year was rung in, it was official: for the first time in more than a decade, the city had recorded fewer than 300 homicides. In a year that had begun with a bloody spate of killings that had surpassed the previous year's pace by nearly three dozen, Baltimore had finished with 262 homicides.

Martin and I were euphoric.

"It's a tremendous morale boost to the Police Department," I told reporters, noting that 262 killings were still "a terrible number. It's nothing to do back-flips over. It doesn't make us the safest city in the country. But it shows that we can make a big difference.

"Now," I added, "we look at the next big milestone: 200."

As promised, Martin and I celebrated in his office by cracking open the bottle of Irish hooch. (Joining us in a toast, interestingly enough, was Catherine Pugh, who was a member of the City Council at the time and is now Baltimore's new mayor.)

A celebratory drink seemed appropriate. It had been a heady first year for the team the newspaper was now calling "Batman and Robin."

Things were certainly looking up for Eddie Norris. Crime was going down. The mayor loved me; it seemed as if the whole city did, too. Soon I was listed in CEO magazine in a feature on the 10 toughest executives in the state.

Another on the list was Baltimore Orioles' owner and super-litigator Peter G. Angelos, who was quoted as saying of me: "I get the impression he's going somewhere, he's going quick and he's taking us with him."

Hell, I was the greatest thing since Cal Ripken, Jr. We were making a ton of arrests. And the naysayers who predicted citizen outrage over our tough, no-nonsense, "zero-tolerance" or "targeted enforcement" approach to crime, were mostly silent.

Going into 2001, we had a lot of momentum on our side. In May, the *Baltimore Sun* ran an editorial titled: "Ed Norris' first year shows gains in policing."

"The dirty little secret among criminologists is that no one quite knows why crime goes up or down," it began. "Virtually the only thing that can be statistically proved is that when crime dips because of crackdowns, citizen complaints against police tend to skyrocket.

"That's why Edward T. Norris' first year as Baltimore's police commissioner is impressive," it continued. "An all-out policing effort has helped curb the city's shockingly high homicide rate without triggering a wave of complaints about excessive law enforcement tactics.

"This is particularly gratifying because alarmists predicted the opposite just a year ago. They argued Mr. Norris' New York training and background . . . virtually guaranteed he would employ cowboy tactics to suppress crime."

I was working my ass off, putting in long hours and then showing up at shootings at 3 in the morning to tell cops they had done a good job. They definitely were not used to that.

During an attempted stick-up of a bar in the Northeast District on a Sunday afternoon, police responded and shot one of the criminals when he raised his gun at them. When the two cops involved in the shooting were brought down to homicide to be de-briefed, I went to talk to them.

As soon as I walked in the room, they jumped up and started apologizing.

"So sorry, sir!" one of them blurted. "We just *had* to shoot and . . ."

"What are you apologizing for?" I said. "I'm just coming here to say 'Good job' and to make sure you're OK. I know it's traumatic to be involved in these things."

It was clearly not the reaction they expected. No, the reaction they expected was the usual angry condemnation: Why'd you fire? Take their guns, suspend them, investigate them, etc.

Around this time, too, we had a young officer arrest a suspect in the suspect's home on an arson warrant. As soon as the suspect was handcuffed, he told the officer: "I gotta pee."

This, you should know, is a routine ploy. Every time somebody's cuffed, the first thing you hear from them is: "I gotta pee! I gotta pee!"

The inexperienced cop fell for it. He un-cuffed the man and allowed him to go relieve himself, a major tactical error.

After a minute or two, the officer went to check on him. When he pushed open the bathroom door, he found the suspect cutting his wrists with a kitchen knife. The man then lunged at the officer with the knife. But the cop managed to draw his service weapon, and shot and killed the man.

When I got to the scene of the incident, a large angry crowd had already gathered outside. Rumors of what had happened were circulating everywhere.

After I was briefed on the details, I went in front of the TV cameras. Right away, the reporters were demanding to know if the officer had committed a violation of department procedure.

"We're going to investigate that and he'll be disciplined for it if he's found guilty of violating any procedure," I said. "But if you jump at *me* with a knife in a tight hallway, I'm going to kill you, too."

The upshot was that police officers now knew they were being supported by their new commissioner. I wasn't going to throw them under the bus every time someone accused them of something.

I was winning the rank-and-file over in another important way, too.

For months, the FBI had been investigating some 20 city police officers – along with a few Baltimore County officers – who had been moonlighting at a Staples. The allegations were that the cops had been working as security guards at the office supply store while also supposedly on-duty. The feds also wanted to know if the cops were being paid for work they never performed.

The investigation finally seemed to be coming to a head. I got a call from the FBI saying, essentially: "Look, we're indicting these officers. You better suspend them."

"I'm not doing it," I told them. "You indict them, I'll suspend them. But until that day comes, I'm not doing it."

Baltimore County would end up suspending their officers involved in the case, but I didn't suspend mine. And eventually, after a two-year federal investigation, prosecutors declined to press charges and quietly dropped the case.

Over and over, I began hearing how the rank-and-file of the department were grateful for my support. But how could I *not* have their backs?

Being a police officer, I knew, was a job unlike any other. With this job, the best thing officers do every day is risk their lives for strangers who might not even like them. As a commissioner, therefore, you really have to know how to motivate people. And one way is to offer them all the encouragement and reassurance you can when they're doing their jobs correctly, and with passion and diligence.

Long ago I learned it's just as easy for an officer to be the fourth car at the scene of a crime as the first car. So if it's a disgruntled officer who's supposed to be racing to save someone's life or respond to a report of a man with a gun, he might think: *Fuck it, the department's not going to support us. So I'm not doing my job and risking my neck.*

Given the aggressive policing I was demanding, it was more important than ever that officers knew I'd back them to the hilt.

When, for example, I heard there was a tradition of people in the city shooting guns in the air when the clock struck midnight on New Year's Eve, I was appalled.

"What do you *do* about this?" I asked some of my officers.

"Well," they said, "we're told to wait in the parking lot until five minutes after midnight."

The message from previous commanders was clear: don't get involved. Stay inside until the bullets stop falling from the sky. Don't rock the boat.

"No, we're not doing that anymore," I said. "We're not hiding. We're the *police.* We're getting *involved.*"

I went out on patrol that first New Year's Eve and within a couple minutes after midnight, three police shootings had already been reported. And from the entire tour that night we confiscated 121 guns throughout the city.

I was in a really good place mentally at this point. I was pushing as hard as possible to help turn the city around, and not for political aspirations. I wasn't looking for the next job.

No, I'm one of those people who are cursed, because I'm a true believer. I really believe in this stuff. I knew I could make a difference in the life of this city. And best of all, what we were doing was working.

But 2001 would also become one of the saddest years of my life, as my best friend, Jack Maple, was losing his battle with colon cancer. I was routinely driving up to New York after work to see him at Memorial Sloan-Kettering Cancer Center, and watching him wither away was agonizing.

Yet his basic personality never changed. He remained a character right up to the end.

One day when Bill Bratton and I visited Jack in his hospital room, Bratton asked gently: "Jack, is there anything I can do for you?"

Jack thought about it for a moment.

"Yeah," he said at last, "*you* can have cancer."

Jack finally passed away in August of that year. I took his death very hard. I was working my ass off. The days were long, crammed with staff meetings, cabinet meetings and meetings with the NAACP, in addition to me going out on patrol and also responding to seemingly every police-related incident in the city.

The nights were long, too, as I found myself drinking too much, trying to unwind after another stressful day so I could turn off all the thoughts pinging through my head and get a few hours sleep.

Jack's death seemed to further my exhaustion. Then came the terrible morning of Sept. 11, 2001, when so many things changed forever.

Photos

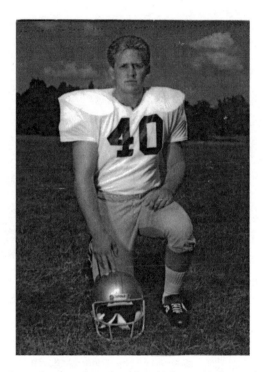

As a handsome, hard-working (and humble!) strong safety on the football team my freshman year at the University of Rochester in 1978. The truth was, I had more heart than talent for the game.

Here's me as the subject of a sports-in-motion photography class at the University of Rochester when I was an amateur light-heavyweight boxer.

Me and my proud father, Edward Norris, on the day of my graduation from the NYPD's Police Academy in January 1981. I couldn't wait to find out for myself what a cop's life was really like.

*Dan Mullin (left), me and Jim LaPiedra on the roof of the NYPD's Mid-
Town South precinct circa 1984. Both were great partners. I always knew
I'd get home safely at the end of my tour when I was with them.*

Yes, I was a mounted cop in the summer of 1984 in the Bronx. Yes, it could make a certain part of your anatomy sore. Training for the mounted patrol involved riding horses for eight hours a day for two straight months.

As a sergeant with the Brooklyn South narcotics unit. The anguished citizen to my right had just been arrested for selling heroin after we broke through his apartment door in the Red Hook neighborhood with a battering ram.

Investigating a Chinese gang murder on Manhattan's Lower East Side circa 1989. The deceased had tried to rob a gambling den at gunpoint – his last very bad idea.

Me pictured between NYPD commissioner Bill Bratton and dapper, bow-tied Jack Maple on the day I was promoted to captain in 1994. Bratton was a terrific leader who re-energized the department in the mid-90's; Maple was a life-long friend and mentor and godfather to my son, Jack.

Leaving the scene of a tense standoff with a serial killer who had barricaded himself in his Queens apartment in the late 1990's. That's Chief of the Department Lou Anemone, a long-time friend and mentor, to my left in the photo.

*One of the happiest days of my life was the day I took my infant son Jack
home from the hospital on June 15, 1999.*

Juggling a fidgety Jack after being sworn in as Baltimore police commissioner May 9, 2000, as Kate and my mom looked on with delight.

Me standing in front of Baltimore Police Department headquarters circa 2001. Is that a great recruiting poster on the building or what?

*Mayor Martin O'Malley reading me the oath of office as I'm sworn in for
my second term as Baltimore's police commissioner in 2002, with Kate and
Jack looking on.*

Me on patrol in a Baltimore alley in 2002. I went on patrol every day and made a point of wearing the same uniform as the street cops, not the dress uniform of the command staff.

Showing off a large cache of illegal drugs and guns found in a traffic stop on I-95. This photo was taken the day I was officially sworn in as State Police superintendent – I had raced up to Harford County earlier that morning to congratulate my troopers for the drug and gun haul and show my support.

Facing the media with Gov. Bob Ehrlich (left) and Lt. Gov. Michael Steele on the day of my official swearing-in as Maryland State Police Superintendent, March 14, 2003. I'm ashen-faced on what should have been one of the happiest days of my life – all the reporters wanted to talk about was the corruption indictment rumored to be coming down.

*My prison ID card, which you were required to hold up whenever there
was a body count inside the fence. I look mean enough to scare a snake,
which was the whole idea. As a former police officer who feared retribution
if his identity were known, I wanted to look like a hardened criminal
when I went in.*

I carried this photo of my son Jack every day of my incarceration, to remind me what I was fighting for.

In my new life as a radio talk show host, I was broadcasting from the site of the Fort Lauderdale Grand Prix in 2006. We were there because Baltimore also hoped to lure the prestigious auto race to its downtown.

Me with "The Wire" actors Michael Williams (left) , who played the notorious Omar, and Lance Reddick, who played Cedric Daniels.

At a screening of "The Wire" in Manhattan with actors Bill Williams and Jim True Frost. I got to walk the red carpet like a real actor!

12

The Darkest Day Yet

A warm, sunny morning, four sleek passenger jets commandeered by terrorists roaring out of a crystalline blue sky to deliver death and destruction – who could have ever imagined such a thing?

I had gone to my office at police headquarters early that day. Like so many other Americans, I watched in horror as images of the Sept. 11 attacks were shown on TV: smoke billowing from the north tower of Manhattan's World Trade Center after the first airliner hit; the second jet plowing into the south tower and igniting a tremendous fireball moments later; the scenes of panic and devastation at the Pentagon outside Washington, D.C. after yet another airliner crashed there; the south tower collapsing in an unholy jumble of noise, rubble and dust; the fourth jetliner after the hijackers crashed it into a muddy field outside Shanksville, Pa., the north tower caving in as crowds of workers, residents and tourists fled in terror.

My hometown had been attacked. So had the nation's capital. Both would have a profound effect on my psyche. Yet in those anxious first hours, with America under siege and thousands of civilians and first-responders already killed, I had no time to put any of it in context.

I had to worry about protecting Baltimore.

Clearly, no one knew what was coming next. No one knew if other cities had been targeted, if this was simply the first wave of deadly attacks and others would follow in the days ahead.

Thankfully, we had prepared for something like this in Baltimore. Immediately, I cancelled all vacation time and time off in the department, and had every police officer in the city mobilized. We called public works and ordered them to fill every dump truck they had with sand, and to position them in front of all our sensitive locations to prevent car bomb attacks.

I was doing hourly press conferences the day of the attacks, trying to look strong before the TV cameras in order to keep everyone calm and assure them that we were ready for anything. Meanwhile, I was worried sick about my father and brother. Both worked near the World Trade Center, and with phone service out, I couldn't find out if they were safe or not.

It was not until the next day, when a couple of my NYPD buddies reached me, that I learned my dad and Robert were OK. By then, I was wearing combat fatigues, carrying an MP-5 submachine gun and patrolling Pratt Street at the Inner Harbor with other officers, marveling at the eerie stillness, with not a car in the streets or a person on the sidewalk. It was a surreal scene that would be repeated in dozens of cities all over the country.

For months after the deadliest attacks on U.S. soil in our nation's history, I would be consumed with survivor's guilt.

I'd lost a number of friends in the World Trade Center attacks. Most were cops and firemen. But two of my dearest friends who died were Danny Richards, a bomb squad detective and karate buddy, and John O'Neill, a former neighbor of mine and an ex-FBI agent who had chased Osama Bin Laden forever.

John had gotten a job as the head of security for the World Trade Center. On the day of the attacks, he had reportedly helped the FBI and the New York Fire Department set up a command center in the lobby of one of the towers while also helping bring people to safety. He was last seen walking toward the north tower when it collapsed.

Making my remorse even worse was my involvement with the

Meir Kahane case years before. The knowledge that we might have stopped future terrorist attacks by cracking down harder on Kahane's cohorts, and paying more attention to the intelligence gathered, would haunt me for a long time.

Still reeling from Sept. 11, the country faced a new threat exactly one week later: letters filled with deadly anthrax spores, mailed anonymously, began arriving at the offices of members of Congress and various media outlets.

Soon, the U.S. was in a full-blown panic. The letters seemed to be popping up in random cities. Over a dozen people suffered from anthrax inhalation. An employee of American Media in Florida died of anthrax poisoning in early October. Less than three weeks later, two postal workers in Washington, D.C., died of the same cause, as did an employee of the Manhattan Eye, Ear and Throat Hospital.

Again, no one knew what was coming next, whether the letters presaged other anthrax attacks in other locations. It was reported that the lethal microscopic spores could be placed in food and water, or released into the air from buildings and planes and trucks.

By this point, though, I was growing increasingly frustrated with federal authorities, feeling they were deliberately keeping local law enforcement agencies out of the loop on these attacks.

Whether it was to protect their sources – or whether they felt they were the only ones smart enough to handle the investigation – they were refusing to share information that I felt could help police departments all over the country protect their citizens.

Finally, on Sept. 25, the local FBI office agreed to hold a briefing for us about the 911 attacks. It took place at Maryland State Police headquarters in Pikesville. The briefing, however, turned out to be a complete charade. Essentially, we were told nothing more than what we'd been reading in the newspapers for days.

The FBI gave us a ho-hum Powerpoint presentation with grainy photos of the suspected hijackers, and little else of substance.

As the meeting wore on, I was getting more and more fed up.

Finally I could keep quiet no longer.

"What else do we have?" I snapped. "Do you even know for certain if these guys were actually on the planes? Have they been identified? Have their bodies been found? Any identifying remnants?"

The agent giving the briefing rolled her eyes.

"Well," she said, "their names were on the flight manifest."

"Yeah?" I said. "You think a terrorist might lie? Or travel under a false name?"

I was furious. Here we were, still shaken from these monstrous attacks, desperate for any nugget of info that might help us anticipate and prevent another one. And we were *still* getting jerked off by the feds.

Just then I got a message on my Blackberry.

"Oh, by the way," I told the assembled agents, "another letter with anthrax was just found at NBC News in New York. Apparently it was mailed to Tom Brokaw. The police are headed there now."

Unreal.

Here we were, not getting squat out of the feds. Yet here I was, giving *them* info on one of the biggest investigations in their long and storied history. Because of my lack of confidence in federal authorities, I had earlier contacted major police agencies on the East Coast and requested to have Baltimore detectives in their operations bureaus, and offered to host their guys in ours. New York and Washington, D.C., did it with us and it worked well. That's why, with our detectives on-site in Manhattan, I had been notified immediately of the latest anthrax threat.

Then early one morning in October, while I was at the Starbucks in Mount Washington fueling up for the long day ahead, I received a call from the FBI.

"We have information that at 1 o'clock this afternoon, there's going to be an anthrax attack in Baltimore," an agent said.

"Have any other cities been mentioned?" I asked.

"No," he said.

"How credible is the information?"

"Credible," was the terse reply.

OK, at least this was a start. At least the feds had given us *something*

No other American city had been mentioned. And the intel had come from a credible source. I didn't give a shit about who the source was. All I wanted was the information. This allowed me to meet with my intelligence people and figure out what we wanted to do.

Finally, a decision was made: we would hold a press conference to let the people of Baltimore know there had been a threat.

But we also decided not to evacuate the city. It was 10 in the morning, we were on full alert, and the folks we were charged to protect had been informed. I was comfortable with the steps we had taken.

One p.m. came and went and nothing happened. We breathed a sigh of relief. There was no attack. And nobody had missed work, nobody had been evacuated, nobody had panicked. With a little help from the feds, I was able to do my job, and I was grateful for that.

But my rift with the government agencies soon grew even larger. For one thing, word got back to me through a friend that the FBI was making fun of me.

"That fucking idiot," the Bureau people were saying, "he's happy with any information we give him. Doesn't even care where it comes from."

Which was true – in its own way.

As I tried to tell the feds: I don't give a shit if you overheard something in a coffee shop in Paris or you beat it out of somebody in Egypt. I don't care how you got it or who your source is. I just need the raw intelligence. After that, I'll make a decision if I think it's credible.

That's all police chiefs really needed to do their jobs. And the feds never got that point.

As the weeks went on, I kept voicing my frustrations. When the government began issuing color-coded terrorist alerts six months after the 911 attacks, I complained that the alerts made no sense, and were more confusing than enlightening.

FBI director Robert Mueller called when he heard about my latest criticisms.

"What's wrong *now*, Eddie?" he asked.

"What's wrong are these stupid alerts," I told him. "What do you want me to do? Do I look up? Do I look down? Where's the threat coming from? And what does it involve?

"Is it my water supply?" I went on. "Is it my infrastructure? Are there going to be guns in schoolyards? I gotta know what to look for!"

Mueller never seemed to have any answers. And neither did anyone else on the federal level.

In early October, Martin O'Malley and I were asked to testify before a subcommittee of the House Committee on Government Reform about our concerns that the feds were freezing out local police departments in the fight against terrorism.

Yet in the days leading up to our appearance before Congress, I was very worried about the repercussions of testifying.

I knew how the government could ruin your life if you took them on. But I had already briefed Maryland Senator Barbara Mikulski on the lack of cooperation we were receiving. And when Barry McCaffrey, the retired general and Vietnam War hero who had served as President Bill Clinton's drug czar, told me it was my duty as an American to testify, I did.

"We have to know what the FBI knows about threats, tips and even just rumors," I told the subcommittee. "Why aren't we all working together to find the people the FBI is looking for?"

At another point, I said: "The FBI has a total of 11,533 agents. There are nearly 650,000 local law enforcement officers in the country. We want to help, and I think the nation needs us to help."

(This was beautiful: when I called the FBI press office before my testimony to find out exactly how many agents they had, they refused to tell me. Instead, I had to Google it. And I found the answer in about 10 seconds.)

I also brought up the Meir Kahane case and talked about all the intelligence that had been unearthed and never pursued because various law enforcement agencies either ignored it or refused to cooperate with each other – and how both World Trade Center attacks might have been stymied if they had.

By all accounts, our frank remarks were well-received by the sub-committee. And our testimony became a huge media story all over the country.

"As we shudder at the certainty that more terrorists lurk among us, a former New York City cop has presented the U.S. Congress with the best and perhaps only effective strategy for preventing another attack," wrote columnist Michael Daly in the next day's *New York Daily News.* "The cop was Edward Norris, once NYPD deputy commissioner and now police commissioner of Baltimore."

I was glad that I'd unburdened myself on a matter that was so important – and that had so many implications for the welfare of the country.

But one thing was certain: the FBI was now rip-shit mad at me. And that was never a good thing for a police chief to have hanging over his head.

Soon enough, I'd wonder how much my candor about the feds had contributed to a campaign of whispers and lies swirling around me.

13

"Too Tony Soprano"

As the months went on, the grinding pressure began to wear me down. I was drinking even more now, not getting enough sleep, not exercising nearly enough.

Not only were we consumed with keeping the city safe from terrorists and the daily fight against crime, but our officers were being killed at an alarming rate. This only deepened my funk.

Officer Kevin McCarthy and Sgt. John Platt had been killed when their patrol car was broadsided by a drunk driver. Officer Kevon M. Gavin had died after a high-speed chase when a budding young hit man — wearing body armor and carrying a 10 mm semiautomatic handgun — plowed his car into the back of Gavin's cruiser and pushed it 100 feet down the street. Officer Michael J. Cowdery, Jr. had been on patrol in East Baltimore when he was fatally shot in an ambush.

(The most brutal killing of all would come months later, when Detective Thomas G. Newman, off-duty at the time, was ambushed and shot outside a bar by three assailants. After Newman died, a doctor in the operating room showed me the detective's heart.

(The sight shook me as few others had. The heart had four bullets sticking straight out of it. Which meant someone had stood directly over his fallen body to pump the last few shots that had ended his life.)

I was so fried after McCarthy and Platt were killed that I was already thinking of quitting the job and going into private industry

– anything to get away from the madness of Baltimore's killings and a police department seemingly beyond repair.

But a train ride to Manhattan quickly disabused me of the notion of leaving.

In my Amtrak car that day, sitting directly in front of me on opposite sides of the aisle, were two smug yuppie businessmen who apparently fancied themselves as towering captains of industry.

Each of these dickheads was carrying on a loud cell phone conversation with his office designed to let the rest of us know how important he was.

"I don't *want* a Cadillac," the first was overheard saying at one point. "I asked for a *Lincoln*."

The other seemed to be talking even more loudly to someone in New York, apparently berating that person for not being the next Al Roker.

"I need to know what the weather up there is right now!" we heard the man bark.

Dude, I thought, *we're in fucking Newark, N.J.! The weather's the same up there as it is here. Look out the fucking window!*

Listening to these two mopes put me in mind of the great line in Shakespeare's Henry V, or at least my paraphrased version: "I could not die in such a man's company."

And I vowed I wouldn't. King Henry V went on to rally the English army before the Battle of Agincourt. And I would go back to rallying my own troops for the battle to save Baltimore.

It was, I realized, still the most noble mission I could undertake.

But nothing about it was easy. As the year 2002 began, I found myself having problems with both Martin O'Malley and his staff.

One incident in particular seemed to begin the downward slide in our relationship. In late February, after a black woman was raped near a bus stop in the Northeastern District, the police department soon found itself engulfed in yet another controversy.

The suspect was described as black and male, around 20 years old. But the next night, Major Donald Healy, the district commander, issued a memo to his officers that read: "Every black male around this Bus Stop is to be stopped until subject is apprehended."

Obviously, it should never have been written that way. You don't stop *all* black men at any time after a crime has been committed. In this case, the only people who should have been stopped were those who fit the description of the rapist.

Knowing Healy as I did, I was sure he hadn't written the memo. I was sure someone had written it for him. Someone who didn't know what they were doing. Or someone who had it in for the white major and had found a way to embarrass him.

When Larry Young, host of a popular talk-radio show with a huge black listenership, got hold of the story a week later, it became a huge deal. Martin summoned me to his office to ask what I knew about it.

"I have no idea – this is the first I've heard of it," I told him. "But I'll find out."

Yet by the time I got back to my office, a three-minute walk, Healy had submitted his resignation. Word was that the mayor had told Sean Malone, his buddy and the police department's legal advisor, to tell Healy he had to retire.

Upon hearing this, I went thermonuclear.

Forcing Healy to quit was absolutely the wrong thing to do. For discipline to be effective, it has to be viewed as fair, even when it's unpopular. *Especially* when it's unpopular.

Had Major Healy made a mistake? Maybe. Had he been set up? Possibly. But we needed to learn more about what had happened before jumping to conclusions.

In the meantime, we needed to remember that Healy was a well-respected commander with a 29-year body of work, a cop's cop, a former SWAT commander and street guy who was still passionate about his job.

Why would you want to lose someone like that? Here I had just lost another terrific commander, John Bergbower. And now *this* was happening.

As so often happened back then, matters quickly got worse.

The mayor called me again. This time he told me the shit had hit the fan, and that he was now taking major heat from black leaders over the department's handling of Healey.

"What are they unhappy about?" I said. "He's already retired. You made him retire."

"They don't feel that's enough," Martin said. "Can you take his pension?"

What?!

I was so white-hot angry I could barely speak.

"Take his pension?" I said finally. "Really, they're not happy with just him losing his job? Hmm, I tell you what. Tell them this: I'm gonna drive down to his house, fuck his wife and burn the place down. Would that satisfy them?"

I slammed the phone down. As to how much my rant and biting wit ended up helping Major Healy, I never knew. But the bottom line was this: his pension remained untouched. And he was allowed to retire normally.

In the months to come, though, I'd have similar fights with the mayor and members of his administration. Martin was definitely not a cop-hater – he had started his career as a prosecutor, after all. But his inner circle was very anti-police.

At one point, Martin's closest advisors wanted to propose that if a police officer got sued, they would only indemnify the officer up to $200,000. This in a city where *everybody* sued, where the courts gave out million-dollar awards for a cop breaking a guy's pinkie.

"No, I'm not doing this," I said. "I'm not putting my cops in jeopardy like that. They'll never do *anything*. And I could be affected, too. I'm a sworn police officer in this state. What if I shoot somebody and get sued for $5 million and I'm covered for 200 grand? I'd be on the hook for $4.8 million! I'll resign before that happens."

Fighting all these battles grew more difficult when I began to hear that Martin's staff was badmouthing me to the mayor. They were telling him I was spending too much time in the gym, that our successes had gone to my head and I was doing whatever I wanted instead of focusing on our mission.

Soon, Martin was showing up unannounced at our ComStat meetings to check up on me, and summoning me to 8 a.m. staff meetings on Monday mornings. I wasn't stupid. No one calls early Monday morning meetings unless they want to send a message.

I began to hear that my popularity was starting to rankle him, too.

I was all over TV in those days, wearing dark shades and black leather jackets and pricey custom suits. At one point Martin told me I was "too Tony Soprano" and suggested I go buy some khakis at Joseph A. Bank. It was a fashion tip I summarily ignored.

One night as Martin and I were leaving the Owl Bar at the venerable Belvedere Hotel after a work meeting that included pints of Guinness, a group of guys at a nearby table spotted us.

"We love you . . .," they yelled, then after a dramatic pause, ". . . Commissioner!"

Martin turned on his heel and walked back to their table.

"What do you mean you love *him?*" he asked. "What about me?"

He seemed serious, and the guys at the table quickly replied: "Oh, we love you, too!"

After we left, Martin turned to me and said: "Nice job, Commissioner Bratton."

He was smiling, but not in a nice, friendly way. More like in a this-is-gonna-stay-in-my-hard-drive kind of smile.

The message was not lost on me.

Years earlier, when Bill Bratton had begun to outshine Rudy Giuliani – appearing on the cover of *Time* without New York's fiery mayor was a tactical mistake – Bratton's days as the city's top cop were numbered.

You never want to upstage your executive. So Martin's dig about Bratton was sobering. *Boy,* I thought, *I really gotta start being careful.*

Yet even though we were having unparalleled success against the bad guys – violent crime was down 14 percent that year alone and overall crime down 29 percent the past three years – Martin's most trusted confidantes continued to view me with suspicion.

My sense was that Sean Malone, deputy mayor Michael Enright and Matt Gallagher, the director of Baltimore's CitiStat program – the data-driven cousin of ComStat that tracked housing problems, trash pickup, snow removal, etc. – thought of themselves as the smart guys.

Me, on the other hand, they viewed as the out-of-towner, a little too rough, not very sophisticated, with an aggressive demeanor they found off-putting.

I was blunt and brash and pushed back when they tried to stick their hands in my department, which didn't win me any friends, either.

With my support from City Hall eroding, I began confiding in people like Lou Anemone and Bill Bratton.

Bratton came down from New York at one point and the two of us talked in my office.

"Eddie," he said, "I want you to look at everything I did with Rudy and do the complete opposite. You've got to learn to manage your boss."

But I was never very good at that, so Bill Bratton's advice mainly went in one ear and out the other.

To give Martin his due, not too many mayors would have put up with a police commissioner who was as in-your-face and plain-spoken as I was. Oh, I wasn't stupid about it. I would never embarrass him in front of others. But I always let him know what was on my mind.

At this point, it seemed almost too late to take Bill Bratton's advice. The gulf between me and the mayor and his advisors was growing ever wider.

It didn't help when, a few weeks later, I began appearing on what would become one of the most critically-acclaimed cable TV series of all time.

If Martin resented the attention I was getting now, this would probably make things even worse.

And that's exactly what it did.

14

"The Best Show Ever on American Television"

"The Wire," HBO's gritty crime drama set on the bleak and forgotten streets of Baltimore, first aired in the summer of 2002. The new show included the unlikeliest of cast members: a certain squat, hard-assed police commissioner who had never taken an acting lesson in his life.

Invited to appear in the series by the show's creator, David Simon, I made my dramatic debut in episode six in early July playing – stay with me here – a hard-bitten homicide detective named Ed Norris.

I know, I know . . . what a stretch, right?

Think about the acting chops needed to pull off such a role!

But my very first line surely hinted at the innate talent about to blossom before the cameras, and the truck-load of Emmys that would certainly come my way.

Walking away from the bloodied corpse of a kid who'd been tortured to death, Detective Ed Norris, lamenting how screwed up things are for a hard-working *poh-leece* like himself, snarls: "Show me the son of a bitch who can fix this department, and I'll give back half my overtime."

Oh, how the critics raved!

OK, actually, I'm not sure the episode was even reviewed, much less that my small role was mentioned. But David Zurawik, the Sun's television critic, *would* later write of my performances: ". . . He has a natural energy and raw anger that are in perfect sync with the dominant sensibility of the series."

(Raw anger? *Moi?* Hey, if that was the best compliment I could get, I'd take it.)

The series, of course, was not kind to Baltimore. This was no gauzy Chamber of Commerce documentary, complete with stirring soundtrack, about the renaissance of a great American city shedding its old blue-collar image in a joyful, head-long rush to embrace the New Millennium.

No, the first season of "The Wire" was all about the brutal drug trade terrorizing the city's worst neighborhoods and the hapless, resource-stressed and often incompetent police force trying to keep it at bay.

Naturally enough, Martin and many of Baltimore's mandarins were appalled to see their beloved Charm City portrayed in such a bleak and desperate light.

"I really don't need an HBO special to tell me what the problems of this city are," O'Malley told reporters. "I do not promote problems. I choose to address them."

But the depiction of Baltimore in "The Wire" was never going to be anything but honest and unsparing about the city's ills – at least those all but crippling its most neglected neighborhoods.

As best-selling horror novelist Stephen King would write: "In David Simon's version of Dante's Inferno, Hell is played by Baltimore and all seven of the deadly sins are doing just fine, thanks."

My involvement with the show began months earlier, when David asked me to lunch not long after I'd been named commissioner.

I knew who David was, having watched "Homicide," the great NBC crime drama of the 90's based on his book by the same name. In fact, I remembered watching it when I first came to Baltimore, looking at the new uniforms the cops wore and listening to their strange lingo and thinking: *I can't believe I'm in charge of a department that's being featured on a television show!*

At that lunch, David explained what "The Wire" was about and that he was just beginning to cast the show. He talked about how much he disliked my predecessor, Tom Frazier, whom he felt was a bumbling bureaucrat who had cluelessly dismantled a solid police department. It was Frazier's dysfunctional police force, David said, that was the inspiration for the new series.

David said he liked the job I'd been doing so far and felt the department was headed in the right direction. But he also made it clear that "The Wire" was going to be very critical of the fictional Baltimore police it depicted.

"The department's not too bad now – I've really tried to correct a lot of the problems," I replied. "The problem is, you guys never miss. HBO always knocks the ball out of the ballpark. So everyone is gonna see it and think nothing's changed. I wish you had picked the LAPD."

But he hadn't, so this was something I would have to live with.

"OK," I asked, "is the police commissioner in the series going to be a black guy or a woman?"

Nope, David said. A white guy.

"OK," I went on, "is it set in the past or the present?"

The present, he said.

"Great," I said, throwing up my hands. "Now *everyone's* going to think it's me."

Yet I wasn't really offended. This was TV. This was entertainment. I totally got it. And I felt the viewers of a sophisticated cable series tackling serious issues of drugs, poverty and urban blight would be enlightened enough to make that distinction, too.

The day after our lunch, a letter arrived for me at police headquarters. It was from David Simon.

After thanking me for my time, he got down to business. Given our discussion, he wrote, would you be willing to appear in a cameo role in "The Wire" playing a detective who criticizes the commissioner?

In effect, he continued, you'd be criticizing yourself. And this would be an inside joke for Baltimoreans that would lessen any ill feelings about the department being cast in a harsh light.

He added that I would get paid – maybe not enough to buy a luxury yacht, but the Screen Actors Guild minimum. And I could save the money, invest it, squander it, give it to charity, or do whatever with it.

I was immediately intrigued. And when Martin signed off on the idea, I told David I was in.

So it was that a few months later, I found myself in a dreary alley in West Baltimore, shooting the scene where Detective Ed Norris studies the mutilated corpse of gay stickup artist Omar's boyfriend and grouses about his non-functioning police radio, the fact that no one has come to collect the body, and how fucked up the department is.

People asked if I was nervous during the filming of the scene, but I wasn't.

My feeling was that everyone already knew I wasn't a real actor, so how humiliating could it be if I screwed up? Plus it actually helped my confidence to know that I was the only one there who had actually *done* this stuff, raced to the scene of a homicide and stood over the stiffening corpse of yet another poor soul gunned down in the city's endless drug wars.

Still, doing the shoot was exciting. So was hanging out with actors like Dominic West and Wendell Pierce, who played Detective Jimmy McNulty and Detective Bunk Moreland, respectively. As I walked off the set that first day, David approached me.

"You know, you're not that bad!" he said. "Want to do it again?"

Sure, I said. And I did, appearing in a total of 22 episodes over five years.

From the very beginning, the reaction within the police department to the new show was mostly positive. Most people thought it was kind of fun having the commissioner appear in a series set in Baltimore, no matter how dark and uncomfortable the subject matter could be.

The public seemed to like it, too – even when some of the things I was doing on-screen were less than savory.

In an episode titled "Dead Soldiers," Detective Norris comes staggering out of a bar as a Pogues tune is blaring from the jukebox and the police are holding a wake for one their dead comrades. Norris is holding two shots of whiskey for McNulty and Moreland, who are equally-hammered, with Bunk slumped wearily on the curb.

"Wake up and die right, you cunts!" Norris barks. And after giving them the shots, he proceeds to puke all over the street.

Oh, yeah, he was all class, that Detective Ed Norris. But years later, on my radio talk show, a caller would remember turning to his girlfriend after watching that scene and exclaiming: "That's our *police commissioner!* How cool is that?!"

Obviously, the spewing scene won't go down as one of the great dramatic moments in television history. But it was fascinating for a novice on the set to get an inside look at how it was filmed.

For one thing, they used 24 cups of tomato soup and corn chowder mixed together to create the fake vomit. They shot the scene from all angles and it required 24 takes. In half of them I was speaking, in the other half I was, um . . hurling.

When we finally finished shooting, Dominic West and Wendell Pierce started laughing, shooting me knowing looks that said: *C'mon, you're too good at this! You've clearly done this in real life!*

Another bit of "Wire" insider trivia: if you ever wondered why the characters didn't speak with that distinctive "Bawlmer" accent, the answer is simple – and hilarious at the same time.

David said they had originally tried having the characters on "Homicide" speak in vintage "Bawlmerese." But the feedback from the public had been almost entirely negative. Apparently viewers hadn't known whether they were supposed to laugh at many of the lines, because the characters using the accent sounded mentally-handicapped.

All in all, "The Wire" was great fun to do and it was an honor to be associated with such a brilliant and timely show.

Jacob Weisberg, writing in Slate, called it "the best show ever broadcast on American television." And Stephen King would add:

"...its take on America's drug war makes 'Miami Vice' look like a Saturday morning cartoon."

Yet as critically-acclaimed as it was, it was hardly watched.

All sorts of theories were put forth for this discrepancy: its subject matter was too disturbing. It had an almost all-black cast, which might have turned off white viewers. Its multiple, inter-woven story-lines and lengthy list of characters were too hard to keep track of. A lot of people didn't have cable or HBO at the time.

Another mystery was how, year after year, a show as groundbreaking as "The Wire" would get shut out for television's top awards.

Not once was it nominated for Outstanding Drama Series, the Emmy's highest honor. And while it was nominated twice for Outstanding Writing for a Drama Series, it never won that, either.

"It's like them never giving a Nobel Prize to Tolstoy," Weisberg wrote in Slate. "It doesn't make Tolstoy look bad, it makes the Nobel Prize look bad."

In a lot of ways, I think TV people simply over-looked David Simon's talent, viewing him in much the same way that a lot of cops had viewed Jack Maple.

With Maple, a lot of cops thought: *The guy was a transit cop, not even a real police. He never even graduated from high school! He has an equivalency diploma! And he doesn't even look like a cop!*

With David, who started as a newspaper staffer for the *Baltimore Sun*, the TV mavens thought: *Who's this fucking baldheaded police reporter from Baltimore? He thinks he's going to break into this industry? Ha!*

As for me, I feel that I owe David in so many ways.

"The Wire" introduced me to so many smart, funny people that I would never have met on my own. People all over the country and in Europe still recognize me from the show, too, which is good not just for my ego, but maybe for any future TV or documentary work.

David's belief in me never wavered. Neither did his support. And just one month after "The Wire" first aired, when my world would begin to crumble – slowly at first and then with astonishing speed – I'd need all the support I could get.

15

The First Rumblings of Trouble

On a warm summer day in 2002, Ragina Averella, the police department's director of communications, came to me with an unusual request.

She said that Del Wilber, a reporter with the *Baltimore Sun,* had heard about something called the commissioner's supplemental account. He wanted to look at our records to learn more about it.

"What do you want to do?" she asked.

"Let him look," I said.

This was in keeping with my policy to be as open and transparent as possible. Unless what the media asked for involved an ongoing investigation or a matter where a crime victim or witness could be jeopardized, my policy was: Give 'em what they want.

I did the same thing here. I had nothing to hide.

"Ed understood the press," Ragina would tell a reporter years later. "He didn't view them as the enemy, as so many bosses do in law enforcement and the private sector."

When Wilbur made his request, all I told Ragina was to make sure he was supervised, and that he didn't take anything out of the building.

Then I forgot about the matter.

What's that old saying about no good deed going unpunished? Sure enough, for his kindness and munificence toward the media,

Commissioner Open and Transparent promptly got whacked upside the head.

On August 13, the *Sun* ran a front-page story with the bombastic headline: "Norris, police spend off-the-books funds on trips, gifts, meals."

The lead paragraph didn't get any cheerier:

"Baltimore Police Commissioner Edward T. Norris has used a loosely-monitored, off-the-books departmental fund to finance more than $178,000 in expenses during the past two years, including trips to New York, gifts to fellow officers and others, and expensive meals at trendy restaurants."

The article went on to detail a number of the expenditures, among them: sweatshirts and jackets I'd bought to keep police commanders warm at a chilly Orioles game. Cheap replica cufflinks I'd given as souvenirs to first-time visitors to Baltimore. Trips I'd taken to New York and other cities, including hotel and restaurant bills. A Palm Pilot I'd bought for work. A Glock pistol I had tested. Holsters I'd bought for my aides. Gifts for members of my staff. Hotel accommodations for out-of-town experts we'd brought to Baltimore to help with our departmental training.

Many receipts, the article said, were missing. Others failed to identify where the expenditure took place.

"I wish better records had been kept," I was quoted as saying. "I thought somebody would be writing this stuff down."

The department's budget and fiscal people had done a poor job of monitoring the fund. But ultimately, I acknowledged: "The buck stops with me."

Martin told the *Sun* he hadn't known about the supplemental account.

"I'm a bit angry there wasn't better and tighter accounting," he was quoted as saying. But he added that he stood behind me and that I was a "terrific police officer and terrific commissioner."

Even when the story broke, though, I still didn't think it was a big deal.

The commissioner's supplemental account had been around since the Great Depression, started as a relief fund for orphans and widows and gradually morphing into a discretionary fund to be used by Baltimore police commissioners.

Apparently, its existence had been little-known outside the department. But I had been briefed on it my first day as commissioner and told that it involved no taxpayer money and was not subject to city review or auditing.

"You can do whatever you want with it," I was told. "It's to be used completely at your discretion."

I saw that my predecessor, Tom Frazier, had refurbished a classic police car for the police museum with money from the fund. He had also bought a tuxedo for a formal function and spent $6,000 on lunches for his staff with fund revenue.

But even after that initial briefing about the fund, I pressed for more clarification on using the fund.

"If I want to buy a thousand dollars worth of bubblegum tomorrow, it's OK?" I asked.

"It's your money," was the answer. "You want to buy bubblegum, it's OK."

Nevertheless, soon after becoming commissioner, I tightened the parameters for the fund's use. From now on, any spending would have to be directly related to furthering the mission of the police department.

After that, though, I had never given the fund a second thought. Never looked into how it operated. Never paid attention to how much money was spent. But after the *Sun* story broke, the media – along with the city comptroller and City Council members – started beating me up about it.

Martin announced that he would turn over control of the fund to the city Finance Department and would hire the accounting firm of Ernst & Young to do an independent audit to investigate the spending.

I told the press I welcomed the move. And I did.

I had done nothing wrong. All of the expenditures under my watch had been for police business.

Yes, the supervision of the account had been shoddy. So had the record-keeping. But consumed as I had been with the never-ending task of trying to make Baltimore safer, it was something that had flown completely under my radar.

Years later, people would ask me: How could you not know what was going on with this fund?

And my answer was: "C'mon! I'm the CEO of a company with 3,200 people under him. The budget was $275 million. I would buy 50 or 60 police cars at a time! I didn't go out and count them. I don't go and check on how much gas is delivered to the precincts.

"It's just preposterous to ask an executive to do that. What executive checks on every single expense incurred on his watch?"

Ultimately, the audit would confirm that most of the roughly $180,000 spent in my three years as commissioner went for legitimate department expenses. Some $20,000 was flagged, mainly because of the lack of receipts and shoddy book-keeping.

But entertaining staff members at Orioles games, handing out cheap trinkets, replica police shields and other items as souvenirs for visiting dignitaries, buying restaurant meals for law enforcement experts in town to help train our department, buying items such as a Palm Pilot for work – all were legitimate expenses that a big-city police commissioner could reasonably be expected to incur.

(Ultimately, after resigning as commissioner, I would pay back some $7,500 in personal expenses rather than fight an endlessly dragged-out accounting battle. And Peggy Watson, the city's finance director, would confide the payback was strictly for show, to make it look as if I hadn't simply received a slap on the wrist for my transgressions.)

For a while, the stories accusing me of misusing the fund went away. A month later, I appeared at a press conference with Thomas

DiBiagio, the U.S. Attorney for Maryland, to announce a drug seizure from a joint operation between the city and the feds.

A *Sun* reporter asked DiBiagio if his office would be looking into the controversy over the police commissioner's supplemental account. DiBiagio said no. Maybe he would have spent the money differently, he told reporters. But since no taxpayer money was involved, there was no need for any investigation.

To my mind, the whole thing was now a dead issue.

But the events of the past year – the never-ending battle to make Baltimore safer, the Sept. 11 attacks and the new concerns about terrorism gripping our cities, the constant drumbeat of negativity from the press over the controversial fund – had definitely taken their toll on me.

I was exhausted, working ridiculous hours and hardly sleeping most nights before going back to work at two or three in the morning.

I began looking around for other jobs, police commissioner posts that were opening up in other cities as well as private consultancy jobs in New York. Big outfits such as American Express, Saloman Brothers and the New York Stock Exchange were always tapping former New York Police Department execs for lucrative positions heading up in-house security operations.

Why couldn't Eddie Norris get in on a gig like that?

Are you kidding? A chance to make a whole lot more money with far fewer headaches? Who wouldn't leap at that?

"It's a good time to leave," my old NYPD buddy John Miller advised. "You could dry-clean yourself of all this stupid fund bullshit. You did a good job in Baltimore. Now you move forward."

Nevertheless, I still had an obligation to the citizens of Baltimore, and I was determined to be the best police commissioner I could for as long as I held the job. But my stress levels were red-lining. I was getting dangerously burned out.

Then came the incident that permanently soured my relations with Martin and led indirectly to my swift departure as the city's top cop.

In November of 2002, I attended the election night party of Maryland's new Republican governor, Robert L. Ehrlich.

I had been invited by Lt. Nick Paros, who headed the union that represented some 1700 state police officers and commanders. Not long after I arrived at the downtown hotel where the celebration was held, the TV cameras zeroed in on me.

Looking back on it now, going there was a dumb move on my part.

I was naïve, and didn't realize how much my boss, a life-long Democrat, hated Ehrlich. Not only that, but I was avowedly apolitical in those days. In my mind, I was a cop and I ran a police department, period. Any decisions I made about whom to associate with were never based on politics or political aspirations.

But none of that mattered in this case. The shit hit the fan immediately.

Martin O'Malley appeared in my office first thing the next morning. To say he was unhappy is putting it mildly. When he gets pissed, his eyes get squinty, like Jack Palance in those old Westerns, when he's getting ready to grab one of the bad guys by the throat.

Martin said I had made him look bad by showing up at the party. Now, he said, he was getting a ton of calls from people essentially asking: what the hell was Norris doing consorting with the enemy?

The conversation with Martin was brief. I didn't fight him on this one. I said "OK, you're right" and I apologized. But a good deal of damage had been done.

Immediately, rumors began swirling that my showing up at Ehrlich's victory gala meant I was about to take the top job with the Maryland State Police. This was patently untrue – there had been no offer on their part and no lobbying on my part to join the agency.

Nevertheless, Martin asked me to go on-camera with Jon Leiberman, a reporter for WBFF-TV in Baltimore, to say I wasn't leaving and dispel the rumors. Dutifully, I did this.

Yet only a few weeks later, I received a call from Gary McLhinney, the former head of the Baltimore police union, who was now part of Bob Ehrlich's transition team.

McLhinney said the governor wanted to invite me to lunch at Harry Browne's Restaurant in Annapolis, the upscale, art-deco dining spot favored by many of the state's movers and shakers.

"He wants to talk about what the state police can do for the city," McLhinney said.

The lunch turned out to be an altogether pleasant affair. The governor made it clear that as a former kid from Arbutus, a Baltimore suburb, the city was important to him.

"I'm not going to forget about the city," Ehrlich told me, "because as the city goes, the state goes. We have to make sure Baltimore continues in the right direction. What can I do to help?"

I laid out a plan that called for state troopers to actually patrol in the city, and to have them do interdiction on highways to help us with drug trafficking, terrorism threats and every other kind of criminal activity.

At the end of our lunch, the governor dropped a bombshell.

"Would you be interested in that job?" he asked. "Running the state police?"

I was stunned. I hadn't seen that coming at all. But, hell, yes, I was interested! I was looking to leave the Baltimore PD anyway. I'd had three very tough years when we had accomplished a lot, but I was just like a peeled nerve at this point.

Heading the state police was like my dream job at this juncture of my career. I had never done that kind of policing, so it was a fresh challenge and a chance to work in the entire state with a very squared-away police agency.

Now I had a chance to get away from the stress and ugly racial politics of policing in Baltimore and still do the job I love. I wouldn't even have to move. I was living in the Mount Washington neighborhood of Baltimore and the drive to state police headquarters in nearby

Pikesville would take 15 minutes at the most.

Another reason to consider the state job was Ehrlich's interest in having me focus on terrorism. Since my testimony in front of Congress following the Sept. 11 attacks, I had become a national figure as someone who had taken the lead on this issue.

Whatever the terrorists were going to bring to hurt people, I told the governor, whether it was bombs, bullets or whatever, they would have to drive it somewhere. And the state police were the people to stop them, because they patrolled the highways.

"I'm definitely interested in the job," I told the governor. "But I've got to talk to the mayor first."

"No, we'll *both* talk to him," Ehrlich said. "I want to assure him we're not going to forget the city. This is going to benefit the city. You running the state police, you're obviously going to take care of Baltimore. And *I* want to take care of Baltimore. So we'll work together."

The next time I could see Martin, a day or two later, I told him all about my lunch meeting with the governor and the unexpected job offer.

"I really want to take it," I said.

Martin was not pleased – another vast understatement. I don't remember if his eyes squinted. I don't remember if he flashed the full Jack Palance death glare.

But he was mad as holy hell at me – *again.*

"If you're going to take a do-nothing job," he grumbled, "can't you do it in another state? Want me to call the governor of New Jersey? I'll see what I can do for you there."

But within minutes, he seemed to accept the inevitable. He got Ehrlich on the phone and we had a three-way conversation.

In a calmer and more playful tone now, the mayor told Ehrlich: "You're stealing my guy." But the governor attempted to paint the move in a rosier hue. Everything would be OK, he kept insisting. Eddie's taking the state police job would be a win-win for both the city and state.

So it was that on New Year's Eve, I made a recorded announcement over the Baltimore police radio, informing the rank-and-file that I was leaving as police commissioner and taking a new job as state police superintendent. I also assured them I was not leaving Baltimore, and I thanked them for all their hard work.

Predictably, the media pummeled me once news of my new job leaked out.

The spin now was: Commissioner Ed Norris is abandoning the city. He came here and talked tough about being the man to help transform Baltimore. But now he was cutting and running.

At a news conference in Pikesville, I was peppered for a half-hour with questions about my motivation for switching jobs and my state of mind, the inference being that I was making a terrible mistake because of cloudy judgment.

"Why would you leave the city?" Terrie Snyder, a reporter for City Paper, asked somewhat incredulously.

"Well, I always looked good in earth tones," I replied.

It was a flippant answer and probably not the best way to endear myself to reporters who might now be covering me in my new role. But by this point, I had had enough of the media piling-on and didn't care.

Not long after, a package was delivered to my house in Mount Washington. It turned out to be a farewell gift from Martin: a beautiful framed photo of General Ulysses S. Grant.

This had been an inside joke between us.

When times were good and crime in Baltimore had decreased, the mayor would address me as Gen. Grant, after the victorious Civil War hero. But when the violence and drug wars spiked, I became Gen. George B. McClellan, the indecisive and ineffective Union commander eventually replaced by President Abraham Lincoln.

On the back of the photo, Martin wrote: "Congratulations on your new job. Thank you for all your work. You saved a lot of lives in Baltimore. Sincerely, Martin."

I was touched by the kind gesture, and the photo would soon grace the walls of my new office at State Police headquarters.

As 2003 began, I was pumped up about my new job, grateful for a fresh start in the business of keeping the citizens of Maryland safe.

Unfortunately, the mood would not last very long. Another shit-storm was lurking just over the horizon, one that would blow in and upend the world of Col. Edward T. Norris, the proud new superintendent of the Maryland State Police.

16

"What Are They Looking For?"

Just a few weeks into the new job, I was attending a police funeral in Snow Hill on Maryland's Eastern Shore when I got a call from Ragina Averella at Baltimore police headquarters.

"I hate to tell you this," she began, "but some people from the U.S. Attorney's office just came by. They're removing all the records of the supplemental fund."

My heart immediately sank.

That's the downside of being in law enforcement and knowing how federal prosecutors work – how the sausage is made, if you will. From the moment I took Ragina's call, I knew, almost intuitively, my career would be over. Because once the feds get interested in something, they never let it go.

Ask yourself this: do they ever come up empty-handed? Have you ever seen a press conference where federal prosecutors announce: "We found nothing, sorry for wasting your time?"

No. Never. They'll find *something*. If you cheat on your taxes, if you leaned on your mailbox as a kid or cherry-bombed it or whatever – they'll find some stupid law you've violated. And owing to a bullshit statute known as U.S. Code 666, they can come in and investigate any entity – such as a police department – that accepts $10,000 in grant money from the federal government.

I went back to the funeral service with my mind racing.

I've been hounded and hounded and hounded since the day I came to Baltimore, I thought. *I'm a fascist, I'm a Nazi, I'm a racist – it never ends. Now they're still chasing me. Why can't I just live a normal life?*

Why can't I just be sad at a funeral like everyone else? Instead, I gotta have this fucking atomic bomb dropped on me . . .

News of the federal investigation was leaked to the media with shocking swiftness. On February 28th, the *Sun* ran another front-page story headlined: "Grand jury probes spending by Norris from city fund."

While I didn't comment directly that day, Major Greg Shipley, the state police spokesman, relayed to the newspaper that I felt the issue was "old news" and that my use of the commissioner's supplemental fund had been thoroughly investigated.

But from that point on, life for me became a nightmare.

The steady drip-drip-drip of leaks to the media seemed to occur on a daily basis. The investigation was all anyone wanted to talk about. Rumors of possible indictments were already out there.

My official swearing-in ceremony as the new state police super-intendent took place in Pikesville on March 14. It was a beautiful, sunny day. My family was there with me and so were many of my old police friends from New York. In the audience were bigwigs from the FBI, Secret Service, U.S. Marshals Service and other law enforcement agencies.

It was supposed to be a joyous occasion. But the photos from that day tell a different story. Flanked on stage by Governor Bob Ehrlich and Lieutenant Governor Michael Steele, I looked stiff and ashen-faced, a shell of myself.

Naturally, in the press conference after the ceremony, all anyone wanted to talk about was the investigation. I'm not sure there was even one question about the state police.

Over and over, the reporters asked a variation on the same theme: "What are the feds looking for?"

And over and over, I gave the same answer: "I have no idea. The last person they're going to tell is me."

The presser turned into this brutal interrogation that went on and on. In the videos that made that night's newscasts, you can see me almost visibly recoiling with each new query.

Obviously, it was hardly the ideal way to begin a new career. Bill Bratton had told me that the first year taking over an agency was the most fun.

"You get to put your people in place," he said. "You get to make your big changes and put your stamp on the agency."

But this was anything but fun.

This was the Department of Justice's version of the Spanish Inquisition, only with English sub-titles.

In the weeks that followed, I learned that many of the people connected to me – friends, relatives, members of my inner circle when I was Baltimore police commissioner – were being subpoenaed and yanked in front of the grand jury.

I tried to focus on the agency, but each new rumor about the investigation had me whipsawing between hope and despair.

"This is all going away," friends would say. "It's all bullshit. They've got nothing."

But just when I'd start to believe them, I'd hear from someone else: "Jesus, they just brought the manager of the Smith & Wollensky steakhouse in to testify."

Meanwhile, my attorney, Andy Graham, was having zero luck getting any information about the investigation from the U.S. Attorney's office.

"This is absolutely Kafkaesque," he would tell me. "They won't tell me what they're looking at. They won't tell me how long it's going to go on. I have no idea what we're doing here."

And this was a guy who had been an assistant U.S. Attorney!

Despite this metaphorical axe now swinging over my head, there were times I could lose myself in my new job and feel almost a sense of normalcy.

One day when I was on patrol near the Maryland-Delaware border, acting on a tip from an informant, John Miller, my old NYPD buddy called.

"How're you holding up?" he asked.

"Couldn't be happier," was my reply. "I'm sitting in a state police car in the median strip of I-95, waiting for a carload of guns to come across the state line. So I'm in heaven."

There were even precious moments of comic relief that I so badly needed. One occurred the day Steve Chaney, chief of operations, and I visited the state police barracks in McHenry, the western-most station before the West Virginia line.

As the new superintendent, I had set out to visit every barracks in the state, mainly to shake hands and introduce myself, but also to keep everyone on their toes. On this visit, Steve and I happened to drop in at the ungodly hour of 4 a.m., both of us dressed in full uniform.

A trooper sat at a desk watching TV. He had his tie off and his feet propped up, the picture of relaxation.

"Hey, how are you?" he greeted us casually.

"Good, good," I said.

"Quiet night," he said.

The two of us continued chatting for a moment. Then I saw him glance at the wall behind me, which contained the official head-shot photos of Gov. Ehrlich, Lt. Gov. Michael Steele and me. The trooper's eyes went from me to my photo a couple more times.

Suddenly he spotted the twin silver eagles affixed to my collar. And with that, he shot to his feet, stood ramrod straight and yelled: "JESUS CHRIST!"

"Relax," I said, as Steve and I burst out laughing.

"*Nobody* ever comes out here!" the poor guy wailed, provoking more laughter.

But as the weeks went by and the investigation dragged on, I became more and more depressed. Now rumors started circulating that the federal prosecutors were looking into women I might have fooled around with.

The feds had questioned John Miller about who I had brought to my NYPD retirement dinner in New York, after I had already started work in Baltimore. They wanted to know whether it was my wife who had accompanied me.

What kind of question is that regarding a federal money case? I wondered. Miller had wondered aloud about the same thing when he was grilled by the feds.

"Oh, this isn't the Ken Starr investigation," one had told him, alluding to the former Whitewater independent counsel who looked into President Bill Clinton's sexual transgressions. "We're just asking."

Just asking. Right. Sure they were.

By August, the *Sun* was reporting that members of my security detail from my police commissioner days had been subpoenaed to testify, which seemed to fan even more conflicting rumors.

"OK, I hear they're announcing Friday that they're dropping the investigation," a friend with connections to the U.S. Attorney's office told me.

But the next day the story had changed.

"I hear the indictment's coming down Tuesday," another friend reported.

Meanwhile I was fielding daily calls from the media and meeting with high-powered lawyers – one was Fred Fielding, former White House Counsel for Presidents Ronald Reagan and George Bush – who assured me I probably wouldn't go to prison if indicted, but would probably lose my job.

I was holding my breath the whole time, going through my workday in a leaden funk, trying to keep my family calm and drinking myself into a stupor every night, just to be able to sleep.

One day, after I ran a meeting with the gun lobby regarding which firearms in the state were to be regulated, it all caught up to me.

When the meeting was over, I stood up, smiled and shook

everyone's hand. Then I went in my office, closed the door and my knees buckled. I literally collapsed in my chair, my head spinning and my breath coming in quick, shallow gasps.

How much longer can I do this? I wondered, staring blankly at the ceiling.

But there was no answer up there, either.

17

The Eight-Point Buck
Goes Down

On a hot day in August, I came home from work to find my wife, Kate, waiting at the foot of the stairs.

She wore a concerned look – well, an even *more* concerned look than the one she usually wore now.

"Let's sit down for a minute," she said. "I have some news."

I groaned and slumped against the banister. By this point, just about everything was freaking me out. I could tell this would be yet another sunny bulletin that neither of us wanted to hear.

Kate said that my parents had called. Federal investigators had shown up at their house in Brooklyn that day and served them with subpoenas to testify about a mortgage application letter, as well as a check found in my bank records.

That's it, I told myself. *They got me. I know exactly what they're going to do with this.*

The thing I had worried about for months was now staring me in the face. Two years earlier, when I had bought my house in Mount Washington, I had borrowed $9,000 for closing costs from my father.

We had both signed a letter saying the nine thou was a gift. But when I paid my father back, the transaction had technically become a loan. Which meant I had lied on a mortgage application, a federal offense.

Sure, it was the wrong thing to do. But just about everybody I knew did this gift-loan maneuver with their folks. And the reason was simple: we did it because we were poor. Because nobody had any money. So you borrowed off your parents. But who the hell ever gets prosecuted for it?

Actually I knew the answer to that from my work with the Department of Investigation in the NYPD.

Back then, we had done a lot of prosecutions with the feds. And if you had a suspect you were targeting and couldn't get him for, say, extortion or murder, there were all sorts of other violations – many of them tax-related – that could put him away.

Now that the tactic was being used on me, I was even more terri-fied of being indicted.

In a private moment with Gov. Ehrlich, not long after my folks had been questioned, I had moaned about the feds: "Why are they doing this to me?"

"'Cause you're the eight-point buck in the state," the governor replied. "Who else are they going to do it to?"

If that was true, the eight-point buck was now squarely in their sights. And they were just itching to pull the trigger.

A couple of months later, while with another trooper on a car-stop on I-95, I got a call from the manager of the Coach store where I had shopped for luggage. She said the feds had called her in to testify and asked her a series of weird, sexually-related questions, including if I had ever taken nude photos of her.

It was so bizarre to think that the U.S. government would be asking citizens these kinds of questions in a financial case. Even if they thought the woman was one of my girlfriends, wouldn't they be asking her whether I had ever taken her on vacations? Or lavished her with gifts?

I was so shaken by her call I almost passed out on the highway.

What the fuck are these guys up to? I kept asking myself.

But that night, as I stood in the shower, I had an epiphany.

Suddenly I started punching the shower walls and screaming at the top of my lungs: "MOTHERFUCKER! MOTHERFUCKER! NOW I GET IT! NOW I KNOW WHAT THEY'RE DOING!"

Thank God my wife and son were on a trip to California, or Kate would have called an ambulance to take me away.

But now it hit me: there wasn't enough with the supplemental fund business for the feds to hang me. Now they had added the whiff of sex. Now they were going to smear me with allegations about my infidelities and use the charge of mortgage fraud as their trump card – a charge that carried a maximum sentence of 30 years.

"Yeah, that's the headshot," attorney Fred Fielding would soon confirm. "They're going to pepper the indictment with things you didn't do. They're going to indict you for bank fraud and mortgage fraud. And they're going to force a plea because they have you on that."

As soon as Kate returned from California, I told her: "I'm done. And there's nothing I can do about it."

At this point, I was so dispirited that I thought about suicide, going so far as to sit in Robert E. Lee Park one day with my gun. Only the thought of my son Jack living without a father kept me from pulling the trigger.

One thing was certain: I wanted to be mobile when the indictments came down. So we put our house up for sale that fall, sold it immediately and moved into the apartments at Harborview downtown.

In early December, I went to Gov. Ehrlich with every intention of resigning. I was still running the state police, going to meetings and dealing with the media, but the pressure of the looming indictment was killing me.

At times, I thought I was going to have a stroke. Day after day, it seemed, the government was leaking allegations that made me look more and more terrible. And the fact that I couldn't defend myself was driving me crazy.

"No, we're going to fight this," Ehrlich said when I tried to quit. He said he still didn't actually believe I'd be charged.

But two days later, on Dec. 10, 2003, as I drove to the Starbucks in Mount Washington to meet my wife, a call from my lawyer made it official. An indictment was being handed up that day.

When I met Kathryn outside of the coffee shop, she was all smiles – until she got a good look at me. I had tears in my eyes as I told her what had happened. And I resigned as superintendent of the Maryland State Police that day.

The sweeping indictment announced by Maryland U.S. Attorney Thomas M. DiBiagio charged me with using the Baltimore Police Department's supplemental fund to pay for personal expenses, including gifts, private travel and liaisons with girlfriends. My former chief of staff, John Stendrini, was also indicted for misapplying police money and obstructing justice by lying to city officials about how the money was spent.

Yet as I studied a copy of the indictment with Kate the night before I was to surrender to a federal magistrate, my hopes were buoyed.

"This is all bullshit," I said as we leafed through the pages. "This is nothing. It's petty stuff and it isn't true, and we'll fight this."

To my mind, this was all a regurgitation of the stuff the city had investigated months earlier.

Personal expenses? The $242 spent on custom-made shirts were *police* uniform shirts, made because I wear a size 50 jacket with an 18-inch neck. With a build like that – like a standup freezer – it was tough to buy clothes off the rack if I wanted to look professional.

The $163 for boots bought at Dan Bros. Discount Shoes? Those were combat boots I bought the day after the Sept. 11 attacks, so I'd have something to tuck my combat fatigues into while on patrol. A $200 knife had actually been a police rescue knife, which we used to cut seat belts out of cars.

On and on it went. Candles? There had been a power failure in my neighborhood and my security detail had brought them to our house. Kate had offered to pay for them, but had been waved off. Same with liquor I'd had delivered to my house. I had offered to pay for that, too, only to be told: "No problem, Commissioner. It's been taken care of."

The pricey restaurant meals and hotel bills they wanted to kill me on were bogus, too.

A $376 meal at Flemings I supposedly had with a girlfriend to celebrate her birthday? I had actually been with a member of the police department and two other men. Bar bills and food bills in Toronto were for my staff when we attended a police chiefs' conference after the Sept. 11 attacks. Trips to New York had all been for legitimate police business, as well as for the wake and funeral of John Stendrini's mother.

Sure enough, though, the last page of the indictment charged me with making a false statement on a mortgage application.

OK, I thought, *they have me on that one. And that could be serious, 'cause they have my father as a co-conspirator. But the rest of it? A joke!*

If you're wondering how Kate reacted to seeing romantic liaisons with other women listed on the document, she was pretty much numb to it by this point.

She had heard the whispers and rumors of my infidelities for months, and had been hurt deeply by them. The truth is, I had lied to her and denied any wrong-doing, trying to protect her from even more pain now that her husband was under siege and her entire world was being turned upside down.

I'm certainly not proud of betraying her. This is no excuse, but the stress of running a big-city police department, the heavy drinking and the number of women who routinely threw themselves at cops – including the new commissioner – created the perfect environment for an affair. And I was too weak to resist it.

Walking into a Canton bar late one night, I heard two women call my name. When I looked over, they smiled, pulled up their T-shirts and flashed me. And that was hardly the first time women let me know they were available.

But spare me your moralizing on the subject of infidelity, please. As recently as September of 2016, the Journal of Marital and Family Therapy reports that 57 percent of men and 54 percent of women admit cheating in a relationship. The bottom line is that this is a common and very personal issue between a man and a woman. The fucking federal government has no business in your bedroom.

But here's the bottom line: I never spent a dime from the fund on these women. Allegations that I bought train tickets from the fund for women to visit me in New York, that I wined and dined them in restaurants and bought gifts for them from Victoria's Secret – none of it was true. (And there's this: when the feds were figuring out my so-called restitution for all these alleged gifts to women, it came to a grand total of $100.)

Yes, I had met other women for a glass of wine or dinner on my trips to Manhattan. But these were *work* trips for the Baltimore PD. Unlike what was alleged, I didn't travel there for the purpose of having trysts.

Understand, even though I felt the government's case was weak as I perused the indictment, I was still terrified.

Believe me, seeing "the United States of America vs. Edward T. Norris" at the top of the page was a sobering sight. This is a country that topples governments! We run the world! And now that chilling phrase was saying, in effect, that I was taking on the legal might – and had incurred the wrath of – the most powerful nation on earth.

Andy Graham and a new, experienced defense attorney, David B. Irwin, recommended by Governor Ehrlich, accompanied me for my hearing before the federal magistrate. (Another heavy hitter, Joseph Murtha, had also joined our legal team. Yes, the same Joe Murtha who had defended Linda Tripp on state wire-tapping charges for her role in the Monica Lewinsky scandal that led to President Bill Clinton's impeachment.)

The prosecutors played hardball from the beginning: they wanted my passport taken and my guns surrendered immediately. But my lawyers emphasized that I was hardly a flight risk – what was I going to do? Take off and leave my family? As for my weapons, they reminded the judge that I had put a lot of people behind bars in Maryland and still had security concerns.

After pleading not guilty, I was allowed to keep both my passport and firearms and was released on my own recognizance. In a brief meeting with the media afterward, I said I very much looked forward to my day in court.

Flashing a thumbs-up sign, I mustered a smile and answered a reporter's shouted question of "How are you doing?" with a simple "Fine." Then, trailed by a platoon of TV camera crews and still photographers, I left the courthouse, seemingly the very picture of confidence.

Of course, it was a complete façade. Inside, I felt totally dead. It was a wonder my brain could even function, and that my rubbery legs could still keep me upright.

"We're going to attack the indictment both on the law and its constitutionality," Andy Graham told the media afterward. "And we're going to attack the facts because many of the facts are just plain wrong.

"You will hear in the final analysis that all these expenditures were appropriate and appropriately related to police business," Andy added.

But I knew leaving that courthouse that my life would never again be the same.

My next move was to get out of Dodge – to move my family somewhere far from the madness that had swirled around us all these months.

Now it was getting scary for us in Baltimore. The day after the indictments were handed down, Kathryn happened to be driving downtown. When she had stopped her car at an intersection, a man selling newspapers had lunged at her, holding up the front page of the *Sun* with a photo of me and the headline: "Chief Lies, Cheats, Steals."

Those had been the stinging words DiBiagio had used to describe my actions to reporters. Later, I'd learn the words would cause him to be hit with an ethics violation, because it made it harder for me to get a fair trial. But now the headline was being thrown in my wife's face by some nutcase running up to her in traffic. No, we were getting the hell out of this town --that much was certain.

"Being at the bottom of the abyss is like hitting the lottery in the sense that you're now free," I told Kate. "Now I have nothing. So we don't have to stay here. The good news is: we can go anywhere we want and start from scratch."

We settled on Tampa, Florida, where I had a friend, Debbie Kurtz, who had worked as a consultant to Rudy Giuliani. My plan was to work with her for Giuliani, who had been hired by the Mexican government to overhaul the notoriously corrupt federal police, or *federales*.

My thinking was this: *Ok, the feds have gotten me to resign. They've humiliated me publicly. But there's no freaking way they're going to move forward with this bullshit case.*

In my more optimistic moments, I assumed I'd be hit with kind of federal misdemeanor charge that would keep me out of law enforcement, but still allow me to carry a firearm and do consulting or security work for private or quasi-governmental agencies.

Luckily, I was still working as an actor on "The Wire." David Simon continued to be incredibly generous toward me. OK, I wasn't getting Brad Pitt money, but I was getting the SAG minimum, which helped. And David was paying for my flights to and from Baltimore, as well as for my hotel stays.

That's how I spent the next few months as we geared up for the trial date, which had yet to be announced. I would try to stay busy, work on the set of "The Wire," do things around our townhouse, go to the beach, listen to music. But the whole time Kathryn and I were worried sick about what lay ahead.

As time went on, I was even more amped up to fight the charges. But my attorneys had been negotiating with the federal prosecutors, both sides trying to see if we could avoid a trial. And ultimately, my legal team convinced me that the best thing to do was take a plea deal.

For one thing, they said, it would cost somewhere in the neighborhood of $500,000 to hire private investigators, forensic accountants and other experts needed to mount a successful defense. Secondly, the feds had assured my lawyers that they were fully prepared to hammer me on the mortgage fraud charge.

"If he doesn't take a plea," one prosecutor said, "he'll never see his son grow up."

My 71-year-old father was also being threatened with jail on the mortgage fraud charge. And the whole ordeal was already taking a considerable toll on him.

After sitting in on one meeting with my lawyers, during which we were told that the *Sun's* negative editorials about me were likely to sway the judge into treating me harshly during a trial, my dad erupted.

On the way home, he began punching the steering wheel of the car and screaming: "THE *BALTIMORE SUN'S* GOING TO INFLUENCE WHETHER YOU GO TO PRISON OR NOT? I CAN'T BELIEVE THIS!"

So it was that on March 8, 2004, I appeared once again in U.S. District Court in Baltimore and pleaded guilty to conspiring to misuse money from the Baltimore police commissioner's supplemental fund and lying on tax returns. In return, the charge of lying on a mortgage loan application would be dropped at sentencing.

That was an awful day for me.

Standing stone-faced in front of the judge, with my hands clasped in front of me, I balked when asked if every word of the indictment was true. (I'd soon learn this was a standard question in such proceedings.)

"I'm not saying that!" I hissed to my attorney, David Irwin. "That's bullshit! It's not true!"

But Irwin squeezed my hand and whispered: "Calm down. You're pleading to a conspiracy to misuse this fund. All they have to do is have one charge be true and you're guilty of the entire conspiracy."

Unbelievable. In other words, if they could prove that I'd done one thing wrong – accepted the candles without paying for them, for instance – I'd be found guilty of the entire conspiracy. Where in God's name is the justice in that?

Addressing the media after I left the courthouse, Irwin said: "He made the decision that a long drawn-out trial would bring too much pain to his family, his friends and the city of Baltimore. Now he'll try to pick up the pieces with his family and put this behind him."

The only good thing – if you could call it that – was this: according to my attorneys, prosecutors were saying they would not recommend jail time. It seemed the worst they would hit me with would be house arrest and probation.

Still, a felony conviction – it was clear prosecutors would accept nothing less – would kill me in other ways. My life depended on my ability to carry a gun and work in law enforcement. No one in that field would hire me now.

Yet at age 44, I was still a relatively young man. I still had many years ahead of in the work force. And now I'd have to start all over again.

After the guilty plea, I went back to BWI airport right away. Waiting for my flight to Tampa, I sat forlornly at the bar, sipping a Manhattan.

When I tried to pay, the bartender shook her head.

"No," she said softly, "when you were here, my street was safe."

When you're as down as I was, you take your little kindnesses wherever you can get them. This was one I would never forget.

Kate and I flew up to Baltimore for my sentencing, and the sentencing of John Stendrini, on June 21, which would prove to be another terrible day. My mother and father drove down from New York to be with me. Standing in front of the packed courtroom, with a huge media throng, I felt my life was over.

John was sentenced first. He received three years probation and was ordered to pay a hefty fine and perform 300 hours of community service. Then it was my turn to face the judge, and now there was a stirring in the room.

John had been the warm-up act for this ugly little farce. But I was the one everyone had come to see.

"This courtroom has seen a vice-president, this courtroom has seen a governor, and now it sees a police commissioner . . .," Judge Richard D. Bennett began, alluding to the infamous corruption trials of Spiro T. Agnew and former Maryland governor Marvin Mandel in the 70's.

At this point, he droned on about the importance of integrity, which was ironic. As a ranking state Republican, Bennett had helped Thomas DiBiagio get the U.S. Attorney job, which meant the judge should have clearly recused himself from the proceedings in the first place. It was just further evidence of how corrupt the whole thing was.

As Bennett continued talking, my father suddenly bolted from the courtroom in tears, in the throes of a massive anxiety attack.

"I knew right then what was going to happen," he would say later.

Sadly, so did I – as much as I hoped I was wrong.

"Eddie is a great father and I need him with me at home, to keep our family together," Kate pleaded to the judge. But it wasn't looking good.

When it was my time to speak, the tears were flowing freely.

"I fully accept responsibility for what happened here," I said. "I know what it's done to the police department. I know what it's done to my family. I said I was sorry for this many, many times. I'll be saying it for the rest of my life."

But ultimately, none of what was said had any effect. Neither did the letters of support from Maryland government officials, and from Rudy Giuliani and Howard Safir, that my lawyers submitted.

"If there was ever a time in the history of this country that we need to depend on the integrity of the police, that time is now," Judge Bennett intoned, referring to the shaky mood of the nation in the wake of the Sept. 11 attacks. "This was the wrong time for two outstanding cops to make a mistake."

When he finally read the sentence, it hit me like a blow to head: six months in federal prison. Six months of home detention after that. A fine of $10,000 and restitution of $12,000 (even though I had no money left from the expense of trying to defend myself.) And 500 hours of community service – 100 hours over the recommended maximum sentence.

Judge Bennett said he would recommend that I serve my time at the minimum-security federal prison at Eglin Air Force Base in the Florida Panhandle. But he said the final decision on where I would go was up to the Federal Bureau of Prisons.

I had 30 days to turn myself in.

And with that, the hearing was over.

Kate and I were devastated. I remember being escorted from the courtroom in a daze and the media mob engulfing me. They were like animals, pushing and climbing over each other to get at me with their microphones.

"WHAT DO YOU SAY TO THE PEOPLE WHO SAY YOU GOT OFF TOO EASY?" someone shouted over the howling din.

But I was through talking. There was nothing left to say – to them or anyone else.

On the flight back to Tampa that day, I don't think Kate and I said a word to each other. We were both too wrapped up in our own gloom, and the terror of not knowing what lay ahead.

When we arrived back at the townhouse, we were greeted by Kate's parents, who had flown in to watch Jack for us while we traveled to Baltimore.

"How did the sentencing go?" they asked as we walked through the door.

"It couldn't have gone any worse," I said.

With that, I went up to our bedroom and closed the door. And I didn't come out for a long time.

18

Preparing for the Unthinkable

I spent the first few days back in Florida in an almost catatonic state.

For hours on end, I would hole up in the little office in my townhouse, brooding about all the ways my life had gone off the rails and second-guessing myself up for all that had happened.

Should I have watched the supplemental fund more closely? Should I have asked to see the books every day?

All those times I asked for the check at a restaurant, only to be told by a staff member "Don't worry about it, Commissioner" – should I have followed up to see how it was paid?

When I'd mentioned that I wanted to stock up on liquor at the house and a detective had appeared at the house with a case of wine or booze, should I have pushed some cash on him even after he said: "It's all taken care of, sir?"

In the days after the sentencing, I must have gone through the indictment a hundred times, trying to remember every trip I took, who I was with, why we went and what we spent. When I wasn't doing that, I was on the computer, researching everything I could about life in a federal prison.

The prison at Eglin Force Base was nicknamed "Club Fed" for the supposedly easy time inmates served there. But that didn't exactly have me breaking out the champagne and party hats.

For one thing, there was no guarantee that I'd be sent to Eglin. Secondly, as a former police officer – and a high-profile, big-city police *commissioner* – I would not be arriving as just any other prisoner.

Ex-cops have a notoriously tough time in prison, with any number of inmates eager to exact revenge on a member of the hated fraternity that put them behind bars. With that in mind, I hired a personal trainer to help me get in the best shape possible. All the eating and drinking I'd done to alleviate the stress of the last few months had taken their toll. I needed to get down to fighting weight – literally – once again.

Dealing with people was stressing me out, too. Whether it was at the gym or at a restaurant or a bar, I would invariably run into some insensitive asshole that had heard about my upcoming sentence and felt compelled to remind me of the horrors I might face.

"Oh, man, prison! That's gotta be terrible," one guy said to me. "Aren't you afraid of getting raped?"

Gee, the thought never occurred to me, I wanted to say. *But thanks for bringing it up. That makes me feel a lot better.*

I saw a psychiatrist for anti-anxiety meds and went into hyper husband-father mode to at least keep the family intact.

To keep life normal while I was gone – or at least as normal as possible – I sold my nice Volvo, gave the money to Kate and told her to use it for a down payment on a house.

There was no question that the entire ordeal was stressing my marriage big-time. I was a basket case and incredibly hard to live with. Even though I had cheated on her, I still loved Kate deeply. And she had been really strong the whole time, when a lot of women would have fallen apart.

Think about all she was dealing with: income gone, husband going to prison, a child who still needed to be raised with love and attention. And now she was living in yet another strange city thousands of miles from any family.

In another attempt at normalization, I also bought 26 little toys for Jack, along with the same number of cards and envelopes, which I filled out and addressed. Jack was five at the time, and the plan was that Kate would give him a toy each week and tell him Daddy had mailed them.

But the thought of leaving him soon was breaking my heart.

One night, as we sat watching a Spiderman animated movie on TV, Jack suddenly pointed at the screen and asked: "Why is Spiderman in jail?"

Say what?!

I had been lost in my usual morose thoughts, barely paying attention. But now I snapped out of it.

What's that?! Spiderman's in the slammer?

What do you say to a kid when he hits you with that one? With why a revered comic-book super-hero is suddenly shown slumped dejectedly behind bars?

"Well," I said, picking up on the story line, "sometimes bad people put good people in jail, Jack."

Yes, the irony was rich here. I had said this just to plant that tiny thought, that chip, in Jack's brain. Someday, I knew, we'd sit down and talk about everything that had happened to me while he was growing up. That's when I'd try to make him understand that the real dangerous people in this world don't always carry guns.

Sometimes they wear suits and ties and frozen smiles.

As crazy as it sounds, I also took to sleeping on the tile floor in my son's bathroom during this time. It was another way to be close to him in the days I had left at home. But I also wanted to get used to sleeping on hard, shitty surfaces, in case the accommodations in prison were as horrible as some had said.

Even when I wasn't obsessing about how depressing my life was now, I couldn't entirely escape it.

One day I went to lunch at a Bar Louie restaurant with my friend Debbie Kurtz. One of the TV's nearby was tuned to CNN. Seconds later I watched incredulously as a crawl at the bottom of the screen flashed by: "Former Maryland State Police Superintendent Edward T. Norris is scheduled to turn himself in soon to begin a six-month . . ."

"I can't fucking believe this!" I said. "I'm that interesting? I'm a national news story? Really?"

A week or so before my reporting date, the government made it official: I was to be incarcerated at Federal Prison Camp, Eglin in Fort Walton Beach, Florida. I didn't want my father or my wife to drive me; the long drive from Tampa would have been too hard on them, and way too emotional for all of us.

Instead, a couple of my old buddies from the NYPD, Rick Burnham and Joe Martinez, offered to fly down and drive me. They rented an SUV and we set out on the morning of July 20, the day before I was scheduled to turn myself in. The plan was to drive to someplace close to the prison and spend the night there, and then I'd report to the facility the next day.

Saying good-bye to my wife and son that morning tore me up inside. I tried to appear strong, smiling at Kate and telling her not to worry, that I'd be back soon and life would get going for us again. I hugged and kissed Jack and told him I had to go on a trip for work, but I'd be sending him something special in the mail each week.

I gave a jaunty wave and walked out. But as soon as the door closed behind me, I began to sob uncontrollably. The next thing I knew, I was doubled over, my whole body heaving as if I were having a convulsion. Thankfully, Rick and Joe made believe that they couldn't see me, giving me a moment's privacy and sparing me from feeling even more embarrassed.

We talked as we drove, but it was awkward for all three of us. They felt terrible for me, a good friend who had also been their boss and their leaders for years. Now, of course, I was relying on them to prop me up emotionally on this horrible journey.

In some ways, though, the trip came to resemble "The Last Detail," the bittersweet Jack Nicholson movie of the 70's. That was the one about two Navy men ordered to bring a young sailor to prison, only they decide to show the kid a good time on the way.

In a way, that's what happened on this trip. We checked into a motel near Eglin, had dinner at a steakhouse and then hit a strip club and an Irish bar as the long night devolved into a boozy blur of wine, bourbon and Manhattans.

Yet I was up early after a fitful few hours of sleep. Brutally hung over, I started banging on the doors of my buddies' rooms screaming: "Wake up! Wake up! Let's get this done! The quicker I get there, the quicker I get out!"

As Rick and Joe got themselves ready, I went back to my room and made a couple of calls to say good-bye.

The first was to Kate, who became so upset she had to put the phone down. We didn't talk long. The second was to Jayne Miller, the veteran investigative reporter for WBAL-TV in Baltimore and one of the few media people I trusted to get my story right.

"I'm checking into prison now," I told her. "You know I didn't do this, right?"

"Yeah, I know, babe," Jayne said in her gravelly voice, her words oddly comforting.

After that we drove over to the prison camp, on the sprawling Air Force base in Eglin, where we ended up at the wrong gate.

"Stay there," a voice on the intercom said. "A prison van will come pick you up."

People always want to know what was going through my head in the moments before surrendering my freedom. I was scared, sure. Afraid for my safety, of course. And I was sad to be leaving my wife and kid.

But the most powerful emotion I felt was basically no emotion at all.

I felt dead inside, like my soul had died. No joy, no hope, just . . . nothing.

When the prison van came to pick me up, Rick and Joe remained in the SUV and stared mournfully at me.

"Just fucking leave! I shouted. "I'm serious! Direct order! Don't look at me! You're just making this worse!"

Finally, the two drove away. Later, they would tell me they were so upset that they didn't say a word to each other for over an hour.

I climbed into the van and we drove slowly to the prison's processing center, where I got my first look at the place that would be my home for the next six months. Wearing a T-shirt, jeans and lace-up logger boots, I walked in carrying a bible and nothing else.

The bible was a gift from the Catholic priests at St. Jude Shrine in Baltimore. I am not a religious person, but I *am* spiritual. St. Jude, I knew, was the patron saint of lost causes.

As the doors clanged shut behind me, I wondered if I'd be calling upon him soon.

19

Locked Up

One of the first things they make you do upon reporting to federal prison is fill out a ton of paperwork, almost as if you're buying a car or applying for a mortgage.

They ask you the usual stuff: date of birth, Social Security number, occupation, etc. But from there the questions quickly get darker and more pointed.

They ask about any gang affiliations. They ask about any martial arts in which you're proficient. They ask about any tattoos you have. They ask about any training you had in the military.

Are you an expert in weapons? Explosives? Hand-to-hand combat?

And that's when it hits you: you're not filling out all these forms to buy a Hyundai Sonata. Or a nice Cape Cod on a quiet cul-de-sac somewhere.

No, you, my friend, are going to prison. And the hard-eyed people running it want to know just how much trouble you're capable of causing while you're their guest.

If there was any lingering doubt about your new life, it quickly disappears when they take your clothes and shoes and make you change into a snappy outfit of khaki shirt, khaki pants and slip-on sneakers. An ID tag is affixed to your shirt with your name and prison number. (Mine was 41115-037, which I'll remember for the rest of my life.)

Then they give you a bedroll and hand you over to a doctor for a cursory physical exam. Naturally, with my luck, the doc turned out to be a dick to the 10th power.

"What health issues are you concerned about?" he asked.

"Well," I said, "I'm having problems with anxiety."

"In prison, you're *supposed* to be anxious," he said.

Thanks, Doc. That's very helpful. Yes, very helpful indeed.

"OK, what else is on your mind?" he continued.

"Well, my weight has spiked," I said.

"OK, then stop eating," he said.

Right. Nice talking to you, Doc. It's been an absolute pleasure.

To my great relief, once I was escorted into the yard, the prison looked more like a college campus than the Big House. There were no fences, no razor wire. Instead, what you saw were a series of low-slung buildings and walkways bordered by grass and palm trees.

It wasn't exactly Club Fed – there weren't any marimba bands playing and bikini-clad waitresses serving frozen cocktails. But it sure didn't look like the photos I'd seen of Attica, either.

Inmates were hanging out everywhere, all of them checking out the new guy as I was led to my building. Instead of prison cells, Eglin featured an open-dormitory setting. Each building housed a couple hundred inmates, with bunk beds everywhere, similar to what you'd see in a military barracks.

When I finally reached my bed, a few of the prisoners came over and introduced themselves. One was a big old guy they called Goat Head.

Finally I asked him: "Why do they call you Goat Head? Your head's not that big."

He explained that when he first arrived at Eglin, they were hurrying him through the processing phase. To speed things along, this one red-neck guard with a thick Southern accent kept shouting what sounded like: "Go 'haid! Go 'haid!"

"Sir, why are you calling me Goat Head?" the confused newcomer asked. But somehow, the nickname stuck.

The other inmates began asking me where I was from and what I did on the outside. I had grown a mustache and beard and shaved my head to disguise myself as best I could. At first I told them I was a government consultant, which would have been partially true if I had landed a job working for Rudy Giuliani.

Hearing this, a thin, dark-haired man said: "Hey, can I talk to you for a second?"

When we were safely out of earshot, he said: "First of all, relax. There's not a lot of violence here. It's pretty laid back for a prison. Second of all, everybody knows who you are. We get newspapers, we watch TV. So we've been waiting for you to get here."

Oh. Hearing this, I chuckled to myself. *Guess I wasn't as slick as I thought.* Then I walked back inside and told them who I really was.

"Look, I know everyone in here is innocent," I said. "But I *really* am." And then I went into my whole sad story and how the feds had managed to put me behind bars for what essentially was a shitty little $9,000 loan.

The thin, dark-haired prisoner who had advised me to come clean would turn out to be Martin L. Grass, the former CEO of Rite Aid, who was serving an eight-year term for conspiring to inflate the value of his company.

But it turned out – big surprise! – that I wasn't the only one in there who'd been screwed over for patently unjust or obscure reasons.

One kid was doing federal time because he'd been busted for marijuana possession while driving through Fort Bragg, N.C. If he'd been popped anywhere outside of a military base, he would have gotten a slap on the wrist at worst. Another guy from Tennessee was in there for "misprision of felony" a little-known "crime" that involves knowing a felony has been committed and not reporting it to the police.

Eglin, I would learn, was mainly populated with drug offenders. Only 20 percent of the inmates had been convicted of so-called "white collar" crimes. The rest were people who had been caught up, in one form or another, in the drug trade.

But there could be no crime of violence in their past, which was one of the reasons disputes among the inmate population rarely rose above the level of occasional fistfights. To avoid those, there was plenty to keep the prisoners occupied: basketball courts, a soccer field used mainly by the Latino prisoners, a weight room, TV room and chapel.

There was even plenty of sex available if you wanted it. My new inmate pals showed me a sandy stretch of ground called Pinga Beach that abutted an inlet. Pinga, they noted helpfully, meant penis in Spanish. And Pinga Beach is where you could go at night to get a blowjob from prostitute prisoners, if you were so inclined.

As a new prisoner, I was assigned a job on a work crew cutting grass with a weed-whacker. Which was when I came face-to-face – literally – with my first dickhead cracker guard.

He was intent on being a hard-ass, laying down the law to a group of us newcomers to Federal Prison Camp, Eglin. In an icy, menacing voice right out of "Cool Hand Luke" or "The Shawshank Redemption," he began: "This isn't Club Fed anymore. There are rules here."

Suddenly he took a step forward, got right in my face and started screaming: "WE DON'T GIVE A SHIT WHERE YOU CAME FROM! WE DON'T GIVE A SHIT WHERE YOU'VE BEEN! THINGS ARE DIFFERENT HERE! WE RUN THIS PLACE, UNDERSTAND?"

When the rant was finally over and he walked away, I turned to another inmate and asked: ""What was *that* all about?"

The inmate shrugged. "He saw that Murder One haircut of yours," he explained.

Great. Apparently my shaved head made the guard think I was some bad-ass who'd been transferred from a hard-core prison to do my final bit at Eglin, where I'd surely attempt to have my way with everything.

As it turned out, though, the guard was a dick to everyone, not just me. Later that day, as our work crew sweltered under the broiling

Florida sun, he kept singing out: "NUTHIN' MAKES ME HAPPIER THAN SEEING GROWN MEN CUT GRASS IN 107-DEGREE WEATHER!"

When I wasn't working, I would often just lay in my bed with a stocking cap pulled low over my face and headphones on, listening to the radio. A lot of the inmates did this. There is very little privacy in prison, and this was a way to isolate yourself from your surroundings.

You didn't want to see what was going on, you didn't want to hear what was going on. You'd just sit there alone with your thoughts, brooding about how far you'd fallen, all the mistakes you made, all the people who'd screwed you over, how much you missed your family and what you planned to do with your godawful life when you got out.

Another way to lose yourself in prison was to read. During my six months behind bars, I would read 70 books. I read Tom Wolfe, Michael Crichton, everything Dan Brown wrote, including "The DaVinci Code."

I read the entire "Lonesome Dove" series by Larry McMurtry. I read philosophy books, obscure works of Russian literature like "The Master and Margarita" and anything else I could get my hands on.

Soon I fell in with a group of guys who would meet every day to smoke cigars and bullshit. One was Tyrone Marks, a drug dealer from New Orleans, who was about my age. He was well-respected in the prison camp and I was happy to befriend him, because if you were OK with him, you were left alone.

Another in the group was Dan Levitan, an investment banker from Fort Lauderdale. He was also an excellent chef who ran the prison kitchen. Soon, he asked me to come work there with him and watch his back, because disputes often flared up.

As I was to learn, the kitchen was the hub around which so much of prison commerce revolved. Inmates would steal things like fried chicken, steaks, peanut butter and potato chips and sell them for cash, drugs, cigarettes or anything else.

No wonder the guards searched you when you left the kitchen, although a lot of stuff still managed to walk out the door. The kitchen was like our own little stock exchange in terms of how many financial transactions it generated.

Another way to acquire things was to do jobs for others. Someone would do your laundry and you'd pay him in whatever the going currency was. At Eglin, it was cans of mackerel. Don't ask me why. I never saw anyone actually eat from the cans. But guys would have the cans stacked up by their bunks – that was their currency.

If you wanted your laundry done, for instance, it would cost you two cans of mackerel. A haircut, on the other hand, would cost you cigarettes. Why? 'Cause that's what the barber wanted instead of mackerel. Maybe he was sick to death of mackerel. That I don't know.

I'm telling you: banks could learn from these places. It was a beautiful system. Nobody's debts ever went unpaid, either.

Despite daily access to all that food, however, I actually lost 40 pounds fairly quickly. I'd walk for miles every day with my cigar smoker friends. I also had Kate send me the Weight Watcher's points book and I'd log everything I ate, sticking with lots of protein and vegetables.

Ironically enough, Eglin was also the most polite place you could ever imagine. People held doors for each other. They said "Good morning" and "How are you?" when they passed on the walkways.

They did this because everyone was angry and somewhat dangerous in their own way. Everyone was operating on a really short fuse. And no one wanted to be the guy who disrespected someone with some stupid slight and ignited an incident that could have easily been prevented with common courtesy.

Yet despite this veneer of politeness, you never forgot where you were. Even a minimum-security camp like Eglin had its prison rituals. One mandated that you knocked twice on the table before getting up after a meal, the traditional signal that you weren't rising suddenly to stick a knife in someone.

Again, this wasn't "Escape From Alcatraz." But it wasn't "Hogan's Heroes, either." Life at Eglin wasn't brutally harsh. But it wasn't a cake-walk, either.

The central fact of your existence was this: you had no freedom. All you had were people telling you what to do, when to go to bed, when to wake up, what to wear, where to work, etc. You were given 300 minutes on the prison telephone each month, which works out to about 10 per day, if you were good. If you weren't, sorry, no phone privileges.

All calls were monitored, too. And when the recipient of your call first answered, the first thing they heard was this cheery message: "This call is being made at the United States Penitentiary, Eglin . . ."

On the other hand, I must have been the only inmate at Eglin who hadn't somehow smuggled in a cell phone. At night, after lights out at 10 p.m., you'd seen the glow of cell phones winking on under blankets all over the room.

But God help you if you ever got caught with a cell phone. In prison, it was like having a gun. The penalty was severe, because inmates could order hits on their rivals and continue to run their criminal enterprises with a contraband cell phone.

Eventually, unless you were the most pissed-off, rebellious inmate in the whole world, you settled into the mind-numbing routine of prison life. You were up early because breakfast was served early – I'd be up at 5:30 every morning because chow was at 6. Then you headed off to your job for the rest of the day.

A really weird part of life in prison is that inmates are counted all the time. At certain times of the day, you were required to stand by your bunk or work place and be counted, which was supposed to ensure that no one had escaped. (A 4 p.m. count, I was told, takes place at nearly every prison in the country.)

It was a de-humanizing and demeaning ritual. But like everything else, you eventually got used to it.

I had been at Eglin a little less than two months when we were suddenly ordered to appear in the cafeteria at 5 p.m. that day.

"Bring your toothbrush and a book," we were told, "and nothing else."

The explanation turned out to be this: two hurricanes had already hit the Panhandle, causing varying degrees of damage. And now, with another powerful storm in Hurricane Ivan on the way, we were being evacuated to another prison, although the exact location was still hush-hush for security reasons.

We were loaded onto buses and we drove for many hours, eventually passing through flatlands with cotton fields as far as the eye could see. Only then were we told our destination: Yazoo City, Mississippi and a new medium-security prison that was actually still under construction.

This would turn out to be a fresh hell of unparalleled dimensions.

For one thing, when we finally arrived at the prison, we discovered there were no beds. No kitchen facilities. No phones. No nothing. Construction workers were actually still on site. It was a giant, half-finished concrete slab, for all intents and purposes.

We were told to pair up and find a cell. Tyrone Marks and I found one on the first floor, and that would turn out to be our new home for the next month or so.

Later that night, two huge box trucks filled with mattresses and bedrolls rumbled up to the prison. This set off a frenzied scene right out of "Lord of the Flies" as hundreds of wild-eyed inmates, under the harsh glare of the prison spotlights, fought each other to get a mattress before the supply ran out.

The prison would prove to be an absolutely miserable place. It made Eglin look like the Ritz Carlton. The cells were unbearably hot and humid and infested with the biggest black bugs any of us had ever seen.

Even though our cells were unlocked during the day, the prison was run like a maximum-security facility. There was razor wire everywhere. We were confined to our cellblock "pods" 23 hours a day and allowed to exercise in the yard for an hour. Also, the prison practiced "controlled movements," meaning prisoners could not walk around freely and were escorted to other areas of the facility only at designated times.

Since there were no phones, there were no phone privileges. This meant our families didn't even know where we were or what had happened to us in the wake of the powerful hurricane that had just roared through the Florida Panhandle.

Eventually we were allowed to call our loved ones and mail began trickling in. But by this time, word came down that we were about to be moved again. The Yazoo prison was simply not ready to adequately house inmates for any length of time without triggering a full-scale riot.

Lists were quickly posted with each prisoner's name and the new facility to which he'd be transferred. The news for me was not good: I was bound for the satellite prison camp at the U.S. Penitentiary, Atlanta.

The word was that Atlanta was a horrible place, an aging facility ringed by razor wire in the middle of the city, with a long history of violence.

Terrific, I told myself. *The ol' Eddie Norris luck is still going strong.*

20

Welcome to the Hole

The bus ride to Atlanta seemed endless as we wound our way through the red-clay fields of Mississippi, dropped a load of prisoners off at the Talladega federal prison in Alabama and continued on into Georgia.

There were 22 of us left on the bus, including a group of my original friends from Eglin, as we rolled on. I grew more and more apprehensive the closer we got to the city.

"Man, there are a lot of bad people in this place we're going to," I said at one point to Dan Levitan. "What if they find out I was a cop?"

Dan nodded thoughtfully. Then he stood and addressed the rest of the guys.

"Listen," he said, "when we get to Atlanta, nobody gives up Eddie's occupation. Everybody got that? It's important."

It was a wonderful gesture. To this day, I get teary-eyed just thinking about it.

People have all these pre-formed opinions of the men and women who are incarcerated. Sure, our prisons are filled with dangerous scumbags who would stab you in the back and take your money in a heartbeat. But there are lots of good people in there, too, good people who made a mistake – or two or three – and are paying for it, sometimes for the rest of their lives.

Anyway, the bottom line was this: I would be imprisoned in

Atlanta for three long months, three of the longest months of my life. Yet during those three months, not one of the 22 men on that bus would breathe a word about me being a cop.

Which is amazing. I can't imagine 22 people from *any* walk of life – police officers, radio talk show hosts, plumbers, lawyers, you name it – keeping a secret for that long.

The U.S. Penitentiary, Atlanta was a medium-security facility with high gray walls, forbidding guard towers and a shadowy glow that made it look like a castle out of a Frankenstein movie.

The satellite prison camp for minimum-security prisoners was next door. But as the bus inched its way down the narrow entrance ramp and the gates swung shut behind us, it was clear that we'd be spending at least the first night in the Big House itself.

It was well after dark when we arrived. We were strip-searched, given new (and horribly mismatched) prison clothes and photographed. Once again, whole forests had been destroyed for the amount of paperwork we were required to fill out during processing.

The kitchen was closed, so we were given Lunchables, the pre-packaged meals of meats, cheeses and crackers busy parents pack for their kids' school lunches. Standing in line with my newly-issued pillow and blanket, I looked down at the picture of Spiderman on the Lunchables box and almost burst into tears.

Lunchables, you see, were what I used to pack for Jack every day for school. But this was definitely not the time for anyone to see me all weepy. Because moments later we were led into the disciplinary segregation unit – the infamous Atlanta "Hole" – and confronted with a scene right out of a San Quentin riot documentary.

As we walked through a narrow corridor, inmates on both sides of us began banging on their cell doors and screaming through the food ports: "GET OUT OF HERE, YOU MOTHERFUCKERS! WE DON'T WANT YOU IN HERE!"

Dan had gone through this before, during an earlier stretch of his incarceration. Amid the horrible clanging din and the shouted oaths, he nodded knowingly at me.

"That's why I didn't tell you earlier what this place is like," he said. "I couldn't really describe it. And I didn't want to freak you out."

It turned out that the prison was already so over-crowded that the last thing these wild-eyed cons in the "Hole" wanted were more bodies crammed into their cells. Which was exactly what was happening: five or six inmates were now being shoe-horned into cells, leading to the altogether pleasant prospect of guys sleeping next to toilets and under sinks.

I was lucky – I ended up in a cell with only two other prisoners, who regarded me warily from their bunk beds. This will surely shock you, but neither of these large, heavily-tattooed gentlemen jumped up to give me a warm handshake or a welcoming hug.

After I exchanged muttered greetings and threw my blanket and pillow on the floor, they tossed me what turned out to be a tube of rolled-up newspaper wrapped in tape.

"Hold that roll under the door with your feet," one said. "It'll keep the rats out."

Rats?!

We gotta deal with rats now?

With that, the two turned away from me. Seconds later, the soft glow of a meth pipe illuminated the cell and two were taking hits off it and blowing the smoke into a vent, beaming up happily to another planet, or maybe an entirely new solar system.

And *that's* when I finally lost it.

Within seconds, a huge wave of self-pity seemed to crash over me, and I found myself laughing hysterically at the absurd depths into which I had fallen.

My God, what had happened?

Just one year earlier, I'd been the head of one of the largest state police agencies in the country! Before that I'd been the highly-regarded police commissioner who had done so much to make Baltimore safer!

Now here I was in the "Hole," clad in a sad clown costume of mismatched prison garb, lying on a dirty cellblock floor with my feet pressing a makeshift rat barrier against the steel bars while my cellies partied on, oblivious to my growing panic.

I stopped laughing soon enough; lurching right up to the brink of madness tends to be sobering after a few minutes. But all night long, the same thought looped over and over in my head:

How the fuck did they ever get away with this?

It was the lowest point of my life, by far. All I could see was darkness and despair, and my future going down the drain.

In the morning, we were marched down to the Atlanta Satellite Prison Camp, re-processed again for what seemed like the 100th time, and given another drab uniform of green pants and shirts.

Compared to leafy and open Eglin, the Atlanta camp was a bleak, forlorn-looking place. While it was still technically considered dormitory housing, we'd be living in a huge concrete enclosure divided into little cubicles with two beds each, giving it all the cozy ambience of a public bathhouse.

They stuck me in a cubicle with a guy named Eddie, a lean, muscular, dark-skinned Floridian who was serving a heavy sentence for drug dealing. When the older guys heard who my new roomie was, they shook their heads and laughed. Because Eddie, it turned out, was a genuine, 100 percent character.

For one thing, Eddie wasn't his real name, although that's what everyone called him. Secondly, he was always high. (Shocked that drugs are so widely available in a federal lock-up? Don't be. It's a fact of life.) He wore sunglasses day or night and talked nonsense to himself and never slept. Finally, Eddie had this singular trait: he wore three baseball caps – simultaneously! – each with the brim set at a different angle, the whole teetering mess perched on a doo-rag.

As it happened, Eddie was also the "Radar" O'Reilly of the camp. Just like the little hyper-active character on the old M*A*S*H TV series who seemed to be everywhere at once, Eddie could get you whatever you wanted, from God knows where.

The first time I met him, he asked if I wanted new Timberlands to replace the worn boots I was wearing.

"No," I said, "I'm good."

"OK then," he said with a shrug, and let the matter drop.

But the more you were around Eddie, the more you were convinced he could smuggle in anything from a case of vintage wine to a John Deere tractor – all for a price, of course.

He was my roomie for my whole stint in Atlanta. And we got along just fine after I laid down one important ground rule.

"Look, you can take whatever you want from my stuff," I told hm. "Just don't steal it. If you need it, just take it. And *tell* me you took it."

As they had at Eglin, random acts of kindness occasionally broke out in Atlanta. This was always amazing to me. You were in prison, you felt like shit, your whole life was fucked up. And yet there was this sense that you needed to help the other guy, both to reinforce your own humanity and because he might return the favor someday.

Case in point: when I first got there, I hadn't shaved in weeks, due to the fact there had been no commissary at Yazoo City to buy toiletries. I had a long beard and my hair had grown out, to the point where I was looking more and more like either Charlie Manson or the Unabomber, take your pick.

One day this Cuban kid came up and asked if I wanted a haircut.

"Sure," I said. "I'd love one. But I can't pay you right now."

"Don't worry about it," he said. And with that, he sat me down and shaved my head clean before trimming my beard with a set of clippers. It wasn't until weeks later that I could pay him back with fried chicken smuggled out of the kitchen.

(Yes, I was again working there with Dan Levitan. Dan's rep as a terrific chef was well-known by the Atlanta prison officials, and they were delighted when he offered his services. It was like a baseball team suddenly hearing that the top free agent on the market wanted to play for them.)

Life went on, but overall it was an edgier existence than at Eglin or Yazoo City. There were some seriously bad people in this camp, as we were to discover.

One inmate had his face slashed during an argument over a TV show. Not long after that, a prisoner standing next to me during a controlled movement began muttering darkly about how much he hated the camp and how much he wanted to go back up the hill to the Big House.

"I can't take this place anymore," he kept mumbling. "I'm going to knock somebody out . . ."

Sure enough, the moment they released us to walk, he clocked another inmate – laid him out cold. For this he was promptly taken away and locked up, presumably in the same cramped, squalid piece of steel-bar real estate he seemed to miss so much.

No, you definitely didn't want to screw around with anyone in this place. Stories abounded about inmates beating each other with soap bars or combination locks stuffed into socks, or heating baby oil in a microwave to throw in an enemy's face.

The inmate who disregarded – or failed to learn – the unspoken rules of the Atlanta prison camp could find himself in a whole lot of hurt.

One day not long after I arrived, for instance, I found myself showering next to this black prisoner. He was very squared-away guy – he might have been ex-military – and always had his beard neatly trimmed, his prison uniform neatly pressed and his shoes shined.

He was also a guy who never cracked a smile, never interacted with anyone and appeared ready and eager to kill someone over the slightest provocation.

Anyway, there were no shower stalls in the camp, only a common area with shower heads installed side by side and plastic curtains you could pull across for privacy. When we were both through showering that day, the black guy discreetly took me aside.

"Look," he said, "I know you don't know what's going on in here yet. But you *never* shower next to anyone."

Huh?

No one, he went on to explain, wanted someone's dirty shower water splashing on them. Therefore you always left a space between you and the other guy in the showers.

It was a valuable lesson learned, and maybe it spared me from getting my ass kicked – or worse somewhere down the line.

Annoying behavior that would simply be ignored or laughed off in the outside world could also get you hurt in Atlanta.

An old Southern con man named Jimmy was a prime example of that. Jimmy was a rumpled sad sack with a perpetually runny nose who was oblivious to social cues, including the possibility that his behavior was pissing people off.

He would do stupid shit like walk all over the floors after the older cons had just waxed them, which would just drive them crazy. But Jimmy's most maddening trait was this: he would never, ever shut up.

Ever.

Once, just before Christmas that year, we were in a controlled movement to go somewhere and Jimmy happened to be next to me.

It was an awfully sad time for me. I missed my wife and kid terribly and the thought of spending the holidays without them was killing me. Now, standing in this sweaty, surly, heaving mass of prisoners, I just wanted to quietly wallow in my misery.

I wanted to be left alone.

But Jimmy wouldn't let me. No, Jimmy wouldn't stop talking.

I asked him nicely to be quiet. He kept jabbering. I asked him again in my most patient and respectful tone. Same thing: he just kept blabbing.

Finally, on the verge of losing it, I barked: "If you don't shut the fuck up, I'm going to go punch the guard and get myself thrown in the Hole, just to get away from you!"

An older black inmate – I'd later learn he was from Harlem – overheard what I said and laughed.

"You must be from New York!" he said. "Only New Yorkers talk like that."

But later, the same inmate would say of Jimmy: "That mother-fucker's gonna get hurt. We tolerate a lot of his shit 'cause he's crazy and we know he's old. But he better watch himself."

No, in prison, you couldn't always walk away from someone who was irritating the crap out of you, which led to an ever-present under-current of tension.

Despite the crowded conditions, intense loneliness was another condition most of us wrestled with in Atlanta.

No one had been able to visit me when we were locked up in Yazoo City, of course. Now, only the visits from my wife, my father and some of my old friends from the NYPD and Baltimore, helped alleviate the gloom.

The visits with Kate, though, could also be singularly humiliating experiences. The first time she came to see me, she was told her skirt was too short, which was against prison regulations. This meant she had to go to a mall to buy a pair of jeans before the let her in.

There was nothing private or intimate about these visits, either. There were guards all around the room, for one thing. You could touch your wife or girlfriend, but the guards watched carefully for any sexual contact. No one was grabbing any pussy or getting a handjob under the table, that's for sure.

Maybe what was most demeaning was that you were still counted during these visits. When it was time for the 10 a.m. count, for instance, you had to stand, line up and be counted off – all while your wife or girlfriend took in the whole dreary ritual.

Fortunately, only twice in Atlanta was my identity as a former cop nearly compromised – and both times I lucked out.

Once, I was walking by the TV room and saw, to my horror, my face suddenly appear on the screen.

What the hell?

It turned out the TV was tuned to ESPN, which was showing a re-run of the Leopard Games, the police Olympics where officers compete in running, shooting, traversing an obstacle course and other events.

Baltimore had hosted the games the year before and now ESPN was running an old clip of me being interviewed in full Maryland State Police uniform, including my Stetson hat.

Seeing this, I froze and mouthed a silent prayer: *Please don't let anyone recognize me! Please don't let my name flash up on that screen!*

Thankfully, the clip ended quickly and no one in the TV room said anything. It helped that my Stetson was pulled low over my eyes in the interview. What helped even more was that I'd been clean-shaven in that clip, whereas I looked like a biker gang leader now with a shaved head and ZZ Top beard.

The other time I almost got burned was while a guard was escorting me and another inmate to another part of the prison.

Somehow, the conversation between the guard and this other con turned to the types of surveillance tools used by law enforcement officials.

I was barely listening, until out of the blue, the guard turned to me and said: "Hey, *you* know. *You* were a cop. Tell him about the surveillance stuff . . ."

Even though my insides were churning, I managed to keep my voice calm.

"I don't know what you're talking about," I said, shooting the guard a dagger look that said: *You dumb motherfucker! Never do that to me again!*

In early December, while I was eating lunch in the dining room, one of the kitchen workers approached carrying a newspaper.

He stabbed a beefy finger at a small article on the front page and said: "Hey, isn't this the guy who did you?"

And there it was: Maryland U.S. Attorney Thomas M. DiBiagio, the man who had railroaded my conviction and ruined my life, was resigning from office under heavy criticism. Months earlier, the *Baltimore Sun* had published damaging emails that DiBiagio had written to his staff, urging them to make "front-page" indictments in political corruption cases.

The U.S. Justice Department had publicly reprimanded DiBiagio, and the *Sun* reported that in an internal review, prosecutors under the U.S. Attorney had said their boss should be removed from office. Well, he was gone now.

The news didn't totally shock me – I had been aware that Justice seemed unhappy with the over-zealousness of their top Maryland prosecutor. It gave me a measure of satisfaction, too. Maybe now people would see how dangerous a ruthless prosecutor out to grab headlines and further his career could be.

The news of his downfall also gave me a tiny glimmer of hope that someday I could be vindicated, even after my career had been de-railed and my life shattered.

Finally, in January of 2005, after what seemed like a lifetime, the day of my release was at hand.

Prison tradition dictates that all your buddies cook you a nice meal on the day before you get out. So some 10 of the guys with whom I played cards and bocce and smoked cigars chipped in a few bucks and bought food from the commissary, and this old Italian guy named Alfredo whipped up a pretty decent pasta meal with fish.

Naturally, though, the federal government found one last way to torture me.

In the middle of the meal, I was told to go see the camp administrator. When I got to his office, he leaned back in his chair and stared at me.

"The news media is here," he said. "And the word has gotten around that they're here for you."

Unbeknownst to me, reporters Richard Sher from WJZ-TV and Jayne Miller from WBAL-TV had flown down from Baltimore to interview me upon my release.

"So we're going to put you up in disciplinary segregation for your own protection," the administrator continued, "in case anyone finds out you're a cop and tries to attack you."

I couldn't believe my ears! They were putting me back in the Hole?! On my last night in this godforsaken place? So that I couldn't even say good-bye to anyone? Really?

"Look," I said, "I've been here for months and pretty much gotten along with everyone. I've had no problems in here. Don't do this to me."

But his mind was made up. I could see by his expression that pleading my case any further was just a waste of breath.

"No," he said, "the guards will come and get you soon and take you up the hill."

When I got back to the dorm, some of my buddies were looking at me strangely. Beyond the fence, they could see the street where a couple of satellite trucks were parked and TV cameras were already set up.

Finally this old Cuban motorcycle gangster, a dead ringer for Fred Flintstone with a thick body and head, turned to me and said: "Dude, who the fuck *are* you?"

My buddies who had been with me at Eglin knew who I was, of course. But the others in the room were stunned when I revealed my identity. Then, after a moment or two, everyone cracked up.

"No! We've been hanging out with the head of the Maryland State Police?!" someone cried.

"Yes," I said, laughing along with them. "Yes, you have."

As promised, a couple of guards appeared not long after to take me up the hill to the disciplinary segregation until. But when I groused about going, they looked at each other and shrugged.

"Oh, you don't want to go?" one said. "All right, I'm a big fan of 'The Wire.' Don't worry about it. You can stay here."

It was another act of kindness from another unexpected quarter in this hard place, another simple gesture of humanity for which I'll be eternally grateful.

Around 9 the next morning, right after breakfast, they processed me out. As I was leaving, a light-skinned black guy dressed in a suit and tie and looking like a buttoned-down professional, was turning himself in.

He was scared shitless, shaking all over and on the verge of tears. A guard kept trying to calm him.

"Dude, don't worry about it," the guard said. "It's not as bad as you think."

"He's right," I said, overhearing the conversation.

"But I didn't *do* anything!" the guy wailed.

The guard shook his head wearily and sighed.

"It's just a game," he said softly. "They do this to people all the time. Just come in and do your time."

To me, it yet another sad commentary on the whole system – this time from someone on the inside. And it reinforced what I'd thought all along: that so many of these incarcerations were not only unjust, but done for the most ridiculous of reasons, destroying families and ruining lives in the process.

Yes, that poor bastard would have to suck it up and do his time. But my time at three different federal prisons, thank God, was over.

My buddies walked me to the main gate. I gave my watch to one of them and my toilet kit to Dan, with instructions to give it to a new inmate who might need it. We said our good-byes with hurried hugs and a tinge of sadness; some of those guys, I knew, would remain there for many more years..

Through the fence, I could see Kate out in the parking lot, smiling and waving and looking drop-dead gorgeous, as always. Then I walked out and gave her a big hug and a kiss. It was January 19, 2005, a sunny and cold morning in Atlanta, and I was a free man for the first time in six months.

Jayne Miller and Richard Sher and their camera crews were across the street to greet me, too.

"When Ed came out," Jayne would later tell a reporter, "I thought: he lost weight! He was smaller! Here was the guy who was the police commissioner for two or three years and, yeah, it was kind of a stark difference to see him kind of stripped of all that authority.

"Prison's humbling. And he was definitely humbled. But he still had that confidence about him when he came out. He still had that swagger."

From there, we all drove to a nearby motel, where Jayne and Richard had rented a room so they could each interview me separately.

We kept the interviews short. They peppered me with questions about what life was like in prison and how did it feel to be out.

It felt *weird* to be out – that was the dominant feeling. But I was incredibly happy and excited, too. Yet all my emotions were still raw, and I broke down when one of them asked: "Do you still think you got screwed?"

"They shouldn't be able to this to people!" I said, the tears flowing freely now. "They just *shouldn't*."

From there, Kate and I drove to a hotel downtown. My father and my good friend Rick Burnham had flown down from New York to celebrate with us, and the two had already checked in. When Kate and I got to our room, she informed me we were all going to lunch at a fancy restaurant in Atlanta's posh Buckhead section.

"Uh, that might have to wait," I said, pushing Kate gently onto the bed.

(Hey, am I smooth or what? Fine, *you* try being the model of restraint after six months in the slammer.)

The meal that afternoon at the award-winning Restaurant Eugene was wonderful: steak, a few Manhattans and a lot of laughs. But nagging at me in the back of my mind was one of the questions Jayne and Richard had asked, namely: "What will you do now?"

The truth was, I had no idea.

I was 44 years old, with not a clue about what lay ahead.

And this terrified me more than anything else.

21

Stranger in an Even Stranger Land

Getting out was a bitch. The first few days were really hard – and *really* weird. It sounds counter-intuitive, but life seemed much tougher on the outside.

Think about it: when you're behind the fence, as they say, so is everybody else. So many of the other cons were angry men locked up for a long time, with far worse problems than I had. But there was a kind of commonality to our lives, too.

When you're locked up, you're all wearing the same drab clothes and eating the same shitty food. You're all not having sex, you all haven't seen your families and you're all living this miserable life.

But you're all living it *together.*

When you get out, now you're viewed as a pariah. You might as well walk around with a big scarlet letter on your forehead. "E" for ex-con, maybe. Because that's how people perceive you.

Maybe it sounds overly-dramatic, but it's not: your life is forever changed after a stretch behind bars. In the days and weeks after my release, that point was driven home to me constantly.

When Kate and I drove back to Tampa, I walked into a house I had never seen before and was greeted with a quizzical stare from a cute little five-year-old boy. I gave Jack a long hug, but the reconnection felt awkward.

He hadn't seen me in six months. Did he even recognize me? I wasn't completely sure. In prison, I would get him on the phone occasionally to say hi. But like most five-year-olds, he mainly wanted to watch cartoons rather than have a long, boring talk with his dad.

Now Dad was back home. And Jack was giving me these skeptical side-long glances that said: *So . . . you gonna be sticking around for a while this time?*

Here's another thing: you don't recognize how institutionalized you've become when you first get out of prison. And I had only been in for a very short time. I can't imagine how people who have been incarcerated for 15 years feel when they get out.

For some of those guys, when they're released, the world must feel like a completely different place. Now people are walking around with cell phones and iPads and watches that monitor sleep patterns and cardiovascular efficiency. Cars look different, fashion is different . . . it must feel like a parallel universe.

Even for a short-timer like me, the transition back to normal life was jolting. For days after I got out, I continued to walk around the house with my ski cap pulled low and headphones on, just the way I had behind the fence.

The weirdness of my new life really hit home when Kate asked me to help her cook dinner one night.

Understand, I'm not one of those guys who likes to do this. You know those guys you see on the TV commercials, the ones who are always smiling and sipping wine and having a great time cooking steamed vegetables or mixing a world-class salad with their wives?

I'm *not* that guy. Not even close.

But I agreed to help her, mainly because I was trying to be as nice and accommodating as possible after all the shit I'd put her through.

"How about peeling some onions?" she asked.

Onions? Sure. I could do that.

So I started peeling. And I kept peeling and peeling. And I didn't *stop* peeling until I had peeled the entire bag of onions.

When she finally looked up and noticed what I'd done, she gasped.

"What the hell are you *doing?*" she cried.

What?! I didn't know what she was talking about. I looked down at the empty bag for a moment. Then it hit me: I'd peeled enough onions to feed the Tampa Bay Buccaneers.

"I'm sorry!" I said. "It's just . . . I'm used to peeling 50 pounds of onions at a time! That's all I did inside!"

We both cracked up at the absurdity of the whole thing. Sitting in the next room, Jack had to be wondering what his mom and the weird dad with the ski cap and headphones were cackling about.

There weren't too many laughs a few days later, though, when a federal probation officer showed up to fit me with an ankle monitor. This was the official beginning of my six months of house arrest.

After a thorough search of my home for any weapons, ammunition and drugs, the officer clamped the ankle bracelet on me. It looked like a big dive watch and was synced to a box that would sound an alarm if I strayed too far from the house.

I was permitted to leave for only three reasons: to go to church, look for a job and work out at a gym. Now imagine what it was like trying to hide the ankle bracelet in a hot, humid part of the country like Tampa, where everyone wears shorts. (I ended up covering it with a plastic ankle brace.)

Trust me, all of these things take a terrible toll on your dignity and self-respect.

Here I had held a number of powerful law enforcement jobs and been an esteemed member of the community for many years. Now I was subjected to any number of horrible rules and indignities as an ex-con.

My probation officer turned out to be a total pro and was never demeaning in any way. But the cop in me noticed that when he visited my house, he always made it a point to park in my driveway in a way that blocked in my car.

Probation officers do this to ensure that no one tries to make a quick getaway during their visit, which often happens. If, for instance, an ex-con is doing drugs or has drugs in the house when the officer pulls up, he's likely to freak out and try to bolt so he's not violated.

But it really hurt to see the officer do this blocking maneuver on me.

Wow, I thought, *this is how I'm viewed now. This is who I am. I'm just another unpredictable bad guy who might cause trouble.*

If all of that wasn't degrading enough, looking for a job as a convicted felon multiplied the humiliation factor by a thousand.

Seeking employment, by the way, isn't something that's simply *suggested* by your friendly neighborhood federal probation agency. No, you're *mandated* to do it upon your release from prison. You must go out every day and document your search for work. And once a month you are required to document how much money you made, how much you have in your checking and savings account, and whether you have acquired any storage space – including a post office box and safe deposit box – that could be used to hide anything.

So here I was, the former boy wonder of the NYPD, the former police commissioner of Baltimore, the former superintendent of the Maryland State Police, applying for all these menial jobs, most of which were meant for kids.

I hit every fast-food place you could imagine: McDonald's, Chick-fil-A, Krispy Kreme, etc. I applied at Harley-Davidson, hoping my knowledge and passion for motorcycles might be an in. I loved to work out, so I applied to every gym in Tampa. And I loved nice clothes, so I hit every men's store in the city, too.

On most of the applications, one question stood out as if flashing in neon on the page: have you ever been convicted of a felony? Of course there was only one way for me to answer.

Filling out the ubiquitous "Employment History" section was even more depressing. How was that going to look? *Yes, even though I was once one of America's top cops, I am now eager to sell jelly doughnuts and watery coffee to surly office workers at your fine establishment! No, really I am!*

Finally, after looking and looking for work, I stumbled into Caswell-Massey at Tampa's upscale International Plaza and Bay Street mall. Caswell-Massey was a high-end perfumery. The company had been in business for hundreds of years; one of its colognes was said to have been a favorite of President George Washington.

That was pretty cool to know. But this was even better: the application didn't ask about prior convictions. So I filled it out.

And somehow I got hired!

The woman who ran the store was really sweet to me, too. I ended up selling men's and women's products and did so well that eventually I was given the keys to the place and allowed to open in the mornings.

As dispiriting as the rest of my life was, I actually enjoyed the job. It felt good to be useful again. And being able to leave the house every day was a godsend.

Yet less than six weeks later, I got a call at home one day from the store manager. The tone of her voice was funereal.

"I don't even know how to say this," she began. "But I have bad news."

Right away, I knew what was coming.

Sure enough, she said someone had called Caswell-Massey's corporate headquarters and told them who I was, and about my past life. Corporate had called the store manager right away and told her to fire me, on the grounds that I had lied about my background on my application.

This was completely untrue. While I had never been asked about a prior conviction, I had noted that I was a retired police officer. But that didn't matter now. The decision had been made. I was history at Caswell-Massey.

"I'm really sorry," the store manager told me. "I know you didn't lie."

"OK," I said, "should I bring my keys in?"

"You don't have to," she said. "They already made me change the locks."

As the realization of what had happened sunk in – *I just got fired from a minimum wage job! At the mall!* – I was devastated.

You wonder why so many ex-cons go back to their criminal behavior? The answer's simple. They have to make money somehow! Now here I was, jobless, broke and required to go back to Baltimore in a few weeks to start my community service.

Which was when the bad luck that had dogged me for so long finally began to turn.

Within days of my perfumery career coming to an abrupt halt, I got a call from Andy Graham, my lawyer. He had just heard from Bob Phillips of CBS Radio in Baltimore.

Phillips had told him that a local station, WQSR, had just polled its listeners, asking this question: "Now that you know the prosecutor in his case was fired for essentially targeting high-profile cases, would you want Ed Norris back as police commissioner?"

The response was over-whelming: some 90 percent of the respondents said yes. Apparently, I was still wildly popular with a large swath of Baltimoreans. Who knew? Now Phillips wanted to know if I'd be interested in doing some sort of call-in talk show with radio station WHFS, providing the details could be worked out.

So what did I do?

Did I leap at this incredibly fortuitous lifeline being thrown to a down-and-out ex-con who'd just been fired from the mall and was drowning in debt?

Did I shout: "HELL, YEAH, ANDY! ASK 'EM WHERE DO I SIGN?"

No, I didn't. At least not right away.

See, I was still white-hot angry at the world. I especially hated everyone and everything that had to do with Baltimore. In fact, I felt so betrayed by the city that I had even gotten rid of all my Ravens and Orioles gear. (Just *looking* at them practically brought on PTSD.)

So, no, the last thing I wanted to do was talk about my train-wreck of a life and how it went off the rails – especially on a stupid radio show with producers and on-air talent I didn't even know. Or trust.

No thanks, I told Andy. Not interested.

Except . . . then I *was* interested.

After a few hours of soul-searching, I realized I was being stupid. *Heck,* I thought, *I'm not doing anything else. No one wants to hire me down here. And God knows I need the money.*

So I called Andy back. He must have thought I was nuts.

"OK," I said, "tell them I'm interested."

The whole thing seemed ludicrous on the face of it. Someone would actually *pay* me to be on the radio? And people would tune in to listen to what I had to say?

What a concept!

The truth was, I didn't know what kind of fresh hell I was getting myself into.

But I knew this: it couldn't be worse than the hell I was already in.

22

Phoenix Rising

The ground rules for my radio segment were simple: I'd call in at noon each day to talk about my dumpster fire of a life and also offer thoughtful and provocative opinions (he said modestly) on the news of the day in Baltimore and everywhere else.

At least that was the plan.

The station had its affiliate engineers in Tampa come to my house and install an ISDN line, which improves the quality of phone conversations. And the next thing I knew, I was a regular on "Out to Lunch" with co-hosts Chad Dukes and Oscar "The Big O" Santana, doing the show from my little office in the back of my 1,050-square-foot house while my crazy Giant Schnauzer, Max, barked wildly in the background.

Even though most of the callers seemed supportive of having me on the air, part of the shtick was for me to engage with the ones bent on tearing me a new one.

Some of them were vicious bastards, too.

Over and over again, the haters would call in to rant that I was a thief, a crook and a despicable human being who should never be allowed to work again.

It was exhausting to keep interacting with these people. But somehow I did. What else did I have going on? We talked about politics, crime, music, sports, my story, Baltimore stuff – the show had no grid whatsoever.

My job was to chime in and be outrageous, which was easy enough. Plus they were paying me $500 a month. Which meant I was employed – I was still doing "The Wire," too – so it kept the feds off my back.

Yet at the same time, something else had me totally freaked out and paranoid for weeks: my ankle bracelet kept going off, even when I was sitting in the house. Which meant I was getting calls at all hours of the night and day from the probation service charged with monitoring that I was home.

"Yes, I'm right here!" I'd say each time they called. "I don't know why this is happening! I haven't moved!"

Naturally, the probation people – who don't exactly deal with choir boys on a regular basis – were suspicious.

"Well, did you go outside?" they would demand. "Did you go to the store?"

"NO!" I'd shout over and over again. "I HAVEN'T LEFT THE HOUSE!"

The more it happened, the more nuts I became, cursing and raging that the government was doing this on purpose just to fuck with me. I was driving Kate crazy with my paranoia, too. Finally we found out, to my immense relief, that it was the radio equipment that was somehow triggering the bracelet alarm. A technical adjustment quickly fixed the problem.

Somehow, my little segment on "Out to Lunch" became so popular I was offered a one-year contract to do a three-hour daily show called – ta-daa! – "The Ed Norris Show." So when my home detention sentence was up and I returned to Baltimore in August to begin doing my community service, I was also launching a new radio show, with producer Maynard Evans soon assuming a bigger on-air role after the firing of the Big O.

That first day back in the city after being away for so long felt totally surreal.

When Bob Phillips and a couple of other station executives took me to a nice steakhouse in the Inner Harbor and we walked around after dinner, people came up and hugged me. Cops on the street smiled and saluted me. I didn't know what kind of reaction to expect, but I sure didn't expect to be greeted like that.

Two days later, I nervously reported for the first time to my new probation officer, Chris Keating. No, "nervously" is putting it too mildly. I was practically jumping out of my skin, pacing back and forth in the waiting room like a leopard in a zoo.

In Tampa, I had felt safe; here in Baltimore, there were enemies all around me. My case had been so contrived and trumped-up, all I could think was: *What will they try to do to me next?*

I was still wildly-paranoid about violating my probation, both from the ankle bracelet mysteriously going off and from getting fired from the perfumery. In Baltimore, if I was living in a house with, say, even one old shotgun shell lying around, they could violate me for possessing *that,* never mind owning a firearm.

Or they could violate me for talking to a stranger in a bar who turned out to have done 10 years in the federal pen in Lewisburg, which meant I was consorting with a disreputable person, a big no-no.

But as soon as I met with Chris, the knot in my gut loosened.

"Relax," he said with a smile. "You were treated very badly. That ends today."

The new radio show went well from the get-go, too. I lined up a bunch of big-shot guests like Gov. Ehrlich and my old NYPD boss Howard Safir, for the debut, and after that we were rolling.

It was classic shock-jock radio. We'd have strippers and porn stars on, including the legendary Ron Jeremy, the world-record-holder for most appearances in adult films, if you follow that sort of thing. But we'd also talk sports, entertainment, politics, the economy, policing in Baltimore – whatever the listeners wanted to chew over.

Trying to do the required 500 hours of community service, on the other hand, was extremely difficult. I worked at first for Catholic Charities, doing maintenance work at a house they ran for drug-addicted kids.

But I was only working there a few hours a day, so I supplemented that by walking dogs for the SPCA. Still, I wasn't getting enough hours doing that, either. How long can you walk dogs every day? I didn't want to find out.

Finally, someone suggested I check with the League for People With Disabilities – and that's when I found my niche.

The League worked with both the permanently disabled and with those recovering from traumatic accidents. My job was to check people in and help them with their rehabilitation, show them how to lift weights safely and work the exercise machines. It was like being a trainer in a gym and I took to it immediately.

All the while, though, it was a lonely and trying time. My family was still living in Tampa and I was flying home every weekend after the Friday show and flying back Sunday night.

The station had been very good to me, doubling my salary before my one-year contract expired, putting me up in an apartment in the suburbs and getting me endorsements (Air Tran, Victory motorcycles) that suited my lifestyle. But the commute back and forth to Florida was killing me, as was not seeing my wife and son nearly enough.

Once I completed my community service, I went to station management and said: "Look, I don't have to be in Baltimore anymore. I'd like to stay, and if you give me a real contract, I'll move my family up here. But I can't handle the travel."

Management was again unfailingly generous, giving me a new two-year deal with an option for a third year. Unfortunately, I had far less luck pursuing something else that would have made my life easier.

In addition to six months of imprisonment, my original sentence had mandated three years of probation. But Chris Keating had told me from the beginning that he thought I was a perfect candidate for early termination of probation.

"Clearly, you're not a criminal," he'd said, which I greatly appreciated.

But when he submitted my name for early termination to the U.S. Attorney's office, it was denied. They said I wasn't a good candidate, which made me absolutely furious.

Let's see, a former big-city police commissioner and state police superintendent who got fucked over with this trumped-up, bullshit mortgage charge – *I'm* not a good candidate?

Who's a good candidate then?

Colin Powell? Mother Theresa?

I still had a lot of anger in me, and hearing about stupid decisions like that from ruthless, vindictive bureaucrats who controlled my life didn't exactly make me more placid. Unfortunately, the anger could come out in ugly ways, too.

One night, I was having dinner and drinks downtown with Maynard and Chad and some others from the station when this young guy in his 20's began hassling me.

He and his friends were standing a few feet away from us at the bar, and he kept looking over at me and muttering "They should have never let that guy out" and "They should have put him away for 10 years."

He'd been drinking, of course, and his voice grew louder and louder. He knew I could hear him, too – that was part of the game plan.

Finally, I had enough.

"If you want to say something to me," I told him, "just fucking say it."

Puffing up his chest, the guy got right in my face and continued his rant. He pushed me and I snapped immediately.

Seconds later, he was on the ground and my friends and I were quickly making our exit.

End of story?

Uh, no, not exactly. That would have been too easy.

Instead, on the show the next day, Chad Dukes suddenly began regaling the listeners with a spirited account of Eddie Norris' run-in with the drunken blowhard.

"Yeah, Eddie knocked this guy out last night after the dude got in his face!" Chad began. Frantically, I gave him the "kill" signal while shooting him with an icy glare that screamed: *Dude, what the fuck are you doing?!*

Sure enough, that night, as I had dinner with an old friend in a suburban restaurant, I got a call from my friendly neighborhood probation officer.

"I heard something on the radio today," Chris Keating began.

Uh-oh.

"I heard about what happened in the bar with that guy," Chris went on. "You know, you can't get involved in assaultive behavior."

I stammered out a lame explanation about my co-host totally exaggerating the incident, spinning a fantastical story for the listening audience just to kill time.

"It was all bullshit, Chris," I said. "Just radio shtick. You know how it is. There was nothing to it."

But when I hung up, I was soaked in sweat. My stomach was doing back-flips. Chris seemed to believe me, but I was already beating myself up

Holy God, I thought, *how stupid can you be? Getting into a bar-fight? In your situation? After all they've done to you?*

Yet after that first year out of prison, as the months passed and my radio career progressed, as my family and friends stuck with me and the good people of Baltimore continued to embrace me, I was feeling better about life.

I was not the Eddie Norris of old – those days were gone forever. And this new version of me was darker, more cynical, less trusting. But somewhere inside, I could feel my soul again. Slowly yet steadily, I began to sense that maybe things would be OK after all.

Not that I ever wanted to erase the memory of what I'd been through. In fact, late in the summer of 2006, I decided I needed a permanent reminder of that awful period of my life, and all that I'd survived.

So I had a big tattoo of a phoenix rising done in the middle of my back. I wanted it to hurt, too. I wanted to feel the pain and the soft trickle of blood that would seep out with every jab of the artist's needle.

Because I never wanted to forget what they put me through.

EPILOGUE

Much has happened – some of it bad, a lot good – in the 12 years since the dark days of my conviction and incarceration. From that terrible night in the Hole in Atlanta, I have almost returned to being someone I recognize in the mirror.

In 2009, I starred in the Discovery Channel documentary "Jack the Ripper in America." The premise was that when the world's most notorious serial killer was finished with all his nasty business in London, he started a fresh killing spree in the U.S.

Partly because of my work on "The Wire," but mostly because of my real-life experience investigating homicides and creating the NYPD Cold Case Squad, I was cast as a detective looking into the plausibility of such a scenario. I flew to London and got to do some cool things, like reading the original case folder and drinking in the same Whitechapel bar where Jack picked up his prostitute victims.

The Discovery people liked the show so much they approached me about working on other unsolved mysteries, such as whether Hitler really did kill himself. But a change of regime at the channel resulted in all those projects getting canned, and that was the end of my documentary career.

Sadly, and yet inevitably, my wife and I grew apart in the years after my imprisonment.

My divorce from Kathryn was finalized in the spring of 2010. It wasn't just the womanizing that caused it. I became impossible to live with after what I'd been through. Anger and depression dogged me. At times, I was so low I couldn't get off the couch.

Anxiety and paranoia were also constant companions. If the government could railroad me that easily, inventing bogus charges fueled by an ambitious and ruthless prosecutor, what was to prevent the feds from circling around and taking another whack at me?

During the divorce proceedings, I was seeing a therapist for all my issues.

One day I sat there and poured out my whole sad story. I ticked off all the things the sham felony conviction had cost me: money, employment, reputation (the dreaded Google hit), family, social life, hobbies.

I'd lost my right to bear arms. All my law enforcement buddies had to stay away from me, because they couldn't be spotted talking to a known felon.

When I was through, the therapist was silent for a moment. Then he shook his head softly.

"I've never seen anyone lose so much in one incident," he said finally.

Ohh-kay, I thought. *Well, that's not really helping me, doc.*

Here was a person who saw broken people every day. And basically he was telling me: "Wow, you got screwed over worse than anyone I've ever seen."

In any event, Kate put up with it all – the surly prolonged silences on my part, the wild emotional swings, the furious eruptions and hours and hours of venting – until she couldn't any more. I will grieve over that loss for the rest of my life. Thankfully, though, we get along better now than we have for years.

As for my son, Jack, Kate and I shared joint custody, but his age and my work hours necessitated that he live with his mother. Jack is a senior in high school now, an A student and a track star who will go on to college in the fall. He's a wonderful kid and I bought a house near Kate's, in a small town in Carroll County, Maryland, so I could stay close to him.

My father died in November of 2016, just a few days before Thanksgiving. He was 82. A New York Police Department honor guard presided at his funeral and I was given the departmental flag that draped his coffin.

It was an incredibly emotional ceremony. Just as with line of duty deaths, my dad's funeral warranted a bagpiper playing a stirring version of "Amazing Grace." As I do every time I hear it, I wept. I've heard that song played way too many times over the course of my lifetime, for too many brave police officers taken far too soon.

As for my mother, she suffers from Alzheimer's and doesn't know my father is gone. Nor does she know who I am. I miss them both.

What else can I tell you about my new life?

I still work in radio all these years later. These days I'm the co-host, along with Rob Long, of "The Norris and Long Show" on Baltimore's leading sports-talk station, 105.7 The Fan.

It's not a bad gig at all. I make more money than I did as police commissioner. My bosses treat me well, and I'm not exactly breaking rocks in the hot sun. I have a nice car. And the people of Baltimore treat me incredibly well.

Case in point: after breakfast in a South Baltimore diner recently, I reached for the check, only to see it snatched from my hand by a man who was eating at the next table with his daughter.

"I'm buying for him," the man announced to the owner. "Because of all he did for the city."

"Uh-uh," the owner replied with a smile. "We already picked it up."

People are always telling me "You're doing great! You gotta be content, right?"

But the answer is no.

I didn't do anything wrong. I'm not a crook. Yet I have to live with the stain of that pejorative forever. (Or until I get a presidential pardon, something I'm actively pursuing, even though the odds are long.)

Worst of all, I can't be a cop anymore. I can no longer work in the profession that I loved, the profession in which I excelled, the profession in which I was respected and admired.

I tell people all the time: "Being a cop is what I was *meant* to do. And I was really good at it. If your mother was the victim of a crime, you'd want me to have the case."

All these years later, I still replay all the events that landed me in a federal prison at what should have been the prime of my life. I'm still convinced it was a political hatchet job. But whether it was spurred in part by my post-911 criticism of the FBI or a mayor envious of my popularity and enraged by my defection to the state police, I'll probably never know.

Most likely, I was simply the victim of an ambitious and unethical prosecutor attempting to further his career by destroying mine.

But what I want people to understand is this: although I've recovered in many ways – at least in a relative sense – 99 percent of the people the government does this to are crushed and never recover.

Shit happens in life, sure, but the feds have no business destroying marriages and families. I want people to understand the viciousness of this process. Essentially, the government used sex to blackmail me into a guilty plea, with the mortgage letter as their trump card.

I want people to compare whose sin was greater, mine or the government's. And I want people to know how common this really is.

Still, there's no question that the entire ordeal has changed me profoundly.

I used to be passionate. I laughed a lot. I loved hard and hated even harder. There was not much gray in my world. Now I laugh less. I don't get sad, but unfortunately I'm never happy, either.

It's been a dozen years. I thought I'd be over it by now.

Now I'm pretty sure this is who I'll be for the rest of my life.

FINAL THOUGHTS

It will come as no surprise to learn that I pay close attention to cases where the miscarriage of justice is glaring. Cases such as the one that shattered the Duke men's lacrosse team, where innocent kids were nearly railroaded into prison by an unscrupulous prosecutor, Mike Nifong, for a rape he knew had never been committed. Cases such as the ones involving the six Baltimore police officers whose lives were offered as a sacrifice to an angry mob following the death of Freddie Gray and the rioting that devastated the city. That is the real reason that I wrote this book.

I wrote it because the American system of justice has been abused by so many for so long it is now broken. But like the mythical frog in the pot of water that's heated a degree at a time so the poor dumb creature doesn't jump out and is instead complacently boiled, our system's decline has taken place over so long that we've just accepted it.

"Justice for all" and all that happy horseshit about the U.S. being the gold standard from criminal justice in the world is simply not true. Sure, it makes for great speeches on the Fourth of July. But in my opinion, we have one of the most corrupt and dangerous systems of justice in the world.

Too often, innocent people are targeted to launch the careers of unethical prosecutors. Yes, as in most professions, the vast majority of prosecutors are good, ethical people who entered their field for pretty much the same reason I became a police officer. The problem is a belief that America can arrest its way out of its problems, which allows evil prosecutors to masquerade as dedicated crusaders for the public good until they're finally exposed, as mine was, and as Mike Nifong was.

Think about the following facts and come to your own conclusions: The U.S. has more people incarcerated than any country on earth. According to the Bureau of Justice Statistics, in 2013, this country had the largest prison population in the world, with 2,220,300 people incarcerated. The U.S. was second in per capita prison population, but only because the nation ahead of us was the tiny Seychelles, which had 735 people incarcerated in a country of 92,000.

More appropriate comparisons are to other developed countries. While the U.S. had an incarceration rate of 698 per 100,000 in 2013, other developed nations weren't even close. Canada had 106 per 100,000. Greece had 120. Spain had 141. Japan had 49. If you compare the U.S. against itself historically, the reason for the high rate becomes clear: imprisoning people has become big business in our country, led by a misguided war on drugs.

Today there are over two million drug offenders in federal and state prisons, as well as in county jails, in the U.S. When the country celebrated its bicentennial, there were 262,833. If the fact that 10 times more people are imprisoned in America now compared to 40 years ago isn't shocking enough, consider what Adam Gopnik wrote in a *New Yorker* article in 2012 titled "The Caging of America": "Over all, there are now more people under 'correctional supervision' in America – more than six million – than were in the Gulag Archipelago under Stalin at its height."

If you couple the rate at which we imprison people with the fact that a defendant has essentially zero chance at a fair trial once indicted, especially in the federal system, then you might understand why I and many other people who believe they were innocent opted to plead guilty to crimes they believe they didn't commit.

Oh, yes, another pertinent fact: nearly 100 percent of people indicted by the federal government are convicted. And be mindful that a grand jury indictment requires the same burden of proof as when a police officer arrests someone on the street: probable cause. That's certainly a low bar, is it not? So if you believe 97-99 percent of people accused by the federal government are guilty, you're living in a fool's paradise.

Just pray your tax returns are in order and you never do anything to piss off someone in a position of power.

The way it really works is this: someone (a prosecutor) decides you're a big enough target to propel his or her career forward and you're investigated. This is important because, while under state laws the police investigate crimes and endeavor to solve them by finding the guilty party, federal prosecutors often find targets (their term, not mine) and then "build" cases using whatever "crimes" they can find or come up with.

In other words, they decide someone is a bad actor and load up enough charges so that the risk of proving one's innocence at trial simply isn't worth it.

In my case, my attorneys were told by the feds that if I didn't take a plea to the bullshit charges they had drawn up, I would never see my son grow up. Faced with the prospect of losing at trial – of the 1-3 percent of people who actually go to trial in federal court, only about 8 percent are found not guilty – I would have pled guilty to killing JFK to be able to raise my son.

It's not supposed to be this way, or at least that's what I naively believed all my life. I thought justice was possible in America. I now no longer do.

Now the lines from the Bob Dylan protest song "Hurricane" keep rattling around in my head. Dylan played fast and loose with the facts of Rubin "Hurricane" Carter's sensational 1966 murder case. But he got this part right:

How can the life of such a man
Be in the palm of some fool's hand?
To see him obviously framed
Couldn't help but make me feel ashamed to live in a land
Where justice is a game.

Acknowledgments

I wrote this book not just for myself, but for the many who taught, mentored and supported me in the darkest of times. This is for them.

Many thanks to Kevin Cowherd, who did such an outstanding job telling my story and in the process became a friend.

Thank you to Lou Anemone, who inspired me my first night on patrol in the New York Police Department as a green 20-year-old and remained an inspiration through my 20 years with that organization.

Thanks to the great Jack Maple, who taught me more about police strategy in three years than I learned in the prior 15. And to John Miller, whose brilliant mind and equally-brilliant sense of humor I've treasured through decades of friendship.

I'm indebted also to Bill Bratton, who turned around a lumbering NYPD, made us proud again and allowed me to be a part of it from his most inner circle. And to Howard Safir, an elite police leader who made me "his guy" in stunning fashion and forever changed my life – and to whom I'll always be grateful.

Special thanks to Rudy Giuliani, whose vision and leadership proved to a skeptical world that crime could be controlled. By allowing us to be the police again, he not only made New York City safer, but provided a blueprint to other cities around the world about how it's done. Despite our differences, thanks, too, to Martin O'Malley for the opportunity to run a major city police department – and for allowing me to do it my way.

I am grateful to Gov. Bob Ehrlich, who gave me command of the Maryland State Police and became a friend who helped and supported me when things turned dark. And to David Simon for not only allowing me to have a small role on the greatest show ever broadcast on American television, but also for keeping me employed as a cast member so I could support my family when everything hit the fan.

An enormous debt of gratitude is also owed to Scott Herman, Bob Philips and Dave Labrozzi of CBS Radio, who took a chance on me when no one else would. The opportunity you provided me with 12 years ago when I was ostracized has allowed me to build a second career and, maybe more importantly, a place in our community again.

Thanks to Jayne Miller and Richard Sher, who covered my story as journalists, but unlike some who saw an opportunity to humiliate a public figure, continued to report it as they saw it. It was all someone in my embattled position could ask for, and what the public deserves. And a special shout-out to Major Anthony Barksdale of the Baltimore Police Department and my outstanding press officer in the department, Ragina Averella, for their help in writing this book.

To the many friends and family members who wrote, called or visited during the tough times, I can't possibly tell you how much that meant to me. The same goes for the handful of truly brave men and women in sensitive government positions, who cannot be named here for fear of hurting their careers, but who reached out with words of comfort and encouragement. You all know who you are, although you will never know how important your friendship and support was to me.

I owe so much to my childhood friend, Mike Rabinowitz – words can never express what's in my heart. The same goes for Dan Mullin, Jim LaPiedra, Dan Oates and Anthony Lombardo of the NYPD, and Steve Chaney, Jeff Gahler, Mike Ziegler and Nick Paros of the Maryland State Police.

A big thank-you, too, to all who opened their homes to me upon my return to Baltimore, and who let me know that I was still welcome.

As for those of you who literally let me live in their homes when I had nowhere to go, know that your kindness will never be forgotten.

A very special appreciation goes out to John Stendrini. He came to Baltimore as my Chief of Staff to provide counsel, watch my back and be my friend, which he remains to this day. The same goes for Rick Burnham and Joe Martinez, who literally carried me when I couldn't walk and did things for me I simply couldn't ask my family to do.

Lastly, to the men and women of the NYPD, the Baltimore Police Department and the Maryland State Police: I was honored to serve with you. Now, as a private citizen, I want to thank you and all American police officers for doing an impossible job at such a turbulent time in our country's history.

About the Authors

ED NORRIS is the former police commissioner of Baltimore and former superintendant of the Maryland State Police. Before that, he had a prestigious 20-year-career with the New York Police Department, beginning as a patrolman and rising to the rank of deputy commissioner of operations at the age of 36.

Norris had a recurring role on the HBO hit police drama "The Wire," appearing in 22 episodes over five years, and was the star of the 2009 Discovery Channel documentary, "Jack the Ripper in America."

He is the co-host of the popular "Norris & Long Show" on Baltimore's sports-talk station 105.7 The Fan.

He lives in Carroll County.

KEVIN COWHERD is the New York Times best-selling author of "Hothead" and five other baseball novels for young readers written with Hall of Famer Cal Ripken, Jr. This is his fourth book of non-fiction for Apprentice House Press.

Cowherd was an award-winning sports and features writer for the *Baltimore Sun* for 32 years and has written for *Men's Health*, *Parenting* and *Baseball Digest* magazines. A collection of his newspaper columns, "Last Call at the 7-Eleven," can still be found in fine remainder bins everywhere.

He lives in northern Baltimore County with his wife, Nancy.

Apprentice House is the country's only campus-based, student-staffed book publishing company. Directed by professors and industry professionals, it is a nonprofit activity of the Communication Department at Loyola University Maryland.

Using state-of-the-art technology and an experiential learning model of education, Apprentice House publishes books in untraditional ways. This dual responsibility as publishers and educators creates an unprecedented collaborative environment among faculty and students, while teaching tomorrow's editors, designers, and marketers.

Outside of class, progress on book projects is carried forth by the AH Book Publishing Club, a co-curricular campus organization supported by Loyola University Maryland's Office of Student Activities.

Eclectic and provocative, Apprentice House titles intend to entertain as well as spark dialogue on a variety of topics. Financial contributions to sustain the press's work are welcomed. Contributions are tax deductible to the fullest extent allowed by the IRS.

To learn more about Apprentice House books or to obtain submission guidelines, please visit www.apprenticehouse.com.

Apprentice House
Communication Department
Loyola University Maryland
4501 N. Charles Street
Baltimore, MD 21210
Ph: 410-617-5265 • Fax: 410-617-2198
info@apprenticehouse.com • www.apprenticehouse.com

CPSIA information can be obtained
at www.ICGtesting.com
Printed in the USA
LVOW12s0504250417
532062LV00003B/346/P

AMERICAN LYRIC
POEMS

From Colonial Times to the Present

GOLDENTREE BOOKS

THOMAS E. CONNOLLY, Editor
Joyce's "Portrait": Criticisms & Critiques

C. DAY LEWIS, Editor
English Lyric Poems, 1500–1900

O. B. HARDISON, JR., Editor
Modern Continental Literary Criticism

O. B. HARDISON, JR., Editor
English Literary Criticism: The Renaissance

SAMUEL HYNES, Editor
English Literary Criticism: Restoration and 18th Century

DANIEL G. HOFFMAN and SAMUEL HYNES, Editors
English Literary Criticism: Romantic and Victorian

KATHERINE LEVER
The Novel and the Reader

MILTON MARX
The Enjoyment of Drama, 2nd Edition

WILLIAM MATTHEWS, Editor
Later Medieval English Prose

ELDER OLSON, Editor
American Lyric Poems: From Colonial Times to the Present

HAROLD OREL, Editor
The World of Victorian Humor

ROBERT L. PETERS, Editor
Victorians on Literature & Art

EDWALD STONE, Editor
Henry James: Seven Stories and Studies

ELDER OLSON

University of Chicago

EDITOR

AMERICAN LYRIC
POEMS

From Colonial Times to the Present

New York

APPLETON-CENTURY-CROFTS

Division of Meredith Publishing Company

Acknowledgments

Doubleday & Company, Inc.—for "The Beast" and "The Voice" from *Words for the Wind* by Theodore Roethke. Copyright © 1955 by Theodore Roethke. Reprinted by permission of Doubleday & Company, Inc. For "The Man with the Hoe" from *The Shoes of Happiness and Other Poems* by Edwin Markham. Reprinted by permission of Doubleday & Company, Inc.

Norma Millay Ellis—for "The Poet and His Book" and "Elegy" from *Collected Poems,* Harper & Row, copyright 1921, 1948 by Edna St. Vincent Millay. For "The Buck in the Snow" from *Collected Poems,* Harper & Row, copyright 1929, 1955 by Edna St. Vincent Millay and Norma Millay Ellis. For "Sonnet XXX" from *Fatal Interview,* Harper & Row, copyright 1931, 1958 by Edna St. Vincent Millay and Norma Millay Ellis.

Farrar, Straus & Co., Inc.—for "Old Countryside," "Song for a Slight Voice," and "Song for the Last Act" reprinted from *Collected Poems 1923–1953* by Louise Bogan, by permission of Farrar, Straus & Co., Inc. Copyright 1949 by The New Yorker Magazine, Inc., 1954 by Louise Bogan. "Song for the Last Act" was originally published in *New Yorker.*

Marguerite Foster Fetcher—for permission to reprint "Love Song" by Harriet Monroe from *You and I,* The Macmillan Company, 1914.

Funk & Wagnalls Company, Inc.—for "Sundown," "Bell Tower," and

"Lullaby" from *Poems:* "A Selection" by Léonie Adams. By permission of the publishers, Funk & Wagnalls, N. Y.

Grove Press, Inc.—for "Lethe" by H. D. which appears in *Selected Poems of H.D.*, published by Grove Press, Inc., copyright © 1957 by Norman Holmes Pearson.

Harcourt, Brace & World, Inc.—for "Chanson Innocente" and "All in green went my love riding" by E. E. Cummings. Copyright, 1923, 1951, by E. E. Cummings. Reprinted from his volume, *Poems, 1923–1954,* by permission of Harcourt, Brace & World, Inc. For "A Black November Turkey" by Richard Wilbur. Copyright, 1952, by The New Yorker Magazine, Inc. Reprinted from Richard Wilbur's volume, *Things of This World,* by permission of Harcourt, Brace & World, Inc. For "The Quaker Graveyard at Nantucket" by Robert Lowell from *Lord Weary's Castle,* copyright, 1944, 1946, by Robert Lowell. Reprinted by permission of Harcourt, Brace & World, Inc. For "Four Preludes on Playthings of the Wind" by Carl Sandburg from *Smoke and Steel* by Carl Sandburg, copyright, 1920, by Harcourt, Brace & World, Inc.; renewed, 1948, by Carl Sandburg. Reprinted by permission of the publishers.

Holt, Rinehart and Winston, Inc.—for "Stopping by Woods on a Snowy Evening," "The Pasture," "Design," "Once by the Pacific," "In Hardwood Groves," "Range-Finding," and "The Gift Outright" from *Complete Poems of Robert Frost.* Copyright 1916, 1921, 1923, 1928, 1930, 1934, 1939 by Holt, Rinehart and Winston, Inc. Copyright 1936, 1942 by Robert Frost. Copyright renewed 1944, 1951, © 1956, 1962 by Robert Frost. Reprinted by permission of Holt, Rinehart and Winston, Inc.

Houghton Mifflin Company—for "Roosters" from Elizabeth Bishop, *Poems, North and South,* copyright 1955 by Elizabeth Bishop which is reprinted by permission of and arrangement with Houghton Mifflin Company, the authorized publishers. For "Madonna of the Evening Flowers" from Amy Lowell, *Pictures of the Floating World,* copyright 1947 by Harvey H. Bundy and G. d'Andelot Belin, Jr., Trustees of the Estate of Amy Lowell which is reprinted by permission of and arrangement with Houghton Mifflin Company, the authorized publishers. For "You, Andrew Marvell" and "L'An Trentiesme de Mon Eage" from Archibald MacLeish, *Collected Poems 1917–1952,* copyright 1952 by Archibald MacLeish which is reprinted by permission of and arrangement with Houghton Mifflin Company, the authorized publishers.

The Kenyon Review—for "Upon the Death of George Santayana" by Anthony Hecht, copyright 1954, The Kenyon Review.

Alfred A. Knopf, Inc.—for "Bells for John Whiteside's Daughter" and "Janet Walking" reprinted from *Selected Poems* by John Crowe Ransom, by permission of Alfred A. Knopf, Inc. Copyright, 1924, 1927 by Alfred A. Knopf, Inc. For "Ploughing on Sunday," "Life Is Motion," "Sunday Morning," "The Idea of Order at Key West," and "The Emperor of Ice-Cream" reprinted from *The Collected Poems of Wallace Stevens* by Wallace Stevens, by permission of Alfred A. Knopf, Inc. Copyright, 1923, 1951 by Wallace Stevens. For "Address to My Soul" and "Lament for Glasgerion" reprinted from *Collected Poems of Elinor Wylie* by Elinor Wylie, by permission of Alfred A. Knopf, Inc. Copyright, 1928 by Alfred A. Knopf, Inc. Renewed, 1956 by Edwina C. Rubenstein. For "Hymn to Earth" and "Fair Annet's Song" reprinted from *Collected Poems of Elinor Wylie* by Elinor Wylie, by permission of Alfred A. Knopf, Inc. Copyright, 1929 by Alfred A. Knopf, Inc. Renewed, 1957 by Edwina C. Rubenstein.

Ira Koenig—for "X Minus X" by Kenneth Fearing from *Poems,* Dynamo Press, 1935. By permission of the Estate of Kenneth F. Fearing, Ira Koenig, Executor.

Little, Brown & Company—for "End of Summer" from *Selected Poems* by Stanley Kunitz, by permission of Little, Brown & Co.-Atlantic Monthly Press. Copyright 1953 by Stanley Kunitz.

Liveright Publishing Corporation—for "Voyages: II," "At Melville's Tomb," and "Atlantis" from *The Collected Poems of Hart Crane.* By permission of Liveright, Publishers, N. Y. Copyright © R, 1961, by Liveright Publishing Corp.

The Macmillan Company—for "General William Booth Enters into Heaven" and "Abraham Lincoln Walks at Midnight." Reprinted with permission of the publisher from *Collected Poems* by Vachel Lindsay. Copyright 1913 by The Macmillan Company and copyright 1914 by The Macmillan Company, renewed 1942 by Elizabeth C. Lindsay. For "Eros Turannos." Reprinted with permission of the publisher from *Collected Poems* by Edwin Arlington Robinson. Copyright 1916 by The Macmillan Company, renewed 1944 by Ruth Nivison. For "Wisdom." Reprinted with permission of the publisher from *Collected Poems* by Sara Teasdale. Copyright 1926 by The Macmillan Company, renewed 1954 by Mamie T. Wheless. For "The Steeple-Jack" and "No Swan So Fine." Reprinted with permission of The Macmillan Company from *Collected Poems* by Marianne Moore. Copyright 1951 and 1935 by Marianne Moore.

Mrs. Edgar Lee Masters—for "The Hill" and "Anne Rutledge" from *Spoon River Anthology* by Edgar Lee Masters; New York, The Macmillan Company, 1914, 1915, 1942. Reprinted by permission of Mrs. Edgar Lee Masters.

New Directions—for "The heavy bear who goes with me" from *In Dreams Begin Responsibilities* by Delmore Schwartz. Copyright 1938 by New Directions. Reprinted by permission of New Directions. For "The Red Wheelbarrow" and "Flowers by the Sea" from *The Collected Earlier Poems of William Carlos Williams.* Copyright 1938, 1951 by William Carlos Williams. Reprinted by permission of New Directions, Publishers.

Oxford University Press, Inc.—for "Priapus and the Pool": III. When trout swim down Great Ormond Street; XVII. Fade, then,—die, depart, and come no more; and "Goya" from *Collected Poems* by Conrad Aiken.

Copyright 1953 by Conrad Aiken. Reprinted by permission of Oxford University Press, Inc. For "The Groundhog" from *Collected Poems 1930–1960* by Richard Eberhart. © 1960 by Richard Eberhart. Reprinted by permission of Oxford University Press, Inc. Published in England by Chatto & Windus.

Random House, Inc.—for "Shine, Perishing Republic." Copyright 1925 and renewed 1953 by Robinson Jeffers. Reprinted from *The Selected Poetry of Robinson Jeffers*, by permission of Random House, Inc. For "The Eye." Copyright 1948 by Robinson Jeffers. Reprinted from *The Double Axe and Other Poems*, by Robinson Jeffers, by permission of Random House, Inc. For "Auto Wreck." Copyright 1941 by Karl Shapiro. Reprinted from *Poems 1940–1953*, by Karl Shapiro, by permission of Random House, Inc. For "Terminal." Copyright 1942 by Karl Shapiro. Reprinted from *Poems 1940–1953*, by Karl Shapiro, by permission of Random House, Inc.

Charles Scribner's Sons—for "On the Death of a Metaphysician" and "Sonnet: O world" reprinted from *Poems* by George Santayana, published by Charles Scribner's Sons. Published in England by Constable & Company Ltd., 1922. For "For a Dead Lady" reprinted with the permission of Charles Scribner's Sons from *The Town Down the River* by Edwin Arlington Robinson. Copyright 1910 Charles Scribner's Sons; renewal copyright 1938 Ruth Nivison. For "Winter Mask to the Memory of W. B. Yeats" (Copyright 1945 Allen Tate) which is reprinted with the permission of Charles Scribner's Sons from *Poems* (1960) by Allen Tate.

University of Pennsylvania Press—for "Sonnets": LXVI; LXXIX; CXV; CLIII; CXCIV by George Henry Boker, from *Sonnets* edited by Edward Sculley Bradley; Philadelphia, University of Pennsylvania Press, 1929.

The Viking Press, Inc.—for "April's amazing meaning," "The world goes turning," and "No Question" from *Boy in the Wind* by George Dillon. Copyright 1927, 1955 by George Dillon. Reprinted by permission of The Viking Press. For "The Constant One" from *The Flowering Stone* by George Dillon. Copyright 1931, 1959 by George Dillon. Reprinted by permission of The Viking Press.

CONTENTS

CONTENTS

AMERICAN LYRIC
POEMS

From Colonial Times to the Present

Introduction

࿖

LYRIC POETRY is of great antiquity, yet literary criticism contains surprisingly little theoretical discussion of it compared with forms which emerge much later—and that little is not very satisfactory. What is a lyric? We are not told. The name *lyric* itself is misleading. Is nothing lyric unless it is sung to the music of the lyre? In that case there has not been any lyric poetry for a long time, and almost certainly there has never been an American lyric. And what has accompaniment by a musical instrument to do with literary form? Almost anything can be set to music for a particular instrument; in any case, that seems a composer's concern, not a poet's.

Older literary criticism scarcely troubles itself about the lyric. Preoccupied with the larger forms, it deals with the lyric only incidentally, or defines it in terms of literary conventions. The more serious attempts to consider the specific nature of the lyric begin in the nineteenth century. They amount, in the end, to this: the lyric is brief; it tends to involve intense emotion; it is the most personal form of literary expression, voicing the poet's innermost feelings; it may involve certain verse-forms rather than others.

All of this collapses the moment we examine it. Brief? How brief? The epigram is briefer. And some pieces which are thought of as lyrics —Shelley's *Adonais*, for example—are quite long. Intense emotion? Don't other kinds involve intense emotion? Shall we say that tragedies like *King Lear* or novels like *Crime and Punishment* do not involve intense emotion? Conversely, do all lyrics involve intense emotion? What is particularly intense about Shakespeare's "When icicles hang by the wall?" The lyric voices the poet's innermost feelings? Precisely how do we know that? This is a historical proposition which in many thousands of instances—such as those of anonymous poems—we cannot possibly verify; what is more, it is frequently controverted in cases where we do know the feelings of the poet. We can and do enjoy

1

lyrics, moreover, without knowing anything about the poet; which is enough to show that reflection on his actual feelings has nothing to do with the recognition of the form or with the pleasure we derive from it *as* a particular form. As to the matter of verse-forms: are the lyrics which do not involve these verse-forms therefore *not lyrics?* No, none of this is satisfactory. If you will compare John Stuart Mill's *Thoughts on Poetry and its Varieties* (1833, revised 1859) with T. S. Eliot's *The Three Voices of Poetry* (1953), both of which are concerned with poetry and its kinds (and so perforce with the lyric), you will see that the study of the question has not advanced much in over a hundred years.

I do not want to attempt to define the lyric here (I should say the kinds of lyric, for there is really a whole variety of different forms under this particular head), but I should like to make a few observations, in the hope that they may be useful. There are certain literary forms, like the novel, the drama, the epic, and the lyric, which depict human behavior. (We need not worry here about whether they also—as in Jack London's *White Fang* or Rostand's *Chantecler* —depict non-human behavior.) They can be differentiated, in part, by the *span* of the human behavior which they depict. Thus the larger forms depict larger spans of human behavior, or if they deal with smaller, depict them on a large scale; and the smaller forms, such as the lyric, do the opposite. The peculiar nature of lyric poetry is related, not to its verbal brevity, but to the brevity of the human behavior which it depicts. Its verbal brevity, in general, is a consequence of the brevity of its action. The larger forms are impossible without extensive actions, as their history indicates, for they came into existence only when men had learned to tie a whole series of incidents together. For example, Greek tragedy came into existence only after conditions permitted the exhibition of an action of a certain length, on a scale proper for the stage. An extended action is likely to require a certain number of characters—which is why the plots of Greek tragedy could not be extended until a certain number of actors were used. (If you still have any doubts about this, try writing a full-length play with only one character; it is difficult to do even with two.) On the other hand, the most common forms of lyric show us a single character behaving in some manner in a single situation—sometimes even a single moment; it is impossible to imagine anything smaller than *that*.

Moreover, the larger forms exhibit the changing *fortunes* of their characters, in relation to their behavior. The lyric does not exhibit the *changes* of fortune; it exhibits the character in a particular condition. The larger forms, too, are primarily concerned with *interpersonal* action—that is, the action of A upon B, and B in turn upon A—since changes in fortune chiefly come about through actions which involve others. The lyric is concerned, primarily, with *personal* action or re-action as such; that is, with how some individual feels or thinks or acts in a given situation; and it is concerned with that behavior in isolation, without reference to its position in a sequence of incidents. Here again the larger forms differ. In them it is the contexture of incident with incident, rather than any single incident by itself, which produces the main effect.

From these differences certain things follow. The lyric cannot depict any and every action, just as drama and the novel cannot. There are certain actions which are best suited to certain forms. The action or passion which lyric depicts must be such as can be made immediately intelligible and moving in itself. That is,—however puzzl-ing it may be on a verbal level, as some obscure modern lyrics are —it cannot be one which requires, for our proper response, any lengthy and elaborate exposition on the part of the poet, or any extended acquaintance with the lyric character. In life we react differently toward persons with whom we are well acquainted and those whom we have just met, and we make quite different judgments of their behavior. The same difference obtains between the longer forms and the lyric. A cry of anguish from a character halfway through a novel or a play may convince us of his agony, and the same cry in a lyric may give us the impression that a character is ridiculously hyper-sensitive. No intense emotion can be depicted at length in the lyric (a point known to Bryant as well as Poe) because of the in-constancy of human nature. Moreover, some emotions, like surprise, can be generated rapidly; others are sluggish and take time to become established. The lyric poet cannot hope to produce the latter in his reader. Certain emotions and mental activities are incompatible with one another—for instance, intense emotion and difficult reasoning; the lyric poet cannot demand both of his reader.

While we speak of lyrics as narrative or dramatic, they are never such in the fullest sense. Anything that is really dramatic is intended to be acted out; it is incomplete without the supplement of physical action and gesture. The lyric uses words alone, together with such embellishments, in the way of rhythm, rhyme, assonance, sound-patterns, and so on, as words may have. Any of the visual effects of drama must appear in lyric only as *images,* and the lyricist has to be careful to ask the imagination only to do what it can do. The imagina-tion cannot, for instance, construct an image which is too elaborate as a whole, or which is composed of too many parts, or of these too intricately related. The more elaborate devices of narrative, so important to the writer of fiction, are closed to the lyricist. Both fiction and drama deal heavily with external incidents; these seldom enter into lyric poetry.

In art, something that is long ought to be something that *should* be long, and something that is short ought to be something that *should* be short. The larger forms are all those of which the fundamental technique is one of expansion; the shorter forms, those of which the fundamental technique is concentration. Novel and drama tend naturally toward the fuller development of invention, a broader scale of depiction, a fuller use of discourse, while the lyric tends toward concise invention, economy of depiction, concision of language.

As the longer and the shorter forms are opposed, so are their problems opposite. Novelist and dramatist must be able to contrive long plots by assembling incidents; the lyricist must be able to refine his action down to the essentials. The former strive for full characterization; the latter strives for essential characterization. The former must know how to build up gradually; the latter, how to strike swiftly and suddenly. In general the former employs devices of synthesis; the latter, devices of analysis.

The very smallness of the lyric demands a much stricter unity than that required in the larger forms. The longer forms permit digression; the lyric does not. The smallness, too, demands evenness of execution. A few bad chapters in a novel, a few bad scenes in a play, will not necessarily ruin the general effect, but an unfortunate line, even a phrase or a word, may utterly mar a lyric. The lyric poet has certain advantages, however. Because he is working for the utmost concision, he may use, even throughout a poem, certain artifices of diction which would be intolerable in a longer work.

Every art, as it develops, tends to try to do everything it can within its own limits. Thus, once the basic conditions which bring it into existence are established, it progresses on the one hand by exploration of its medium and devices, and on the other, by exploration of the subjects which these can be used to depict and of the effects which can be achieved by their depiction. The first process is one of differentiation and recombination. For example, the discovery that narration is possible leads to the discovery that there are several basic methods of narration; these in turn are found to include several more special methods, and so on. At various times combinations of these are used to produce whatever effect is desired. The second process is simply one of trying to depict what has not been depicted, or what has not been depicted in the same way, before.

The fact that an art is not, from the technical point of view, highly developed at a given time does not imply that the works of that time are worthless, any more than the fact that an art is highly developed at a given time means that the works of that time are of a high quality. A genius may always leap beyond his age; a bungler is a bungler in any circumstances. The high development of an art does imply, however, that the artist who avails himself of its development is likely to find many of his problems solved for him by others; and to this extent there is a connection between the condition of an art and the quality of artistic productions.

II

Before the mid-eighteenth century, little verse of any kind was produced in the colonies outside of New England; and New England, when it was concerned with poetry, was not primarily concerned with the lyric. Its poetic productions were descriptive or historical pieces, hymns, versified scripture, and memorial eulogies. The purpose of these has been well described as utilitarian. I have included an excerpt from Anne Bradstreet which seems to me, and has seemed to others before me, a lyric, and a fine one; it is, however, an excerpt, and if it indeed is a lyric, is so by accident. The poems of Edward Taylor contain pieces which are unquestionably lyrics. Their excellence need not, however, blind us to the fact that they do not present any particular advancement of lyric art, and in any case, they are not characteristic of American verse in the seventeenth century. The poets of the century were more concerned with catching up with what had been done than with moving forward. During the eighteenth century it was the long poem—descriptive, didactic, or satiric— which was dominant even in England; any notable development of lyrical forms was, therefore, scarcely to be expected from Americans who were imitating English models.

A great deal has been said about the imitativeness of the earlier American poets. There is no doubt that English models and even— belatedly at first, and later more promptly—English literary fashions molded American poetry and poetic taste. In their turn, the influences of Quarles, Sylvester, Waller, Butler, Dryden, Milton, Pope, Thomson, and others are readily to be traced. But this was perfectly natural. It is naive to suppose that such imitativeness makes good poetry impossible.

What is more significant about imitation is that the imitator is likely to restrict himself to the kinds of poetry practiced by the poet who is his model, and that he is not likely to develop even these beyond the sanctions of his master. Lyric poetry was indeed written in eighteenth-century America, though sparsely, and that was because it was written, though sparsely, in England. Gay, Prior, Shenstone, Gray, Collins, and Goldsmith were the principal models. Chloes, Delias, Celias, blushing charms, genial views, etc., abound—in short, the whole apparatus of ideas, attitudes, devices, verse, and diction was brought over. The general imitativeness did not, however, prevent the production of a few charming pieces.

It is Bryant, I think, who marks the first definite development. He is often regarded as an inferior imitator of Wordsworth; but the characteristic *Thanatopsis* was probably written while he was sixteen, and before he had read the *Lyrical Ballads*. His influences were more probably Thomson, Akenside, and Cowper; but he assimilated them to the point where it is possible only to say that he is in their general tradition. He has a few ideas, a few characteristic processes of thought, a few emotional and moral attitudes. He does not develop much, if at all, as an artist; but he should not be disesteemed because he found his poetic limits, and perfected his particular instrument, more rapidly than most poets. He marks a beginning because he had his own perceptions, his own conceptions, and because he developed his own vehicles for their expression. When he writes a lyric, it is not because someone else has, and he does not write it as he does because someone else has done so; he works in a lyric form because his conception requires it.

Bryant's ideas were few and simple; Emerson's were not, and he showed how to handle complex ideas in lyrical form, in particular, how to fine down an argument to an image or a metaphor and how to present abstractions concretely. Longfellow performed much the same service for his age that T. S. Eliot has performed for ours, as an importer of European forms and techniques. Unlike Eliot, however, Longfellow invaded form after form, and worked with a vast diversity of subjects. A great poet he may not have been, but he had the range of one. It is possible to dislike what he does; it is hardly possible to doubt that he had the technical power to do whatever he wished to do. Finally, Poe developed the purely musical resources of the lyric to a perhaps unprecedented degree.

At mid-nineteenth century, thus, the situation of the lyrical art in America was such that one might reasonably have expected a flood of masterpieces. The range of subjects had been vastly extended, a diversity of poetic techniques and devices had been introduced, both stylistic and metrical, and a good number of outworn poetic conventions had been discarded. It is true that there was still much to do. Poets were still hampered by the notion that poetic diction consisted in a certain kind of style and a certain vocabulary, particularly of archaisms. They still had to learn to use words with sharper precision and greater economy, to use metaphors, similes, and images significantly and organically rather than ornamentally. Most important of all, as far as diction was concerned, they had to learn that everything did not need to be made explicit, particularly if it was obvious—in a word, to learn the use of suggestion, implication, and innuendo. In the matter of versification, they had to learn the uses of incomplete rhyme, false rhyme, "analyzed" rhyme, misplaced rhyme, and to use verse more expressively—either to use the old meters more flexibly and meaningfully, or to break away from them altogether toward something that *was* more flexible and meaningful. Finally, in the matter of invention, they had yet to discard certain posturings which stemmed from stock notions of the poetic character; to depend less on conventional predispositions of their readers in producing their effects; and to seek greater and greater diversity of effect.

In general, however, the poets, rather than pressing forward, retreated. Some, like Bayard Taylor, put their trust in exotic subjects; some, like Stoddard and Hayne, took courses that had been repeatedly proven safe; others depended upon pious sentiments. It was left to two very different poets—Walt Whitman and Emily Dickinson—to develop the art further. Between them they did nearly everything that, as stated in the long list above, poetry had still to do; and their innovations were so startling that at first these were considered either eccentricities or faults in craftsmanship. Whitman and Dickinson differ as macrocosm and microcosm. The former strives constantly to identify himself with the whole universe and everything within it; the latter finds the universe reflected in herself and in the narrow limits of her daily life. The former uses an expansive technique which depends upon the accumulation of detail; the latter condenses to the point where a few sparse details are pregnant with implication or suggestion. The former breaks the bounds of meter; the latter shows the innumerable variations possible within a few simple metrical patterns. The former escapes the conventions of trite and obvious rhyme by doing away —almost altogether—with rhyme itself; the latter, by the use of incomplete or missed rhyme.

. Incalculable as the influence of these two poets is in the present day, their effect on the main course of American lyric poetry was—for quite different reasons—negligible. Poets continued to move in grooves already well-worn, and when they did not, they imitated the more recently emerging English poets. The brief flurry caused by Hovey and Carman in the 90's, however much it impressed its contemporaries as a revolt, was in no sense a change; it amounted as a whole to the profound observation that poetry might as well be written out-of-doors as within.

Indeed, toward the end of the century, the more enterprising American poets no longer looked to the poets of their own nation for guidance. The veins worked by the Founding Fathers of American poetry were obviously exhausted; Whitman was repugned or ignored; the influence of Dickinson was still to be felt. Robinson was working out his own way, as Frost and Masters were to work out theirs; the mood of the others must have been that of Eliot a decade later. "The question was," he says, " 'Where do we go after Swinburne?' And the answer appeared to be, 'Nowhere.' "

The great advance came with the New Poetry in the second decade of the twentieth century. Mr. Eliot, whom I scarcely need to indicate as one of the pioneers of that poetry, has said that it was basically a matter of reforming poetic diction. Perhaps so; but I think that Whitman gave the ground for the reform when he said, "The new times, the new people need a tongue according, yes, and what is more, they will have such a tongue—will not be satisfied until it is evolved." For with the passing of the Victorian era, the powerful conventions of that era were losing their force, the structures of belief were changing, together with the emotional attitudes based upon both of these. In a word, what was thought and felt was now different, and had to be said differently.

And the reform of—perhaps the assault upon—language was certainly prodigious. Thus far—with the exception of Dickinson and Whitman, and possibly Poe—American poets had worked out only styles *generally* appropriate; they now set out to make them specifically so, even to forge out individual styles. "A new and distinctive voice" became, and has remained, one of the favorite catch-phrases of the reviewers. The old "poetic diction," with its Basic English vocabulary for poets, its formal style, its generalities, its abstractions, its personifications, its everlasting apostrophes, and well-worn rhetoric, was junked. The poets took words from anywhere and everywhere, coined them, forced them into strange compounds. They struck at English syntax itself, used one part of speech as another, broke up devices of transition, disrupted logical relation, borrowed constructions from other languages (sometimes with lovely effects, as in Pound's use of Greek participial constructions). They went in for associational relation rather than logical, used the connotations of words rather than the denotations, and sought to convey concepts through images. Since grammar and syntax imply the ordering of ideas by the conscious mind, some of these innovations permitted the poets to express subconscious processes. Figures of language were also used differently. Implied or suggested metaphors and similes were employed; what I shall call "subjective" metaphors, in that they are based upon no real likeness but only upon a likeness apparent to someone in a given frame of mind, were used; and also metaphors which subsumed other metaphors. It was inevitable too that the conceit should come back into fashion. Of course verse itself was altered: free verse, verse based on phrasal or intonational rhythms, on syllabism, verse with initial rhyme, sporadic internal rhyme, off-rhyme, eye-rhyme, assonance— all these were used in experimentation. All of this was accompanied by an immense extension of the subject-matter of poetry in a general effort to make art commensurate with the experiences of life.

The consequence is that the technical resources of the lyric poet have never been greater, that devices exist for nearly everything the modern poet wishes to say. Does this mean that the poetry is finer? Is the twentieth century the great age, so far, of American poetry? That is a difficult question which I have not the authority to answer. My own opinion is that in the matter of the lyric the twentieth century *is* the great age so far, but that fine work was done in almost every period of our history, even those in which the art itself was little developed, and those in which the lyric was of less concern than it is now. The justification of this view I must leave to the poets whose works make up this volume.

Poems

⋙§§⋘

from

Contemplations

When I behold the heavens as in their prime,
    And then the earth, though old, still clad in green,
The stones and trees insensible of time,
    Nor age nor wrinkle on their front are seen;
If winter come, and greenness then doth fade,
A spring returns, and they're more youthful made.
But man grows old, lies down, remains where once he's laid.

By birth more noble than those creatures all,
    Yet seems by nature and by custom cursed—
No sooner born but grief and care make fall
    That state obliterate he had at first;
Nor youth, nor strength, nor wisdom spring again,
Nor habitations long their names retain,
But in oblivion to the final day remain.

Shall I then praise the heavens, the trees, the earth,
    Because their beauty and their strength last longer?
Shall I wish there or never to had birth,
    Because they're bigger and their bodies stronger?
Nay, they shall darken, perish, fade, and die,
And when unmade so ever shall they lie;
But man was made for endless immortality.

ANNE BRADSTREET

11

from

Gods Determinations Touching His Elect

THE PREFACE

Infinity, when all things it beheld,
In Nothing, and of Nothing all did build,
Upon what Base was fixt the Lath, wherein
He turn'd this Globe, and riggalld it so trim?
Who blew the Bellows of his Furnace Vast?
Or held the Mould wherein the world was Cast?
Who laid its Corner Stone? Or whose Command?
Where stand the Pillars upon which it stands?
Who Lac'de and Fillitted the earth so fine,
With Rivers like green Ribbons Smaragdine?
Who made the Sea's its Selvedge, and it locks
Like a Quilt Ball within a Silver Box?
Who Spread its Canopy? Or Curtains Spun?
Who in this Bowling Alley bowld the Sun?
Who made it always when it rises set:
To go at once both down, and up to get?
Who th' Curtain rods made for this Tapistry?
Who hung the twinckling Lanthorns in the Sky?
Who? who did this? or who is he? Why, know
It's Onely Might Almighty this did doe.
His hand hath made this noble worke which Stands
His Glorious Handywork not made by hands.
Who spake all things from nothing; and with ease
Can speake all things to nothing, if he please.
Whose Little finger at his pleasure Can
Out mete ten thousand worlds with halfe a Span:
Whose Might Almighty can by half a looks
Root up the rocks and rock the hills by th' roots.
Can take this mighty World up in his hande,
And shake it like a Squitchen or a Wand.
Whose single Frown will make the Heavens shake
Like as an aspen leafe the Winde makes quake.
Oh! what a might is this! Whose single frown
Doth shake the world as it would shake it down?
Which All from Nothing fet, from Nothing, All:
Hath All on Nothing set, lets Nothing fall.
Gave All to nothing Man indeed, whereby

Through nothing man all might him Glorify.
In Nothing is imbosst the brightest Gem
More pretious than all pretiousness in them.
But Nothing man did throw down all by sin:
And darkened that lightsom Gem in him,
    That now his Brightest Diamond is grown
    Darker by far than any Coalpit Stone.

PROLOGUE

Lord, Can a Crumb of Earth the Earth outweigh:
    Outmatch all mountains, nay the Chrystall Sky?
Imbosom in't designs that shall Display
    And trace into the Boundless Deity?
    Yea, hand a Pen whose moysture doth guild ore
    Eternall Glory with a glorious glore.

If it its Pen had of an Angels Quill,
    And sharpened on a Pretious Stone ground tite,
And dipt in Liquid Gold, and mov'de by skill
    In Christall leaves should golden Letters write,
    It would but blot and blur: yea, jag and jar,
    Unless thou mak'st the Pen and Scribener.

I am this Crumb of Dust which is design'd
    To make my Pen unto thy Praise alone,
And my dull Phancy I would gladly grinde
    Unto an Edge on Zions Pretious Stone:
    And Write in Liquid Gold upon thy Name
    My Letters till thy glory forth doth flame.

Let not th' attempts breake down my Dust I pray,
    Nor laugh thou them to scorn, but pardon give.
Inspire this Crumb of Dust till it display
    Thy Glory through 't: and then thy dust shall live.
    Its failings then thou'lt overlook I trust,
    They being Slips slipt from thy Crumb of Dust.

Thy Crumb of Dust breaths two words from its breast;
    That thou wilt guide its pen to write aright
To Prove thou art, and that thou art the best,
    And shew thy Properties to shine most bright.
    And then thy Works will shine as flowers on Stems
    Or as in Jewellary Shops, do jems.

MEDITATION SIX

Canticles II, 1: I am . . . the lily of the valleys.

Am I thy gold? Or Purse, Lord, for thy Wealth;
    Whether in mine or mint refinde for thee?
Ime counted so, but count me o're thyselfe,
    Lest gold washt face, and brass in Heart I bee.
    I Feare my Touchstone touches when I try
    Mee, and my Counted Gold too overly.

Am I new minted by thy Stamp indeed?
    Mine Eyes are dim; I cannot clearly see.
Be thou my Spectacles that I may read
    Thine Image and Inscription stampt on mee.
    If thy bright Image do upon me stand,
    I am a Golden Angell in thy hand.

Lord, make my Soule thy Plate: thine Image bright
    Within the Circle of the same enfoile.
And on its brims in golden Letters write
    Thy Superscription in an Holy style.
    Then I shall be thy Money, thou my Hord:
    Let me thy Angell bee, bee thou my Lord.

EDWARD TAYLOR

The Wild Honey Suckle

Fair flower, that dost so comely grow,
Hid in this silent, dull retreat,
Untouched thy honied blossoms blow,
Unseen thy little branches greet:
    No roving foot shall crush thee here,
    No busy hand provoke a tear.

By Nature's self in white arrayed,
She bade thee shun the vulgar eye,
And planted here the guardian shade,
And sent soft waters murmuring by;
    Thus quietly thy summer goes,
    Thy days declining to repose.

Smit with those charms that must decay,
I grieve to see your future doom;
They died—nor were those flowers more gay,
The flowers that did in Eden bloom;
    Unpitying frosts, and Autumn's power
    Shall leave no vestige of this flower.

From morning suns and evening dews
At first thy little being came:
If nothing once, you nothing lose,
For when you die you arc the same;
    The space between is but an hour,
    The frail duration of a flower.

PHILIP FRENEAU

Advice to a Raven in Russia December, 1812

Black fool, why winter here? These frozen skies,
Worn by your wings and deafen'd by your cries,
Should warn you hence, where milder suns invite,
And day alternates with his mother night.
    You fear perhaps your food will fail you there,
Your human carnage, that delicious fare
That lured you hither, following still your friend,
The great Napoleon, to the world's bleak end.
You fear, because the southern climes pour'd forth
Their clustering nations to infest the north,
Bavarians, Austrians, those who Drink the Po
And those who skirt the Tuscan seas below,
With all Germania, Neustria, Belgia, Gaul,
Doom'd here to wade through slaughter to their fall,
You fear he left behind no wars, to feed
His feather'd cannibals and nurse the breed.
    Fear not, my screamer, call your greedy train,
Sweep over Europe, hurry back to Spain,
You'll find his legions there; the valliant crew
Please best their master when they toil for you.
Abundant there they spread the country o'er
And taint the breeze with every nation's gore,
Iberian, Lusian, British widely strown,

But still more wide and copious flows their own.
　　Go where you will; Calabria, Malta, Greece,
Egypt and Syria still his fame increase,
Domingo's fatten'd isle and India's plains
Glow deep with purple drawn from Gallic veins.
No Raven's wing can stretch the flight so far
As the torn bandrols of Napoleon's war.
Choose then your climate, fix your best abode,
He'll make you deserts and he'll bring you blood.
　　How could you fear a dearth? have not mankind,
Though slain by millions, millions left behind?
Has not CONSCRIPTION still the power to wield
Her annual falchion o'er the human field?
A faithful harvester; or if a man
Escape that gleaner, shall he scape the BAN?
The triple BAN, that like the hound of hell
Gripes with three jowls, to hold his victim well.
　　Fear nothing then, hatch fast your ravenous brood,
Teach them to cry to Bonaparte for food;
They'll be like you, of all his suppliant train,
The only class that never cries in vain.
For see what mutual benefits you lend!
(The surest way to fix the mutual friend)
While on his slaughter'd troops your tribes are fed,
You cleanse his camp and carry off his dead.
Imperial Scavenger! But now you know
Your work is vain amid these hills of snow.
His tentless troops are marbled through with frost
And change to crystal when the breath is lost.
Mere trunks of ice, though limb'd like human frames
And lately warm'd with life's endearing flames,
They cannot taint the air, the world impest,
Nor can you tear one fiber from their breast.
No! from their visual sockets, as they lie,
With beak and claws you cannot pluck an eye.
The frozen orb, preserving still its form,
Defies your talons as it braves the storm,
But stands and stares to God, as if to know
In what curst hands he leaves his world below.
　　Fly then, or starve; though all the dreadful road
From Minsk to Moskow with their bodies strow'd
May count some myriads, yet they can't suffice

To feed you more beneath these dreary skies.
Go back, and winter in the wilds of Spain;
Feast there awhile, and in the next campaign
Rejoin your master; for you'll find him then,
With his new million of the race of men,
Clothed in his thunders, all his flags unfurl'd,
Raging and storming o'er the prostrate world.
　　War after war his hungry soul requires,
State after State shall sink beneath his fires,
Yet other Spains in victim smoke shall rise
And other Moskows suffocate the skies,
Each land lie reeking with its people's slain
And not a stream run bloodless to the main.
Till men resume their souls, and dare to shed
Earth's total vengeance on the monster's head,
Hurl from his blood-built throne this king of woes,
Dash him to dust, and let the world repose.

Joel Barlow

The Lip and the Heart

One day between the Lip and the Heart
　　A wordless strife arose
Which was expertest in the art
　　His purpose to disclose.

The Lip called forth the vassal Tongue,
　　And made him vouch—a lie!
The slave his servile anthem sung
　　And braved the listening sky.

The Heart to speak in vain essayed,
　　Nor could his purpose reach—
His will nor voice nor tongue obeyed,
　　His silence was his speech.

Mark thou their difference, child of earth!
　　While each performs his part

Not all the lip can speak is worth
The silence of the Heart.

JOHN QUINCEY ADAMS

On Snow-Flakes Melting on His Lady's Breast

To kiss my Celia's fairer breast,
    The snow forsakes its native skies,
By proving an unwelcome guest,
    It grieves, dissolves in tears, and dies.

Its touch, like mine, but serves to wake
    Through all her frame a death-like chill—
Its tears, like those I shed, to make
    That icy bosom colder still.

I blame her not; from Celia's eyes
    A common fate beholders prove—
Each swain, each fair one, weeps and dies—
    With envy these, and those with love!

WILLIAM MARTIN JOHNSON

Song

Who has robbed the ocean wave
    To tinge thy lips with coral hue?
Who from India's distant wave
    For thee those pearly treasures drew?
        Who, from yonder orient sky,
        Stole the morning of thine eye?

Thousand charms, thy form to deck,
    From sea, and earth, and air are torn;
Roses bloom upon thy cheek,
    On thy breath their fragrance borne.
        Guard thy bosom from the day,
        Lest thy snows should melt away.

But one charm remains behind,
    Which mute earth can ne'er impart;
Nor in ocean wilt thou find,
    Nor in the circling air, a heart.
        Fairest! wouldst thou perfect be,
        Take, oh take that heart from me.

JOHN SHAW

The Little Beach Bird

Thou little bird, thou dweller by the sea,
    Why takest thou its melancholy voice?
        Why with that boding cry
        O'er the waves dost thou fly?
O, rather, bird, with me
    Through the fair land rejoice!

Thy flitting form comes ghostly dim and pale,
    As driven by a beating storm at sea;
        Thy cry is weak and scared,
        As if thy mates had shared
The doom of us. Thy wail—
    What does it bring to me?

Thou call'st along the sand, and haunt'st the surge,
    Restless and sad; as if, in strange accord
        With motion and with roar
        Of waves that drive to shore,
One spirit did ye urge—
    The Mystery—the Word.

Of thousands thou both sepulchre and pall,
    Old ocean, art! A requiem o'er the dead,
        From out thy gloomy cells,
        A tale of mourning tells,—
Tells of man's woe and fall,
    His sinless glory fled.

Then turn thee, little bird, and take thy flight
    Where the complaining sea shall sadness bring

Thy spirit nevermore.
Come, quit with me the shore,
For gladness and the light,
Where birds of summer sing.

RICHARD HENRY DANA

On the Death of Joseph Rodman Drake

Green be the turf above thee,
    Friend of my better days!
None knew thee but to love thee,
    Nor named thee but to praise.

Tears fell when thou wert dying,
    From eyes unused to weep,
And long, where thou art lying,
    Will tears the cold turf steep.

When hearts, whose truth was proven,
    Like thine, are laid in earth,
There should a wreath be woven
    To tell the world their worth;

And I who woke each morrow
    To clasp thy hand in mine,
Who shared thy joy and sorrow,
    Whose weal and woe were thine;

It should be mine to braid it
    Around thy faded brow,
But I've in vain essayed it,
    And feel I cannot now.

While memory bids me weep thee,
    Nor thoughts nor words are free,—
The grief is fixed too deeply
    That mourns a man like thee.

FITZ-GREENE HALLECK

Niagara

Flow on forever, in thy glorious robe
Of terror and of beauty. Yea, flow on
Unfathomed and resistless. God hath set
His rainbow on thy forehead: and the cloud
Mantled around thy feet. And He doth give
Thy voice of thunder, power to speak of Him
Eternally—bidding the lip of man
Keep silence—and upon thy rocky altar pour
Incense of awe-struck praise.
                         Ah! who can dare
To lift the insect-trump of earthly hope,
Or love, or sorrow—'mid the peal sublime
Of thy tremendous hymn? Even Ocean shrinks
Back from thy brotherhood; and all his waves
Retire abashed. For he doth sometimes seem
To sleep like a spent labourer—and recall
His wearied billows from their vexing play,
And lull them to a cradle calm: but thou,
With everlasting, undecaying tide,
Dost rest not, night or day. The morning stars,
When first they sang o'er young creation's birth,
Heard thy deep anthem; and those wrecking fires,
That wait the archangel's signal to dissolve
This solid earth, shall find Jehovah's name
Graven, as with a thousand diamond spears,
On thine unending volume.
                         Every leaf,
That lifts itself within thy wide domain,
Doth gather greenness from thy living spray,
Yet tremble at the baptism. Lo! —yon birds
Do boldly venture near, and bathe their wing
Amid thy mist and foam. 'Tis meet for them
To touch thy garment's hem, and lightly stir
The snowy leaflets of thy vapor-wreath,
For they may sport unharmed amid the cloud,
Or listen at the echoing gate of heaven,
Without reproof. But as for us, it seems
Scarce lawful, with our broken tones, to speak
Familiarly of thee. Methinks, to tint
Thy glorious features with our pencil's point,

Or woo thee to the tablet of our song,
Were profanation.
                    Thou dost make the soul
A wondering witness of thy majesty,
But as it presses with delirious joy
To pierce thy vestibule, dost chain its step,
And tame its rapture with the humbling view
Of its own nothingness, bidding it stand
In the dread presence of the Invisible,
As if to answer to its God through thee.

Lydia Huntley Sigourney

Thanatopsis

To him who in the love of Nature holds
Communion with her visible forms, she speaks
A various language; for his gayer hours
She has a voice of gladness, and a smile
And eloquence of beauty, and she glides
Into his darker musings, with a mild
And healing sympathy, that steals away
Their sharpness ere he is aware. When thoughts
Of the last bitter hour come like a blight
Over thy spirit, and sad images
Of the stern agony, and shroud, and pall,
And breathless darkness, and the narrow house,
Make thee to shudder, and grow sick at heart;—
Go forth, under the open sky, and list
To Nature's teachings, while from all around—
Earth and her waters, and the depths of air,—
Comes a still voice—Yet a few days, and thee
The all-beholding sun shall see no more
In all his course; nor yet in the cold ground,
Where thy pale form was laid, with many tears,
Nor in the embrace of ocean, shall exist
Thy image. Earth, that nourished thee, shall claim
Thy growth, to be resolved to earth again,
And, lost each human trace, surrendering up
Thine individual being, shalt thou go
To mix for ever with the elements,

To be a brother to the insensible rock
And to the sluggish clod, which the rude swain
Turns with his share, and treads upon. The oak
Shall send his roots abroad, and pierce thy mould.

     Yet not to thine eternal resting-place
Shalt thou retire alone,—nor couldst thou wish
Couch more magnificent. Thou shalt lie down
With patriarchs of the infant world—with kings,
The powerful of the earth—the wise, the good,
Fair forms, and hoary seers of ages past,
All in one mighty sepulchre. The hills
Rock-ribbed and ancient as the sun; the vales
Stretching in pensive quietness between;
The venerable woods; rivers that move
In majesty, and the complaining brooks
That make the meadows green; and, poured round all,
Old ocean's grey and melancholy waste—
Are but the solemn decorations all
Of the great tomb of man. The golden sun,
The planets, all the infinite host of heaven,
Are shining on the sad abodes of death,
Through the still lapse of ages. All that tread
The globe are but a handful to the tribes
That slumber in its bosom.—Take the wings
Of morning, traverse Barca's desert sands,
Or lose thyself in the continuous woods
Where rolls the Oregon, and hears no sound,
Save his own dashings—yet—the dead are there:
And millions in those solitudes, since first
The flight of years began, have laid them down
In their last sleep—the dead reign there alone.
So shalt thou rest, and what if thou withdraw
In silence from the living, and no friend
Take note of thy departure? All that breathe
Will share thy destiny. The gay will laugh
When thou are gone, the solemn brood of care
Plod on, and each one as before will chase
His favourite phantom; yet all these shall leave
Their mirth and their employments, and shall come,
And make their bed with thee. As the long train
Of ages glide away, the sons of men,

The youth in life's green spring, and he who goes
In the full strength of years, matron, and maid,
And the sweet babe, and the grey-headed man—
Shall one by one be gathered to thy side,
By those, who in their turn shall follow them.

So live, that when thy summons comes to join
The innumerable caravan, which moves
To that mysterious realm, where each shall take
His chamber in the silent halls of death,
Thou go not, like the quarry-slave at night,
Scourged to his dungeon, but, sustained and soothed
By an unfaltering trust, approach thy grave
Like one who wraps the drapery of his couch
About him, and lies down to pleasant dreams.

WILLIAM CULLEN BRYANT

To a Waterfowl

Whither, midst falling dew,
While glow the heavens with the last steps of day
Far, through their rosy depths, dost thou pursue
Thy solitary way?

Vainly the fowler's eye
Might mark thy distant flight to do thee wrong
As, darkly seen against the crimson sky,
Thy figure floats along.

Seek'st thou the plashy brink
Of weedy lake, or marge of river wide,
Or where the rocking billows rise and sink
On the chafed ocean-side?

There is a Power whose care
Teaches thy way along that pathless coast—
The desert and illimitable air—
Lone wandering, but not lost.

All day thy wings have fanned,
At that far height, the cold, thin atmosphere,
Yet stoop not, weary, to the welcome land,
    Though the dark night is near.

And soon that toil shall end;
Soon shalt thou find a summer home, and rest,
And scream among thy fellows; reeds shall bend,
    Soon, o'er thy sheltered nest.

Thou'rt gone, the abyss of heaven
Hath swallowed up thy form; yet, on my heart
Deeply has sunk the lesson thou hast given,
    And shall not soon depart.

He who, from zone to zone,
Guides through the boundless sky thy certain flight,
In the long way that I must tread alone,
    Will lead my steps aright.

              WILLIAM CULLEN BRYANT

"O, fairest of the rural maids!"

O, fairest of the rural maids!
Thy birth was in the forest shades;
Green boughs, and glimpses of the sky,
Were all that met thine infant eye.

Thy sports, thy wanderings, when a child,
Were ever in the sylvan wild,
And all the beauty of the place
Is in thy heart and on thy face.

The twilight of the trees and rocks
Is in the light shade of thy locks;
Thy step is as the wind, that weaves
Its playful way among the leaves.

Thine eyes are springs, in whose serene
And silent waters heaven is seen;

Their lashes are the herbs that look
On their young figures in the brook.

The forest depths, by foot unpressed,
Are not more sinless than thy breast;
The holy peace, that fills the air
Of those calm solitudes, is there.

WILLIAM CULLEN BRYANT

Inscription for the Entrance to a Wood

Stranger, if thou hast learned a truth which needs
No school of long experience, that the world
Is full of guilt and misery, and hast seen
Enough of all its sorrows, crimes, and cares,
To tire thee of it, enter this wild wood
And view the haunts of Nature. The calm shade
Shall bring a kindred calm, and the sweet breeze
That makes the green leaves dance, shall waft a balm
To thy sick heart. Thou wilt find nothing here
Of all that pained thee in the haunts of men,
And made thee loathe thy life. The primal curse
Fell, it is true, upon the unsinning earth,
But not in vengeance. God hath yoked to Guilt
Her pale tormentor, Misery. Hence these shades
Are still the abodes of gladness; the thick roof
Of green and stirring branches is alive
And musical with birds, that sing and sport
In wantonness of spirit; while below
The squirrel, with raised paws and form erect,
Chirps merrily. Throngs of insects in the shade
Try their thin wings and dance in the warm beam
That waked them into life. Even the green trees
Partake the deep contentment; as they bend
To the soft winds, the sun from the blue sky
Looks in and sheds a blessing on the scene.
Scarce less the cleft-born wild-flower seems to enjoy
Existence, than the winged plunderer
That sucks its sweets. The mossy rocks themselves,
And the old and ponderous trunks of prostrate trees

That lead from knoll to knoll a causey rude,
Or bridge the sunken brook, and their dark roots,
With all their earth upon them, twisting high,
Breathe fixed tranquillity. The rivulet
Sends forth glad sounds, and tripping o'er its bed
Of pebbly sands, or leaping down the rocks,
Seems, with continuous laughter, to rejoice
In its own being. Softly tread the marge,
Lest from her midway perch thou scare the wren
That dips her bill in water. The cool wind,
That stirs the stream in play, shall come to thee,
Like one that loves thee nor will let thee pass
Ungreeted, and shall give its light embrace.

WILLIAM CULLEN BRYANT

The Coral Grove

Deep in the wave is a coral grove,
Where the purple mullet and gold-fish rove;
Where the sea-flower spreads its leaves of blue
That never are wet with falling dew,
But in bright and changeful beauty shine
Far down in the green and glassy brine.
The floor is of sand, like the mountain drift,
And the pearl-shells spangle the flinty snow;
From coral rocks the sea-plants lift
Their boughs, where the tides and billows flow:
The water is calm and still below,
For the winds and waves are absent there,
And the sands are bright as the stars that glow
In the motionless fields of upper air.
There, with its waving blade of green,
The sea-flag streams through the silent water,
And the crimson leaf of the dulse is seen
To blush, like a banner bathed in slaughter.
There, with a light and easy motion,
The fan-coral sweeps through the clear deep sea;
And the yellow and scarlet tufts of ocean
Are bending like corn on the upland lea:
And life, in rare and beautiful forms,

Is sporting amid those bowers of stone,
And is safe when the wrathful Spirit of storms
Has made the top of the wave his own.
And when the ship from his fury flies,
Where the myriad voices of Ocean roar;
When the wind-god frowns in the murky skies,
And demons are waiting the wreck on shore;
Then, far below, in the peaceful sea,
The purple mullet and gold-fish rove,
Where the waters murmur tranquilly,
Through the bending twigs of the coral grove.

JAMES GATES PERCIVAL

The American Flag

I

When Freedom from her mountain height
    Unfurl'd her standard to the air,
She tore the azure robe of night,
    And set the stars of glory there.
She mingled with its gorgeous dyes
The milky baldric of the skies,
And striped its pure celestial white
With streakings of the morning light;
Then from his mansion in the sun
She call'd her eagle bearer down,
And gave into his mighty hand
The symbol of her chosen land.

II

Majestic monarch of the cloud,
    Who rear'st aloft thy regal form,
To hear the tempest trumpings loud
And see the lightning lances driven,
    When strive the warriors of the storm,
And rolls the thunder-drum of heaven,
Child of the sun! to thee 'tis given
    To guard the banner of the free,

To hover in the sulphur smoke,
To ward away the battle stroke,
And bid its blendings shine afar,
Like rainbows on the cloud of war,
    The harbingers of victory!

III

Flag of the brave! thy folds shall fly,
    The sign of hope and triumph high,
When speaks the signal trumpet tone,
    And the long line comes gleaming on.
Ere yet the life-blood, warm and wet,
    Has dimm'd the glistening bayonet,
Each soldier eye shall brightly turn
    To where thy sky-born glories burn;
And, as his springing steps advance,
Catch war and vengeance from the glance.
And when the cannon-mouthings loud
    Heave in wild wreaths the battle-shroud
And gory sabres rise and fall
Like shoots of flame on midnight's pall;
    Then shall thy meteor glances glow,
And cowering foes shall shrink beneath
    Each gallant arm that strikes below
That lovely messenger of death.

IV

Flag of the seas! on ocean wave
Thy stars shall glitter o'er the brave;
When death, careering on the gale,
Sweeps darkly round the bellied sail,
And freighted waves rush wildly back
Before the broadside's reeling rack,
Each dying wanderer of the sea
Shall look at once to heaven and thee,
And smile to see thy splendour fly
In triumph o'er his closing eye.

V

Flag of the free heart's hope and home!
    By angel hands to valor given;

The stars have lit the welkin dome,
    And all thy hues were born in heaven.
Forever float that standard sheet!
    Where breathes the foe but falls before us,
With Freedom's soil beneath our feet,
    And Freedom's banner streaming o'er us!

JOSEPH RODMAN DRAKE

Leila

When first you look upon her face,
    You little note beside
The timidness that still betrays
    The beauties it would hide:
But one by one, they look out from
    Her blushes and her eyes;
And still the last the loveliest,
    Like stars from twilight skies.

And thoughts go sporting through her mind,
    Like children among flowers;
And deeds of gentle goodness are
    The measure of her hours.
In soul or face, she bears no trace
    Of one from Eden driven;
But, like the rainbow, seems, though born
    Of earth, a part of heaven.

GEORGE HILL

A Serenade

Look out upon the stars, my love,
    And shame them with thine eyes,
On which, than on the lights above,
    There hang more destinies.
Night's beauty is the harmony
    Of blending shades and light;

Then, lady, up,—look out, and be
    A sister to the night!

Sleep not! thine image wakes for aye
    Within my watching breast:
Sleep not! from her soft sleep should fly
    Who robs all hearts of rest.
Nay, lady, from thy slumbers break,
    And make this darkness gay
With looks, whose brightness well might make
    Of darker nights a day.

EDWARD COOTE PINKNEY

Song

We break the glass, whose sacred wine,
    To some beloved health we drain,
Lest future pledges, less divine,
    Should e'er the hallowed toy profane;
And thus I broke a heart that poured
    Its tide of feelings out for thee,
In draught, by after-times deplored,
    Yet dear to memory.

But still the old impassioned ways
    And habits of my mind remain,
And still unhappy light displays
    Thine image chambered in my brain,
And still it looks as when the hours
    Went by like flights of singing birds,
Or that soft chain of spoken flowers
    And airy gems,—thy words.

EDWARD COOTE PINKNEY

The Rhodora

On being asked, Whence is the flower?

In May, when sea-winds pierced our solitudes,
I found the fresh Rhodora in the woods,

Spreading its leafless blooms in a damp nook,
To please the desert and the sluggish brook.
The purple petals, fallen in the pool,
Made the black water with their beauty gay;
Here might the red-bird come his plumes to cool,
And court the flower that cheapens his array.
Rhodora! if the sages ask thee why
This charm is wasted on the earth and sky,
Tell them, dear, that if eyes were made for seeing,
Then Beauty is its own excuse for being:
Why thou wert there, O rival of the rose!
I never thought to ask, I never knew;
But, in my simple ignorance, suppose
The self-same Power that brought me there brought you.

RALPH WALDO EMERSON

Two Rivers

Thy summer voice, Musketaquit,
Repeats the music of the rain;
But sweeter rivers pulsing flit
Through thee, as thou through Concord Plain.

Thou in thy narrow banks art pent:
The stream I love unbounded goes
Through flood and sea and firmament;
Through light, through life, it forward flows.

I see the inundation sweet,
I hear the spending of the stream
Through years, through men, through Nature fleet,
Through love and thought, through power and dream.

Musketaquit, a goblin strong,
Of shard and flint makes jewels gay;
They lose their grief who hear his song,
And where he winds is the day of day.

So forth and brighter fares my stream,—
Who drink it shall not thirst again;

No darkness stains its equal gleam
And ages drop in it like rain.

RALPH WALDO EMERSON

Brahma

If the red slayer think he slays,
    Or if the slain think he is slain,
They know not well the subtle ways
    I keep, and pass, and turn again.

Far or forgot to me is near;
    Shadow and sunlight are the same;
The vanquished gods to me appear;
    And one to me are shame and fame.

They reckon ill who leave me out;
    When me they fly, I am the wings;
I am the doubter and the doubt,
    And I the hymn the Brahmin sings.

The strong gods pine for my abode,
    And pine in vain the sacred Seven;
But thou, meek lover of the good!
    Find me, and turn thy back on heaven.

RALPH WALDO EMERSON

History

There is no great and no small
To the Soul that maketh all:
And where it cometh, all things are;
And it cometh every where.

I am owner of the sphere,
Of the seven stars and the solar year,

Of Caesar's hand, and Plato's brain,
Of Lord Christ's heart, and Shakespeare's strain.

RALPH WALDO EMERSON

Nature

A subtle chain of countless rings
The next unto the farthest brings;
The eye reads omens where it goes,
And speaks all languages the rose;
And, striving to be man, the worm
Mounts through all the spires of form.

RALPH WALDO EMERSON

To Giulia Grisi

When the rose is brightest,
    Its bloom will soonest die;
When burns the meteor brightest,
    'T will vanish from the sky.
If Death but wait until delight
    O'errun the heart like wine,
And break the cup with brimming quite,
I die—for thou hast poured to-night
    The last drop into mine.

NATHANIEL PARKER WILLIS

Hymn to the Night

'Ασπασίη, τρίλλιστος

I heard the trailing garments of the Night
    Sweep through her marble halls!
I saw her sable skirts all fringed with light
    From the celestial walls!

I felt her presence, by its spell of might,
    Stoop o'er me from above;
The calm, majestic presence of the Night,
    As of the one I love.

I heard the sounds of sorrow and delight,
    The manifold, soft chimes,
That fill the haunted chambers of the Night,
    Like some old poet's rhymes.

From the cool cisterns of the midnight air
    My spirit drank repose;
The fountain of perpetual peace flows there,—
    From those deep cisterns flows.

O holy Night! from thee I learn to bear
    What man has borne before!
Thou layest thy finger on the lips of Care,
    And they complain no more.

Peace! Peace! Orestes-like I breathe this prayer!
    Descend with broad-winged flight,
The welcome, the thrice-prayed-for, the most fair,
    The best-beloved Night!

        HENRY WADSWORTH LONGFELLOW

Snow-Flakes

Out of the bosom of the Air,
    Out of the cloud-folds of her garments shaken,
Over the woodlands brown and bare,
    Over the harvest-fields forsaken,
        Silent and soft and slow
        Descends the snow.

Even as our cloudy fancies take
    Suddenly shape in some divine expression,
Even as the troubled heart doth make
    In the white countenance confession,
        The troubled sky reveals
        The grief it feels.

This is the poem of the air,
    Slowly in silent syllables recorded;
This is the secret of despair,
    Long in its cloudy bosom hoarded,
        Now whispered and revealed
        To wood and field.

HENRY WADSWORTH LONGFELLOW

"The tide rises, the tide falls"

The tide rises, the tide falls,
The twilight darkens, the curlew calls;
Along the sea-sands damp and brown
The traveller hastens toward the town,
    And the tide rises, the tide falls.

Darkness settles on roofs and walls,
But the sea, the sea in the darkness calls;
The little waves, with their soft, white hands,
Efface the footprints in the sands,
    And the tide rises, the tide falls.

The morning breaks; the steeds in their stalls
Stamp and neigh, as the hostler calls;
The day returns, but nevermore
Returns the traveller to the shore,
    And the tide rises, the tide falls.

HENRY WADSWORTH LONGFELLOW

Chaucer

An old man in a lodge within a park;
The chamber walls depicted all around
With portraitures of huntsman, hawk, and hound,
And the hurt deer. He listeneth to the lark,
Whose song comes with the sunshine through the dark
Of painted glass in leaden lattice bound;
He listeneth and he laugheth at the sound,

Then writeth in a book like any clerk.
He is the poet of the dawn, who wrote
The Canterbury Tales, and his old age
Made beautiful with song; and as I read
I hear the crowing cock, I hear the note
Of lark and linnet, and from every page
Rise odors of plowed field or flowery mead.

HENRY WADSWORTH LONGFELLOW

Milton

I pace the sounding sea-beach and behold
How the voluminous billows roll and run,
Upheaving and subsiding, while the sun
Shines through their sheeted emerald far unrolled
And the ninth wave, slow gathering fold on fold
All its loose-flowing garments into one,
Plunges upon the shore, and floods the dun
Pale reach of sands, and changes them to gold.
So in majestic cadence rise and fall
The mighty undulations of thy song,
O sightless bard, England's Maeonides!
And ever and anon, high over all
Uplifted, a ninth wave superb and strong,
Floods all the soul with its melodious seas.

HENRY WADSWORTH LONGFELLOW

The Pageant

A sound as if from bells of silver,
    Or elfin cymbals smitten clear,
    Through the frost-pictured panes I hear.

A brightness which outshines the morning,
    A splendor brooking no delay,
    Beckons and tempts my feet away.

I leave the trodden village highway
    For virgin snow-paths glimmering through
    A jewelled elm-tree avenue;

Where, keen against the walls of sapphire,
    The gleaming tree-bolls, ice-embossed,
    Hold up their chandeliers of frost.

I tread in Orient halls enchanted,
    I dream the Saga's dream of caves
    Gem-lit beneath the North Sea waves!

I walk the land of Eldorado,
    I touch its mimic garden bowers,
    Its silver leaves and diamond flowers!

The flora of the mystic mine-world
    Around me lifts on crystal stems
    The petals of its clustered gems!

What miracle of weird transforming
    In this wild work of frost and light,
    This glimpse of glory infinite!

This foregleam of the Holy City
    Like that to him of Patmos given,
    The white bride coming down from heaven!

How flash the ranked and mail-clad alders,
    Through what sharp-glancing spears of reeds
    The brook its muffled water leads!

Yon maple, like the bush of Horeb,
    Burns unconsumed: a white, cold fire
    Rays out from every grassy spire.

Each slender rush and spike of mullein,
    Low laurel shrub and drooping fern,
    Transfigured, blaze where'er I turn.

How yonder Ethiopian hemlock
    Crowned with his glistening circlet stands!
    What jewels light his swarthy hands!

Here, where the forest opens southward,
   Between its hospitable pines,
   As through a door, the warm sun shines.

The jewels loosen on the branches,
   And lightly, as the soft winds blow,
   Fall, tinkling, on the ice below.

And through the clashing of their cymbals
   I hear the old familiar fall
   Of water down the rocky wall,

Where, from its wintry prison breaking,
   In dark and silence hidden long,
   The brook repeats its summer song.

One instant flashing in the sunshine,
   Keen as a sabre from its sheath,
   Then lost again the ice beneath.

I hear the rabbit lightly leaping,
   The foolish screaming of the jay,
   The chopper's axe-stroke far away;

The clamor of some neighboring barnyard,
   The lazy cock's belated crow,
   Or cattle-tramp in crispy snow.

And, as in some enchanted forest
   The lost knight hears his comrades sing,
   And, near at hand, their bridles ring,—

So welcome I these sounds and voices,
   These airs from far-off summer blown,
   This life that leaves me not alone.

For the white glory overawes me;
   The crystal terror of the seer
   Of Chebar's vision blinds me here.

Rebuke me not, O sapphire heaven!
   Thou stainless earth, lay not on me
   Thy keen reproach of purity,

If, in this august presence-chamber,
    I sigh for summer's leaf-green gloom
    And warm airs thick with odorous bloom!

Let the strange frost-work sink and crumble,
    And let the loosened tree-boughs swing,
    Till all their bells of silver ring.

Shine warmly down, thou sun of noontime,
    On this chill pageant, melt and move
    The winter's frozen heart with love.

And, soft and low, thou wind south-blowing,
    Breathe through a veil of tenderest haze
    Thy prophecy of summer days.

Come with thy green relief of promise,
    And to this dead, cold splendor bring
    The living jewels of the spring!

JOHN GREENLEAF WHITTIER

The Last Leaf

I saw him once before,
As he passed by the door,
    And again
The pavement stones resound,
As he totters o'er the ground
    With his cane.

They say that in his prime,
Ere the pruning-knife of Time
    Cut him down,
Not a better man was found
By the Crier on his round
    Through the town.

But now he walks the streets,
And he looks at all he meets
    Sad and wan,

And he shakes his feeble head,
That it seems as if he said,
   "They are gone."

The mossy marbles rest
On the lips that he has prest
   In their bloom,
And the names he loved to hear
Have been carved for many a year
   On the tomb.

My grandmamma has said—
Poor old lady, she is dead
   Long ago—
That he had a Roman nose,
And his cheek was like a rose
   In the snow.

But now his nose is thin,
And it rests upon his chin
   Like a staff,
And a crook is in his back,
And a melancholy crack
   In his laugh.

I know it is a sin
For me to sit and grin
   At him here;
But the old three-cornered hat,
And the breeches, and all that,
   Are so queer!

And if I should live to be
The last leaf upon the tree
   In the spring,
Let them smile, as I do now,
At the old forsaken bough
   Where I cling.

OLIVER WENDELL HOLMES

The Chambered Nautilus

This is the ship of pearl, which, poets feign,
    Sails the unshadowed main,—
    The venturous bark that flings
On the sweet summer wind its purpled wings
In gulfs enchanted, where the Siren sings,
    And coral reefs lie bare,
Where the cold sea-maids rise to sun their streaming hair.

Its webs of living gauze no more unfurl;
    Wrecked is the ship of pearl!
    And every chambered cell,
Where its dim dreaming life was wont to dwell,
As the frail tenant shaped his growing shell,
    Before thee lies revealed,—
Its irised ceiling rent, its sunless crypt unsealed!

Year after year beheld the silent toil
    That spread his lustrous coil;
    Still, as the spiral grew,
He left the past year's dwelling for the new,
Stole with soft step its shining archway through,
    Built up its idle door,
Stretched in his last-found home, and knew the old no more.

Thanks for the heavenly message brought by thee,
    Child of the wandering sea,
    Cast from her lap, forlorn!
From thy dead lips a clear note is born
Than ever Triton blew from wreathèd horn!
    While on mine ear it rings,
Through the deep caves of thought I hear a voice that sings:—

Build thee more stately mansions, O my soul,
    As the swift seasons roll!
    Leave thy low-vaulted past!
Let each new temple, nobler than the last,
Shut thee from heaven with a dome more vast,
    Till thou at length art free,
Leaving thine outgrown shell by life's unresting sea!

                    OLIVER WENDELL HOLMES

Old Ironsides

September 14, 1830

Ay, tear her tattered ensign down!
    Long has it waved on high,
And many an eye has danced to see
    That banner in the sky;
Beneath it rung the battle shout,
    And burst the cannon's roar—
The meteor of the ocean air
    Shall sweep the clouds no more.

Her deck, once red with heroes' blood,
    Where knelt the vanquished foe,
When winds were hurrying o'er the flood,
    And waves were white below,
No more shall feel the victor's tread,
    Or know the conquered knee—
The harpies of the shore shall pluck
    The eagle of the sea!

Oh, better that her shattered hulk
    Should sink beneath the wave;
Her thunders shook the mighty deep,
    And there should be her grave;
Nail to the mast her holy flag,
    Set every threadbare sail,
And give her to the god of storms,
    The lightning and the gale!

OLIVER WENDELL HOLMES

To One in Paradise

Thou wast that all to me, love,
    For which my soul did pine—
A green isle in the sea, love,
    A fountain and a shrine,
All wreathed with fairy fruits and flowers,
    And all the flowers were mine.

Ah, dream too bright to last!
    Ah, starry Hope! that didst arise
But to be overcast!
    A voice from out the Future cries,
'On! on!'—but o'er the Past
    (Dim gulf!) my spirit hovering lies
Mute, motionless, aghast!

For, alas! alas! with me
    The light of Life is o'er!
No more—no more—no more—
    (Such language holds the solemn sea
To the sands upon the shore)
    Shall bloom the thunder-blasted tree,
Or the stricken eagle soar!

And all my days are trances,
    And all my nightly dreams
And where thy grey eye glances,
    And where thy footstep gleams—
In what ethereal dances,
    By what eternal streams.

EDGAR ALLAN POE

The City in the Sea

Lo! Death has reared himself a throne
In a strange city lying alone
Far down within the dim West,
Where the good and the bad and the worst and the best
Have gone to their eternal rest.
There shrines and palaces and towers
(Time-eaten towers that tremble not!)
Resemble nothing that is ours.
Around, by lifting winds forgot,
Resignedly beneath the sky
The melancholy waters lie.

No rays from the holy heaven come down
On the long night-time of that town;

But light from out the lurid sea
Streams up the turrets silently—
Gleams up the pinnacles far and free—
Up domes—up spires—up kingly halls—
Up fanes—up Babylon-like walls—
Up shadowy long-forgotten bowers
Of sculptured ivy and stone flowers—
Up many and many a marvellous shrine
Whose wreathèd friezes intertwine
The viol, the violet, and the vine.

Resignedly beneath the sky
The melancholy waters lie.
So blend the turrets and shadows there
That all seem pendulous in air,
While from a proud tower in the town
Death looks gigantically down.

There open fanes and gaping graves
Yawn level with the luminous waves;
But not the riches there that lie
In each idol's diamond eye—
Not the gaily-jewelled dead
Tempt the waters from their bed;
For no ripples curl, alas!
Along that wilderness of glass—
No swellings tell that winds may be
Upon some far-off happier sea—
No heavings hint that winds have been
On seas less hideously serene.

But lo, a stir is in the air!
The wave—there is a movement there!
As if the towers had thrust aside,
In slightly sinking, the dull tide—
As if their tops had feebly given
A void within the filmy Heaven.
The waves have now a redder glow—
The hours are breathing faint and low—
And when, amid no earthly moans,
Down, down that town shall settle hence,

Hell, rising from a thousand thrones,
Shall do it reverence.

EDGAR ALLAN POE

The Haunted Palace

In the greenest of our valleys
    By good angels tenanted,
Once a fair and stately palace—
    Radiant palace—reared its head.
In the monarch Thought's dominion,
    It stood there!
Never seraph spread a pinion
    Over fabric half so fair!

Banners yellow, glorious, golden,
    On its roof did float and flow
(This—all this—was in the olden
    Time, long ago,)
And every gentle air that dallied,
    In that sweet day,
Along the ramparts plumed and pallid,
    A wingèd odor went away.

Wanderers in that happy valley,
    Through two luminous windows, saw
Spirits moving musically
    To a lute's well-tunèd law,
Round about a throne where, sitting,
    (Porphyrogene!)
In state his glory well befitting,
    The ruler of the realm was seen.

And all with pearl and ruby glowing
    Was the fair palace door,
Through which came flowing, flowing, flowing
    And sparkling evermore,
A troop of Echoes, whose sweet duty
    Was but to sing,

In voices of surpassing beauty,
    The wit and wisdom of their king.

But evil things, in robes of sorrow,
    Assailed the monarch's high estate.
(Ah, let us mourn!—for never morrow
    Shall dawn upon him, desolate!)
And round about his home the glory
    That blushed and bloomed,
Is but a dim-remembered story
    Of the old time entombed.

And travellers, now, within that valley,
    Through the red-litten windows see
Vast forms that move fantastically
    To a discordant melody,
While, like a ghastly rapid river,
    Through the pale door
A hideous throng rush out forever,
    And laugh—but smile no more.

EDGAR ALLAN POE

Dream-Land

By a route obscure and lonely,
Haunted by ill angels only,
Where an Eidolon, named NIGHT,
On a black throne reigns upright,
I have reached these lands but newly
From an ultimate dim Thule—
From a wild weird clime that lieth, sublime,
    Out of SPACE—out of TIME.

Bottomless vales and boundless floods,
And chasms, and caves, and Titan woods,
With forms that no man can discover
For the dews that drip all over;
Mountains toppling evermore
Into seas without a shore;
Seas that restlessly aspire,

Surging, unto skies of fire;
Lakes that endlessly outspread
Their lone waters, lone and dead,—
Their still waters, still and chilly
With the snows of the lolling lily.

By the lakes that thus outspread
Their lone waters, lone and dead,—
Their sad waters, sad and chilly
With the snows of the lolling lily,—
By the mountains—near the river
Murmuring lowly murmuring ever,—
By the grey woods,—by the swamp
Where the toad and the newt encamp,—
By the dismal tarns and pools
  Where dwell the Ghouls,—
By each spot the most unholy—
In each nook most melancholy,—
There the traveller meets, aghast,
Sheeted Memories of the Past—
Shrouded forms that start and sigh
As they pass the wanderer by—
White-robed forms of friends long given,
In agony, to the Earth—and Heaven.

For the heart whose woes are legion
'T is a peaceful, soothing region—
For the spirit that walks in shadow
'T is—oh, 't is an Eldorado!
But the traveller, travelling through it,
May not—dare not openly view it;
Never its mysteries are exposed
To the weak human eye unclosed;
So wills its King, who hath forbid
The uplifting of the fringèd lid;
And thus the sad Soul that here passes
Beholds it but through darkened glasses.

By a route obscure and lonely,
Haunted by ill angels only,
Where an Eidolon, named NIGHT,
On a black throne reigns upright,

I have wandered home but newly
From this ultimate dim Thule.

EDGAR ALLAN POE

A Proem

When in my walks I meet some ruddy lad
    Or swarthy man, with tray-beladen head,
Whose smile entreats me, or his visage sad,
    To buy the images he moulds for bread,

I think that,—though his poor Greek Slave in chains,
    His Venus and her Boy with plaster dart,
Be, like the organ-grinder's quavering strains,
    But farthings in the currency of art,—

Such coins a kingly effigy still wear,
    Let metals base or precious in them mix:
The painted vellum hallows not the Prayer,
    Nor ivory nor gold the Crucifix.

SAMUEL WARD

Stanza From an Early Poem

Thought is deeper than all speech,
    Feeling deeper than all thought;
Souls to souls can never teach
    What unto themselves was taught.

CHRISTOPHER PEARSE CRANCH

The Pines and the Sea

Beyond the low marsh-meadows and the beach,
Seen through the hoary trunks of windy pines,
The long blue level of the ocean shines.
The distant surf, with hoarse, complaining speech,

Out from its sandy barrier seems to reach;
And while the sun behind the woods declines,
The moaning sea with sighing boughs combines,
And waves and pines make answer, each to each.
O melancholy soul, whom far and near,
In life, faith, hope, the same sad undertone
Pursues from thought to thought! thou needs must hear
An old refrain, too much, too long thine own:
'Tis thy mortality infects thine ear;
The mournful strain was in thyself alone.

CHRISTOPHER PEARSE CRANCH

The Spirit-Land

Father! thy wonders do not singly stand,
Nor far removed where feet have seldom strayed;
Around us ever lies the enchanted land,
In marvels rich to thine own sons displayed.
In finding thee are all things round us found;
In losing thee are all things lost beside;
Ears have we, but in vain strange voices sound;
And to our eyes the vision is denied.
We wander in the country far remote,
Mid tombs and ruined piles in death to dwell;
Or on the records of past greatness dote,
And for a buried soul the living sell;
While on our path bewildered falls the night
That ne'er returns us to the fields of light.

JONES VERY

The Hand and Foot

The hand and foot that stir not, they shall find
Sooner than all the rightful place to go:
Now in their motion free as roving wind,
Though first no snail so limited and slow;
I mark them full of labor all the day,
Each active motion made in perfect rest;

They cannot from their path mistaken stray,
Though 't is not theirs, yet in it they are blest;
The bird has not their hidden track found out,
The cunning fox though full of art he be;
It is the way unseen, the certain route,
Where ever bound, yet thou art ever free;
The path of Him, whose perfect law of love
Bids spheres and atoms in just order move.

JONES VERY

Yourself

'Tis to yourself I speak; you cannot know
Him whom I call in speaking such a one,
For you beneath the earth lie buried low,
Which he alone as living walks upon:
You may at times have heard him speak to you,
And often wished perchance that you were he;
And I must ever wish that it were true,
For then you could hold fellowship with me:
But now you hear us talk as strangers, met
Above the room wherein you lie abed;
A word perhaps loud spoken you may get,
Or hear our feet when heavily they tread;
But he who speaks, or him who's spoken to,
Must both remain as strangers still to you.

JONES VERY

Mist

Low-anchored cloud,
Newfoundland air,
Fountain-head and source of rivers
Dew-cloth, dream-drapery,
And napkin spread by fays;
Drifting meadow of the air,

Where bloom the daisied banks and violets
And in whose fenny labyrinth
The bittern booms and heron wades;
Spirit of lakes and seas and rivers,—
Bear only perfumes and the scent
Of healing herbs to just men's fields.

HENRY DAVID THOREAU

Smoke

Light-wingèd Smoke! Icarian bird,
Melting thy pinions in thy upward flight;
Lark without song, and messenger of dawn,
Circling above the hamlets as thy nest;
Or else, departing dream, and shadowy form
Of midnight vision, gathering up thy skirts;
By night star-veiling, and by day
Darkening the light and blotting out the sun;
Go thou, my incense, upward from this hearth,
And ask the gods to pardon this clear flame.

HENRY DAVID THOREAU

Stanzas

Nature doth have her dawn each day,
But mine are far between;
Content, I cry, for, sooth to say,
Mine brightest are, I ween.

For when my sun doth deign to rise,
Though it be her noontide,
Her fairest field in shadow lies,
Nor can my light abide.

Sometimes I bask me in her day,
Conversing with my mate,
But if we interchange one ray,
Forthwith her heats abate.

Through his discourse I climb and see
  As from some eastern hill,
A brighter morrow rise to me
  Than lieth in her still.

As 't were two summer days in one,
  Two Sundays come together,
Our rays united make one sun,
  With fairest summer weather.

HENRY DAVID THOREAU

Winter Memories

Within the circuit of this plodding life
There enter moments of an azure hue,
Untarnished fair as is the violet
Or anemone, when the spring strews them
By some meandering rivulet, which make
The best philosophy untrue that aims
But to console man for his grievances.
I have remembered when the winter came,
High in my chamber in the frosty nights,
When in the still light of the cheerful moon,
On every twig and rail and jutting spout,
The icy spears were adding to their length
Against the arrows of the coming sun,
How in the shimmering noon of summer past
Some unrecorded beam slanted across
The upland pastures where the Johnswort grew;
Or heard, amid the verdure of my mind,
The bee's long smothered hum, on the blue flag
Loitering amidst the mead; or busy rill,
Which now through all its course stands still and dumb
Its own memorial,—purling at its play
Along the slopes, and through the meadows next,
Until its youthful sound was hushed at last
In the staid current of the lowland stream;
Or seen the furrows shine but late upturned,
And where the fieldfare followed in the rear;
When all the fields around lay bound and hoar

Beneath a thick integument of snow.
So by God's cheap economy made rich
To go upon my winter's task again.

HENRY DAVID THOREAU

Auspex

My heart, I cannot still it,
Nest that had song-birds in it;
And when the last shall go,
The dreary days, to fill it,
Instead of lark or linnet,
Shall whirl dead leaves and snow.

Had they been swallows only,
Without the passion stronger
That skyward longs and sings,—
Woe's me, I shall be lonely
When I can feel no longer
The impatience of their wings!

A moment, sweet delusion,
Like birds the brown leaves hover;
But it will not be long
Before their wild confusion
Fall wavering down to cover
The poet and his song.

JAMES RUSSELL LOWELL

from the Prelude to

The Vision of Sir Launfal

And what is so rare as a day in June?
    Then, if ever, come perfect days;
Then Heaven tries the earth if it be in tune,
    And over it softly her warm ear lays:
Whether we look, or whether we listen,

We hear life murmur, or see it glisten;
Every clod feels a stir of might,
    An instinct within it that reaches and towers
And, groping blindly above it for light,
    Climbs to a soul in grass and flowers;
The flush of life may well be seen
    Thrilling back over hills and valleys;
The cowslip startles in meadows green,
    The buttercup catches the sun in its chalice
And there's never a leaf or a blade too mean
    To be some happy creature's palace;
The little bird sits at his door in the sun,
    Atilt like a blossom among the leaves,
And lets his illumined being o'errun
    With the deluge of summer it receives;
His mate feels the eggs beneath her wings,
And the heart in her dumb breast flutters and sings;
He sings to the wide world, and she to her nest,—
In the nice ear of Nature, which song is the best?

Now is the high-tide of the year,
    And whatever of life hath ebbed away
Comes flooding back, with a ripply cheer,
    Into every bare inlet and creek and bay;
Now the heart is so full that a drop overfills it,
We are happy now because God wills it;
No matter how barren the past may have been,
'Tis enough for us now that the leaves are green;
We sit in the warm shade and feel right well
How the sap creeps up and the blossoms swell;
We may shut our eyes, but we cannot help knowing
That skies are clear and grass is growing;
That breeze comes whispering in our ear,
That dandelions are blossoming near,
    That maize has sprouted, that streams are flowing,
That the river is bluer than the sky,
That the robin is plastering his house hard by;
And if the breeze kept the good news back,
For other couriers we should not lack;
    We could guess it all by yon heifer's lowing,—
And hark! how clear bold chanticleer,
Warmed with the new wine of the year,
    Tells all his lusty crowing!

Joy comes, grief goes, we know not how;
Everything is happy now,
     Everything is upward striving;
'Tis as easy now for the heart to be true
As for grass to be green or skies to be blue,—
     'Tis the natural way of living:
Who knows whither the clouds have fled?
     In the unscarred heaven they leave no wake,
And the eyes forget the tears they have shed,
     The heart forgets its sorrow and ache;
The soul partakes the season's youth,
     And the sulphurous rifts of passion and woe
Lie deep 'neath a silence pure and smooth,
     Like burnt-out craters healed with snow.

                    JAMES RUSSELL LOWELL

Monna Lisa

     She gave me all that woman can,
     Nor her soul's nunnery forego,
     A confidence that man to man
     Without remorse can never show.

     Rare art, that can the sense refine
     Till not a pulse rebellious stirs,
     And, since she never can be mine,
     Makes it seem sweeter to be hers!

               JAMES RUSSELL LOWELL

Battle-Hymn of the Republic

Mine eyes have seen the glory of the coming of the Lord:
He is trampling out the vintage where the grapes of wrath are stored;
He hath loosed the fateful lightning of his terrible swift sword:
     His truth is marching on.

I have seen him in the watch-fires of a hundred circling camps;
They have builded him an altar in the evening dews and damps;

I can read his righteous sentence by the dim and flaring lamps:
   His day is marching on.

I have read a fiery gospel, writ in burnished rows of steel:
"As ye deal with my contemners, so with you my grace shall deal;
Let the Hero, born of woman, crush the serpent with his heel,
   Since God is marching on."

He has sounded forth the trumpet that shall never call retreat;
He is sifting out the hearts of men before his judgment-seat:
O, be swift, my soul, to answer him! be jubilant, my feet!
   Our God is marching on.

In the beauty of the lilies Christ was born across the sea,
With a glory in his bosom that transfigures you and me;
As he died to make men holy, let us die to make men free,
   While God is marching on.

He is coming like the glory of the morning on the wave,
He is wisdom to the mighty, he is honor to the brave,
So the world shall be his footstool, the soul of wrong his slave,
   Our God is marching on!

                       JULIA WARD HOWE

"Darest thou now O soul"

Darest thou now O soul,
Walk out with me toward the unknown region,
Where neither ground is for the feet nor any path to follow?

No map there, nor guide,
Nor voice sounding, nor touch of human hand,
Nor face with blooming flesh, nor lips, nor eyes, are in that land.

I know it not O soul,
Nor dost thou, all is a blank before us,
All waits undream'd of in that region, that inaccessible land.

Till when the ties loosen,
All but the ties eternal, Time and Space,
Nor darkness, gravitation, sense, nor any bounds bounding us.

Then we burst forth, we float,
In Time and Space O soul, prepared for them,
Equal, equipt at last, (O joy! O fruit of all!) them to fulfil O soul.

WALT WHITMAN

"The world below the brine"

The world below the brine,
Forests at the bottom of the sea, the branches and leaves,
Sea-lettuce, vast lichens, strange flowers and seeds, the thick
        tangle, openings, and pink turf,
Different colors, pale gray and green, purple, white, and gold,
        the play of light through the water,
Dumb swimmers there among the rocks, coral, gluten, grass,
        rushes, and the aliment of the swimmers,
Sluggish existences grazing there suspended, or slowly crawl-
        ing close to the bottom,
The sperm-whale at the surface blowing air and spray, or
        disporting with his flukes,
The leaden-eyed shark, the walrus, the turtle, the hairy sea-
        leopard, and the sting-ray,
Passions there, wars, pursuits, tribes, sight in those ocean-
        depths, breathing that thick-breathing air, as so many do,
The change thence to the sight here, and to the subtle air
        breathed by beings like us who walk this sphere,
The change onward from ours to that of beings who walk
        other spheres.

WALT WHITMAN

To a Locomotive in Winter

Thee for my recitative,
Thee in the driving storm even as now, the snow, the winter-
        day declining,
Thee in thy panoply, thy measur'd dual throbbing and thy
        beat convulsive,
Thy black cylindric body, golden brass and silvery steel,
Thy ponderous side-bars, parallel and connecting rods, gyrat-
        ing, shuttling at thy sides,

Thy metrical, now swelling pant and roar, now tapering in
    the distance,
Thy great protruding head-light fix'd in front,
Thy long, pale, floating vapor-pennants, tinged with delicate
    purple,
The dense and murky clouds out-belching from thy smoke-
    stack,
Thy knitted frame, thy springs and valves, the tremulous
    twinkle of thy wheels,
Thy train of cars behind, obedient, merrily following,
Through gale or calm, now swift, now slack, yet steadily
    careering;
Type of the modern—emblem of motion and power—pulse
    of the continent,
For once come serve the Muse and merge in verse, even as
    here I see thee,
With storm and buffeting gusts of wind and falling snow,
By day thy warning ringing bell to sound its notes,
By night thy silent signal lamps to swing.

Fierce-throated beauty!
Roll through my chant with all thy lawless music, thy swing-
    ing lamps at night,
Thy madly-whistled laughter, echoing, rumbling like an earth-
    quake, rousing all,
Law of thyself complete, thine own track firmly holding,
(No sweetness debonair of tearful harp or glib piano thine,)
Thy trills of shrieks by rocks and hills return'd,
Launch'd o'er the prairies wide, across the lakes,
To the free skies unpent and glad and strong.

WALT WHITMAN

An Uninscribed Monument
on One of the Battlefields of the Wilderness

Silence and Solitude may hint
    (Whose home is in yon piny wood)
What I, though tableted, could never tell—
    The din which here befell,
    And striving of the multitude.

The iron cones and spheres of death
    Set round me in their rust,—
        These, too, if just,
Shall speak with more than animated breath.
    Thou who beholdest, if thy thought,
Not narrowed down to personal cheer,
Take in the import of the quiet here—
    The after-quiet—the calm full fraught;
Thou too wilt silent stand,—
Silent as I, and lonesome as the land.

HERMAN MELVILLE

The Enviable Isles

Through storms you reach them and from storms are free.
    Afar descried, the foremost drear in hue,
But, nearer, green; and on the marge, the sea
    Makes thunder low and mist of rainbowed dew.

But, inland,—where the sleep that folds the hills
A dreamier sleep, the trance of God, instils—
    On uplands hazed, in wandering airs aswoon,
Slow-swaying palms salute love's cypress tree
    Adown in vale where pebbly runlets croon
A song to lull all sorrow and all glee.

Sweet-fern and moss in many a glade are here,
    Where, strown in flocks, what cheek-flushed myriads lie
Dimpling in dream, unconscious slumberers mere,
    Where billows endless round the beaches lie.

HERMAN MELVILLE

Sonnets

LXVI

Tonight I walked with the grim Florentine
Through all the woes of his material hell;

And wondered greatly of the joy which fell
On his stern spirit o'er the foes who pine
Forever in those waves of fiery brine
Beneath the malediction of his spell.
Yet wondered more he nowhere chose to tell
Of such a dreary destiny as mine.
He paints no lover with a weary sense
That what he loves is just beyond his sight,
Towards which in vain he wings his wistful flight,
Drawn ever backward by omnipotence:
Perhaps his hatred was not so intense
As to curse any with such cruel despite.

LXXIX

Oh! sigh no more, no longer paint the air
With the distempered pictures of thy brain!
The sighs are idle, and the shapes are vain
Before thy reason's cold, unwinking stare.
Why wound thy heart with arrows of despair,
By love's shrewd shaft already cleft in twain?
Why drag and drag a still unfolding chain,
If rest will make thy shackles less to bear?
Thus with myself I sometimes strive in thought,
To reason down the love that preys upon
Heart, mind, life, soul, and feeds on all as one.
As well might poor Prometheus, distraught
With the fierce eagle's hungry claws, be brought
To turn his face and smile against the sun.

CXV

Oh spring, that hides the wrinkled earth in green,
And decorates the cracked and rugged bark
Of trees with lichens pale and mosses dark:
That makes the canker of decay unseen
Beneath the shadow of thy leafy screen;
Till from the hillside and the rolling park
Are razed the traces of Time's fatal mark,
And all things glitter with creation's sheen;—
Restoring Spring, hast thou no mask to spread
Above the wrinkles of this drooping brow?
No skill to hide these limbs that crook and bow,

No purple tints of youth to grace this head
Ashen with years and sorrows? Why should'st thou
So trim the scene in the poor actor's stead?

CLIII

You say my Love no marvel is to you.
As she sedately treads the dust and stir
Of earthly ways, a brightness follows her,
Like morning's track across the shaking dew.
How shall you judge, who see her beauty through
The haze of distance, how your sight may err?
Or what delights her presence may confer
Upon the privilege of a nearer view?
But keep your judgment; you may rail as well
Against the moon, and hope to dim her rays,
Which the great ocean follows and obeys.
Ring out your censure with the crier's bell;
For beauty lives not by your blame or praise;
But, as you rate it, thus your worth you tell.

CXCIV

Three seasons only in his calendar
My love has counted. First came opening spring,
When love put forth, a weak and timid thing,
Shy of the cowslip's nod, or violet's stir.
Then summer caught him with the rush and whir
Of many wings; and proudly caroling,
He brushed the lilies, made the roses swing,
And trod the land a smiling conqueror.
With autumn's fruitages ripened at his feet,
He pauses now. Is this the end of all—
The consummation, boundless and complete?
Or shall the starving raven sound his call
Through days to come, when every leaf shall fall,
And dismal winter's snows and tempest beat?

GEORGE HENRY BOKER

Charleston

April, 1863

Calm as that second summer which precedes
    The first fall of the snow,
In the broad sunlight of heroic deeds,
    The city bides the foe.

As yet, behind their ramparts, stern and proud,
    Her bolted thunders sleep,—
Dark Sumter, like a battlemented cloud,
    Looms o'er the solemn deep.

No Calpe frowns from lofty cliff or scaur
    To guard the holy strand;
But Moultrie holds in leash her dogs of war
    Above the level sand.

And down the dunes a thousand guns lie couched,
    Unseen, beside the flood,—
Like tigers in some Orient jungle crouched,
    That wait and watch for blood.

Meanwhile, through streets still echoing with trade,
    Walk grave and thoughtful men,
Whose hands may one day wield the patriot's blade
    As lightly as the pen.

And maidens, with such eyes as would go dim
    Over a bleeding hound,
Seem each one to have caught the strength of him
    Whose sword she sadly bound.

Thus girt without and garrisoned at home,
    Day patient following day,
Old Charleston looks from roof and spire and dome,
    Across her tranquil bay.

Ships, through a hundred foes, from Saxon lands
    And spicy Indian ports,
Bring Saxon steel and iron to her hands,
    And summer to her courts.

But still, along yon dim Atlantic line,
    The only hostile smoke
Creeps like a harmless mist above the brine,
    From some frail floating oak.

Shall the spring dawn, and she, still clad in smiles,
    And with an unscathed brow,
Rest in the strong arms of her palm-crowned isles,
    As fair and free as now?

We know not; in the temple of the Fates
    God has inscribed her doom:
And, all untroubled in her faith, she waits
    The triumph or the tomb.

HENRY TIMROD

"The wind took up the northern things"

The wind took up the northern things
And piled them in the south,
Then bent the east unto the west
And, opening his mouth,

The four divisions of the earth
Did make as to devour,
While everything to corners slunk
Behind the awful power.

The wind unto his chambers went,
And nature ventured out,
Her subjects scattered into place,
Her systems ranged about;

Again the smoke from dwellings rose
The day abroad was heard.
How intimate, a tempest past,
The transport of the bird!

EMILY DICKINSON

"I like to see it lap the miles"

I like to see it lap the miles,
And lick the valleys up,
And stop to feed itself at tanks;
And then, prodigious, step

Around a pile of mountains,
And, supercilious, peer
In shanties by the sides of roads;
And then a quarry pare

To fit its sides, and crawl between,
Complaining all the while
In horrid, hooting stanza;
Then chase itself down hill

And neigh like Boanerges;
Then, punctual as a star,
Stop—docile and omnipotent—
At its own stable door.

EMILY DICKINSON

"Because I could not stop for Death"

Because I could not stop for Death,
He kindly stopped for me;
The carriage held but just ourselves
And Immortality.

We slowly drove, he knew no haste,
And I had put away
My labour, and my leisure too,
For his civility.

We passed the school where children played,
Their lessons scarcely done;
We passed the fields of grazing grain,
We passed the setting sun.

We paused before a house that seemed
A swelling on the ground;
The roof was scarcely visible,
The cornice but a mound.

Since then 'tis centuries; but each
Feels shorter than the day
I first surmised the horses' heads
Were toward eternity.

EMILY DICKINSON

"Whole gulfs of red and fleets of red"

Whole gulfs of red and fleets of red
And crews of solid blood
Did place about the west tonight
As 'twere a signal ground,

And they, appointed creatures
In authorized arrays
Due, promptly as a drama
That bows and disappears.

EMILY DICKINSON

"I heard a fly buzz when I died"

I heard a fly buzz when I died;
The stillness in the room
Was like the stillness in the air
Between the heaves of storm.

The eyes around had wrung them dry,
And breaths were gathering firm
For that last onset, when the king
Be witnessed in the room.

I willed my keepsakes, signed away
What portion of me be
Assignable—and then it was
There interposed a fly,

With blue, uncertain, stumbling buzz,
Between the light and me;
And then the windows failed, and then
I could not see to see.

EMILY DICKINSON

"A narrow fellow in the grass"

A narrow fellow in the grass
Occasionally rides;
You may have met him,—did you not?
His notice sudden is.

The grass divides as with a comb,
A spotted shaft is seen;
And then it closes at your feet
And opens further on.

He likes a boggy acre,
A floor too cool for corn.
Yet when a child, & barefoot,
I more than once, at morn,

Have passed, I thought, a whip-lash
Unbraiding in the sun,—
When, stooping to secure it,
It wrinkled, and was gone.

Several of nature's people
I know, and they know me;
I feel for them a transport
Of cordiality;

But never met this fellow,
Attended or alone,

Without a tighter breathing,
And zero at the bone.

EMILY DICKINSON

"At half-past three"

At half-past three a single bird
Unto a silent sky
Propounded but a single term
Of cautious melody.

At half-past four, experiment
Had subjugated test,
And lo! her silver principle
Supplanted all the rest.

At half-past seven, element
Nor implement was seen,
And place was where the presence was,
Circumference between.

EMILY DICKINSON

"A bird came down the walk"

A bird came down the walk:
He did not know I saw;
He bit an angle-worm in halves
And ate the fellow, raw.

And then he drank a dew
From a convenient grass,
And then hopped sideways to the wall
To let a beetle pass.

He glanced with rapid eyes
That hurried all abroad,—
They looked like frightened beads, I thought
He stirred his velvet head

Like one in danger; cautious,
I offered him a crumb,
And he unrolled his feathers
And rowed him softer home

Than oars divide the ocean,
Too silver for a seam,
Or butterflies, off banks of noon,
Leap, plashless, as they swim.

EMILY DICKINSON

"The bustle in a house"

The bustle in a house
The morning after death
Is solemnest of industries
Enacted upon earth,—

The sweeping up the heart,
And putting love away
We shall not want to use again
Until eternity.

EMILY DICKINSON

"A route of evanescence"

A route of evanescence
With a revolving wheel;
A resonance of emerald,
A rush of cochineal;
And every blossom on the bush
Adjusts its tumbled head—
The mail from Tunis, probably,
An easy morning's ride.

EMILY DICKINSON

The Scarlet Tanager

A ball of fire shoots through the tamarack
In scarlet splendor, on voluptuous wings;
Delirious joy the pyrotechnist brings,
Who marks for us high summer's almanac.
How instantly the red-coat hurtles back!
No fiercer flame has flashed beneath the sky.
Note now the rapture in his cautious eye,
The conflagration lit along his track.
Winged soul of beauty, tropic in desire,
Thy love seems alien in our northern zone;
Thou giv'st to our green lands a burst of fire
And callest back the fables we disown.
The hot equator thou mightst well inspire,
Or stand above some Eastern monarch's throne.

JOEL BENTON

The Word

O Earth! thou hast not any wind that blows
Which is not music; every weed of thine
Pressed rightly flows in aromatic wine;
And every humble hedgerow flower that grows,
And every little brown bird that doth sing,
Hath something greater than itself, and bears
A living Word to every living thing,
Albeit it hold the Message unawares.
All shapes and sounds have something which is not
Of them: a Spirit broods amid the grass;
Vague outlines of the Everlasting Thought
Lie in the melting shadows as they pass;
The touch of an Eternal Presence thrills
The fringes of the sunsets and the hills.

RICHARD REALF

Memory

My mind lets go a thousand things,
Like dates of wars and deaths of kings,
And yet recalls the very hour—
'Twas noon by yonder village tower,
And on the last blue noon in May—
The wind came briskly up this way,
Crisping the brook beside the road;
Then, pausing here, set down its load
Of pine-scents, and shook listlessly
Two petals from that wild-rose tree.

THOMAS BAILEY ALDRICH

Crossing the Plains

What great yoked brutes with briskets low,
With wrinkled necks like buffalo,
With round, brown, liquid, pleading eyes,
That turned so slow and sad to you,
That shone like love's eyes soft with tears,
That seemed to plead and make replies,
The while they bowed their necks and drew
The creaking load; and looked at you.
Their sable briskets swept the ground,
Their cloven feet kept solemn sound.

Two sullen bullocks led the line,
Their great eyes shining bright like wine;
Two sullen captive kings were they,
That had in time held herds at bay,
And even now they crushed the sod
With stolid sense of majesty,
And stately stepped and stately trod,
As if't were something still to be
Kings even in captivity.

JOAQUIN MILLER

Fame

Their noonday never knows
    What names immortal are:
'Tis night alone that shows
    How star surpasseth star.

JOHN BANNISTER TABB

Biftek aux Champignons

Mimi, do you remember—
    Don't get behind your fan—
That morning in September
    On the cliffs of Grand Manan,
Where to the shock of Fundy
    The topmost harebells sway
(*Campanula rotundi-
    folia: cf.* Gray)?

On the pastures high and level,
    That overlook the sea,
Where I wondered what the devil
    Those little things could be
That Mimi stooped to gather
    As she strolled across the down,
And held her dress skirt rather—
    Oh, now, you needn't frown.

For you know the dew was heavy
    And your boots, *I* know, were thin;
So a little extra brevi-
    ty in skirts was, sure, no sin.
Besides, who minds a cousin?
    First, second, even third,—
I've kissed 'em by the dozen,
    And they never once demurred.

"If one's allowed to ask it,"
    Quoth I, "*Ma belle cousine,*

What have you in your basket?"
    (Those baskets white and green
The brave Passamaquoddies
    Weave out of scented grass,
And sell to tourist bodies
    Who through Mt. Desert pass.)

You answered, slightly frowning,
    "Put down your stupid book—
That everlasting Browning!—
    And come and help me look.
Mushroom you spik him English,
    I call him *champignon:*
I'll teach you to distinguish
    The right kind from the wrong."

There was no fog on Fundy
    That blue September day;
The west wind, for that one day,
    Had swept it all away.
The lighthouse glasses twinkled,
    The white gulls screamed and flew,
The merry sheep-bells tinkled,
    The merry breezes blew.

The bayberry aromatic,
    The papery immortelles
(That give our grandma's attic
    That sentimental smell,
Tied up in little brush-brooms)
    Were sweet as new-mown hay,
While we went hunting mushrooms
    That blue September day.

HENRY AUGUSTIN BEERS

"It is in Winter that we dream of Spring"

It is in Winter that we dream of Spring;
    For all the barren bleakness and the cold,
    The longing fancy sees the frozen mould
Decked with sweet blossoming.

Though all the birds be silent,—though
    The fettered stream's soft voice be still,
And on the leafless bough the snow
    Be rested, marble-like and chill,—

Yet will the fancy build, from these,
    The transient but well-pleasing dream
Of leaf and bloom among the trees,
    And sunlight glancing on the stream.

Though, to the eye, the joyless landscape yields
    No faintest sign to which the hope might cling,—
Amidst the pallid desert of the fields,—
    It is in Winter that we dream of Spring.

ROBERT BURNS WILSON

A Dutch Lullaby

Wynken, Blynken, and Nod one night
    Sailed off in a wooden shoe,—
Sailed on a river of crystal light
    Into a sea of dew.
"Where are you going, and what do you wish?"
    The old moon asked the three.
"We have come to fish for the herring fish
    That live in this beautiful sea;
    Nets of silver and gold have we!"
        Said Wynken,
        Blynken,
        And Nod.

The old moon laughed and sang a song,
    As they rocked in the wooden shoe;
And the wind that sped them all night long
    Ruffled the waves of dew.
The little stars were the herring fish
    That lived in that beautiful sea—
"Now cast your nets wherever you wish,—
    Never afeard are we!"

So cried the stars to the fishermen three,
    Wynken,
    Blynken,
    And Nod.

All night long their nets they threw
    To the stars in the twinkling foam,—
Then down from the skies came the wooden shoe,
    Bringing the fishermen home:
'Twas all so pretty a sail, it seemed
    As if it could not be;
And some folk thought 'twas a dream they'd dreamed
    Of sailing that beautiful sea;
    But I shall name you the fishermen three:
    Wynken,
    Blynken,
    And Nod.

Wynken and Blynken are two little eyes,
    And Nod is a little head,
And the wooden shoe that sailed the skies
    Is a wee one's trundle-bed;
So shut your eyes while Mother sings
    Of wonderful sights that be,
And you shall see the beautiful things
    As you rock in the misty sea
    Where the old shoe rocked the fishermen three:—
    Wynken,
    Blynken,
    And Nod.

                              EUGENE FIELD

The Man with the Hoe

Written after seeing Millet's world-famous painting

Bowed by the weight of centuries he leans
Upon his hoe and gazes on the ground,
The emptiness of ages in his face,

And on his back the burden of the world.
Who made him dead to rapture and despair,
A thing that grieves not and that never hopes,
Stolid and stunned, a brother to the ox?
Who loosened and let down this brutal jaw?
Whose was the hand that slanted back this brow?
Whose breath blew out the light within this brain?

Is this the Thing the Lord God made and gave
To have dominion over sea and land;
To trace the stars and search the heavens for power;
To feel the passion of Eternity?
Is this the dream He dreamed who shaped the suns
And marked their ways upon the ancient deep?
Down all the caverns of Hell to their last gulf
There is no shape more terrible than this—
More tongued with censure of the world's blind greed—
More filled with signs and portents for the soul—
More packed with danger to the universe.

What gulfs between him and the seraphim!
Slave of the wheel of labor, what to him
Are Plato and the swing of Pleiades?
What the long reaches of the peaks of song,
The rift of dawn, the reddening of the rose?
Through this dread shape the suffering ages look;
Time's tragedy is in that aching stoop;
Through this dread shape humanity betrayed,
Plundered, profaned, and disinherited,
Cries protest to the Judges of the World,
A protest that is also prophecy.

O masters, lords and rulers in all lands,
Is this the handiwork you give to God,
This monstrous thing distorted and soul-quenched?
How will you ever straighten up this shape;
Touch it again with immortality;
Give back the upward looking and the light;
Rebuild in it the music and the dream;
Make right the immemorial infamies,
Perfidious wrongs, immedicable woes?

O masters, lords and rulers in all lands,
How will the Future reckon with this man?
How answer his brute question in that hour
When whirlwinds of rebellion shake all shores?
How will it be with kingdoms and with kings—
With those who shaped him to the thing he is—
When this dumb terror shall rise to judge the world,
After the silence of the centuries?

EDWIN MARKHAM

Love Song

I love my life, but not too well
        To give it to thee like a flower,
So it may pleasure thee to dwell
        Deep in its perfume but an hour.
I love my life, but not too well.

I love my life, but not too well
        To sing it note by note away,
So to thy soul the song may tell
        The beauty of the desolate day.
I love my life, but not too well.

I love my life, but not too well
        To cast it like a cloak on thine,
Against the storms that sound and swell
        Between thy lonely heart and mine.
I love my life, but not too well.

HARRIET MONROE

On the Death of a Metaphysician

Unhappy dreamer, who outwinged in flight
The pleasant region of the things I love,
And soared beyond the sunshine, and above
The golden cornfields and the dear and bright

Warmth of the hearth,—blasphemer of delight,
Was your proud bosom not at peace with Jove,
That you sought, thankless for his guarded grove,
The empty horror of abysmal night?
Ah, the thin air is cold above the moon!
I stood and saw you fall, befooled in death,
As in your numbëd spirit's fatal swoon,
You cried you were a god, or were to be;
I heard with feeble moan your boastful breath
Bubble from depths of the Icarian sea.

GEORGE SANTAYANA

Sonnet: O world

O world, thou choosest not the better part!
It is not wisdom to be only wise,
And on the inward vision close the eyes,
But it is wisdom to believe the heart.
Columbus found a world, and had no chart,
Save one that faith deciphered in the skies;
To trust the soul's invincible surmise
Was all his science and his only art.
Our knowledge is a torch of smoky pine
That lights the pathway but one step ahead
Across a void of mystery and dread.
Bid, then, the tender light of faith to shine
By which alone the mortal heart is led
Unto the thinking of the thought divine.

GEORGE SANTAYANA

The Black Vulture

Aloof upon the day's immeasured dome,
He holds unshared the silence of the sky.
Far down his bleak, relentless eyes descry
The eagle's empire and the falcon's home—

Far down, the galleons of sunset roam;
   His hazards on the sea of morning lie;
   Serene, he hears the broken tempest sigh
Where cold sierras gleam like scattered foam.

And least of all he holds the human swarm—
   Unwitting now that envious men prepare
      To make their dream and its fulfillment one,
When, poised above the caldrons of the storm,
   Their hearts, contemptuous of death, shall dare
      His roads between the thunder and the sun.

GEORGE STERLING

Eros Turannos

She fears him, and will always ask
   What fated her to choose him;
She meets in his engaging mask
   All reasons to refuse him;
But what she meets and what she fears
Are less than are the downward years,
Drawn slowly to the foamless weirs
   Of age, were she to lose him.

Between a blurred sagacity
   That once had power to sound him,
And Love, that will not let him be
   The Judas that she found him,
Her pride assuages her almost,
As if it were alone the cost.—
He sees that he will not be lost,
   And waits and looks around him.

A sense of ocean and old trees
   Envelops and allures him;
Tradition, touching all he sees,
   Beguiles and reassures him;
And all her doubts of what he says
Are dimmed with what she knows of days—

Till even prejudice delays
    And fades, and she secures him.

The falling leaf inaugurates
    The reign of her confusion;
The pounding wave reverberates
    The dirge of her illusion;
And home, where passion lived and died,
Becomes a place where she can hide,
While all the town and harbor side
    Vibrate with her seclusion.

We tell you, tapping on our brows,
    The story as it should be,—
As if the story of a house
    Were told, or ever could be;
We'll have no kindly veil between
Her visions and those we have seen,—
As if we guessed what hers have been,
    Or what they are or would be.

Meanwhile we do no harm; for they
    That with a god have striven,
Not hearing much of what we say,
    Take what the god has given;
Though like waves breaking it may be,
Or like a changed familiar tree,
Or like a stairway to the sea
    Where down the blind are driven.

EDWIN ARLINGTON ROBINSON

For a Dead Lady

No more with overflowing light
Shall fill the eyes that now are faded,
Nor shall another's fringe with night
Their woman-hidden world as they did.
No more shall quiver down the days
The flowing wonder of her ways,

Whereof no language may requite
The shifting and the many-shaded.

The grace, divine, definitive,
Clings only as a faint forestalling;
The laugh that love could not forgive
Is hushed, and answers to no calling;
The forehead and the little ears
Have gone where Saturn keeps the years;
The breast where roses could not live
Has done with rising and with falling.

The beauty, shattered by the laws
That have creation in their keeping,
No longer trembles at applause,
Or over children that are sleeping;
And we who delve in beauty's lore
Know all that we have known before
Of what inexorable cause
Makes Time so vicious in his reaping.

EDWIN ARLINGTON ROBINSON

The Hill

Where are Elmer, Herman, Bert, Tom and Charley,
The weak of will, the strong of arm, the clown, the boozer, the fighter?
All, all, are sleeping on the hill.

One passed in a fever,
One was burned in a mine,
One was killed in a brawl,
One died in a jail,
One fell from a bridge toiling for children and wife—
All, all are sleeping, sleeping, sleeping on the hill.

Where are Ella, Kate, Mag, Lizzie and Edith,
The tender heart, the simple soul, the loud, the proud, the happy one?—
All, all, are sleeping on the hill.

One died in shameful child-birth,
One of a thwarted love,
One at the hands of a brute in a brothel,
One of a broken pride, in search for heart's desire,
One after life in far-away London and Paris
Was brought to her little space by Ella and Kate and Mag—
All, all are sleeping, sleeping, sleeping on the hill.

Where are Uncle Isaac and Aunt Emily,
And old Towny Kincaid and Sevigne Houghton,
And Major Walker who had talked
With venerable men of the revolution?—
All, all, are sleeping on the hill.

They brought them dead sons from the war,
And daughters whom life had crushed,
And their children fatherless, crying—
All, all are sleeping, sleeping, sleeping on the hill.

Where is Old Fiddler Jones
Who played with life all his ninety years,
Braving the sleet with bared breast,
Drinking, rioting, thinking neither of wife nor kin,
Nor gold, nor love, nor heaven?
Lo! he babbles of the fish-frys of long ago,
Of the horse-races of long ago at Clary's Grove,
Of what Abe Lincoln said
One time at Springfield.

EDGAR LEE MASTERS

Anne Rutledge

Out of me unworthy and unknown
The vibrations of deathless music;
"With malice toward none, with charity for all."
Out of me the forgiveness of millions toward millions,
And the beneficent face of a nation
Shining with justice and truth.

I am Anne Rutledge who sleep beneath these weeds,
Beloved in life of Abraham Lincoln,
Wedded to him, not through union,
But through separation.
Bloom forever, O Republic,
From the dust of my bosom!

EDGAR LEE MASTERS

Mt. Lykaion

Alone on Lykaion since man hath been
Stand on the height two columns, where at rest
Two eagles hewn of gold sit looking East
Forever; and the sun goes up between.
Far down around the mountain's oval green
An order keeps the falling stones abreast.
Below within the chaos last and least
A river like a curl of light is seen.
Beyond the river lies the even sea,
Beyond the sea another ghost of sky,—
O God, support the sickness of my eye
Lest the far space and long antiquity
Suck out my heart, and on this awful ground
The great wind kill my little shell with sound.

TRUMBULL STICKNEY

"Be still. The Hanging Gardens were a dream"

Be still. The Hanging Gardens were a dream
That over Persian roses flew to kiss
The curlèd lashes of Semiramis.
Troy never was, nor green Skamander stream.
Provence and Troubadour are merest lies,
The glorious hair of Venice was a beam
Made within Titian's eye. The sunsets seem,
The world is very old and nothing is.
Be still. Thou foolish thing, thou canst not wake,
Nor thy tears wedge thy soldered lids apart,

But patter in the darkness of thy heart.
Thy brain is plagued. Thou art a frighted owl
Blind with the light of life thou'ldst not forsake,
And error loves and nourishes thy soul.

TRUMBULL STICKNEY

Live Blindly

Live blindly and upon the hour. The Lord,
Who was the Future, died full long ago.
Knowledge which is the Past is folly. Go,
Poor child, and be not to thyself abhorred.
Around thine earth sun-wingèd winds do blow
And planets roll; a meteor draws his sword;
The rainbow breaks his seven-coloured chord
And the long strips of river-silver flow:
Awake! Give thyself to the lovely hours.
Drinking their lips, catch thou the dream in flight
About their fragile hairs' aërial gold.
Thou art divine, thou livest,—as of old
Apollo springing naked to the light,
And all his island shivered into flowers.

TRUMBULL STICKNEY

Madonna of the Evening Flowers

All day long I have been working,
Now I am tired.
I call: "Where are you?"
But there is only the oak tree rustling in the wind.
The house is very quiet,
The sun shines in on your books,
On your scissors and thimble just put down,
But you are not there.
Suddenly I am lonely:
Where are you?
I go about searching.

Then I see you,
Standing under a spire of pale blue larkspur,
With a basket of roses on your arm.
You are cool, like silver,
And you smile.
I think the Canterbury bells are playing little tunes,
You tell me that the peonies need spraying,
That the columbines have overrun all bounds,
That the pyrus japonica should be cut back and rounded.
You tell me these things.
But I look at you, heart of silver,
White heart-flame of polished silver,
Burning beneath the blue steeples of the larkspur,
And I long to kneel instantly at your feet,
While all about us peal the loud, sweet, Te Deums of the
    Canterbury bells.

                                        AMY LOWELL

Stopping by Woods on a Snowy Evening

Whose woods these are I think I know.
His house is in the village though;
He will not see me stopping here
To watch his woods fill up with snow.

My little horse must think it queer
To stop without a farmhouse near
Between the woods and frozen lake
The darkest evening of the year.

He gives his harness bells a shake
To ask if there is some mistake.
The only other sound's the sweep
Of easy wind and downy flake.

The woods are lovely, dark and deep.
But I have promises to keep,
And miles to go before I sleep,
And miles to go before I sleep.

                              ROBERT FROST

The Pasture

I'm going out to clean the pasture spring;
I'll only stop to rake the leaves away
(And wait to watch the water clear, I may):
I sha'n't be gone long.—You come too.

I'm going out to fetch the little calf
That's standing by the mother. It's so young,
It totters when she licks it with her tongue.
I sha'n't be gone long.—You come too.

ROBERT FROST

Design

I found a dimpled spider, fat and white,
On a white heal-all, holding up a moth
Like a white piece of rigid satin cloth—
Assorted characters of death and blight
Mixed ready to begin the morning right,
Like the ingredients of a witches' broth—
A snow-drop spider, a flower like froth,
And dead wings carried like a paper kite.
What had that flower to do with being white,
The wayside blue and innocent heal-all?
What brought the kindred spider to that height,
Then steered the white moth thither in the night?
What but design of darkness to appall?—
If design govern in a thing so small.

ROBERT FROST

Once by the Pacific

The shattered water made a misty din.
Great waves looked over others coming in,
And thought of doing something to the shore
That water never did to land before.

The clouds were low and hairy in the skies,
Like locks blown forward in the gleam of eyes.
You could not tell, and yot it looked as If
The shore was lucky in being backed by cliff,
The cliff in being backed by continent;
It looked as if a night of dark intent
Was coming, and not only a night, an age.
Someone had better be prepared for rage.
There would be more than ocean-water broken
Before God's last *Put out the Light* was spoken.

ROBERT FROST

In Hardwood Groves

The same leaves over and over again!
They fall from giving shade above
To make one texture of faded brown
And fit the earth like a leather glove.

Before the leaves can mount again
To fill the trees with another shade,
They must go down past things coming up
They must go down into the dark decayed.

They *must* be pierced by flowers and put
Beneath the feet of dancing flowers.
However it is in some other world
I know that this is the way in ours.

ROBERT FROST

Range-Finding

The battle rent a cobweb diamond-strung
And cut a flower beside a ground bird's nest
Before it stained a single human breast.
The stricken flower bent double and so hung.
And still the bird revisited her young.
A butterfly its fall had dispossessed

A moment sought in air his flower of rest,
Then lightly stooped to it and fluttering clung.

On the bare upland pasture there had spread
O'ernight 'twixt mullein stalks a wheel of thread
And straining cables wet with silver dew.
A sudden passing bullet shook it dry.
The indwelling spider ran to greet the fly,
But finding nothing, sullenly withdrew.

ROBERT FROST

The Gift Outright

The land was ours before we were the land's.
She was our land more than a hundred years
Before we were her people. She was ours
In Massachusetts, in Virginia,
But we were England's, still colonials,
Possessing what we still were unpossessed by,
Possessed by what we now no more possessed.
Something we were withholding made us weak
Until we found out that it was ourselves
We were withholding from our land of living,
And forthwith found salvation in surrender.
Such as we were we gave ourselves outright
(The deed of gift was many deeds of war)
To the land vaguely realizing westward,
But still unstoried, artless, unenhanced,
Such as she was, such as she would become.

ROBERT FROST

Song

I make my shroud but no one knows,
So shimmering fine it is and fair,

With stitches set in even rows.
I make my shroud but no one knows.

In door-way where the lilac blows,
Humming a little wandering air,
I make my shroud but no one knows,
So shimmering fine it is and fair.

ADELAIDE CRAPSEY

Four Preludes on Playthings of the Wind

I

The woman named Tomorrow
sits with a hairpin in her teeth
and takes her time
and does her hair the way she wants it
and fastens at last the last braid and coil
and puts the hairpin where it belongs
and turns and drawls: Well, what of it?
My grandmother, Yesterday, is gone.
What of it? Let the dead be dead.

II

The doors were cedar
and the panel strips of gold
and the girls were golden girls
and the panels read and the girls chanted:
        We are the greatest city,
        and the greatest nation:
        nothing like us ever was.
The doors are twisted on broken hinges.
Sheets of rain swish through on the wind
        where the golden girls ran and the panels
            read:
        We are the greatest city,
        the greatest nation,
        nothing like us ever was.

III

It has happened before.
Strong men put up a city and got
    a nation together,
And paid singers to sing and women
    to warble: We are the greatest city,
        the greatest nation,
        nothing like us ever was.
And while the singers sang
and the strong men listened
and paid the singers well,
    there were rats and lizards who listened
    . . . and the only listeners left now
    . . . are . . . the rats . . . and the lizards.
    And there are black crows
    crying, "Caw, caw,"
    bringing mud and sticks
    building a nest
    over the words carved
    on the doors where the panels were cedar
    and the strips on the panels were gold
    and the golden girls came singing:
        We are the greatest city,
        the greatest nation:
        nothing like us ever was.

The only singers now are crows crying, "Caw, caw,"
And the sheets of rain whine in the wind and doorways.
And the only listeners now are . . . the rats . . . and the lizards.

IV

The feet of the rats
scribble on the doorsills;
the hieroglyphs of the rat footprints
chatter the pedigrees of the rats
and babble of the blood
and gabble of the breed
of the grandfathers and the great-grandfathers
of the rats.
And the wind shifts
and the dust on a doorsill shifts

and even the writing of the rat footprints
tells us nothing, nothing at all
about the greatest city, the greatest nation
where the strong men listened
and the women warbled: Nothing like us ever was.

CARL SANDBURG

General William Booth Enters into Heaven

(To be sung to the tune of "The Blood of the Lamb" with indicated instrument.)

I

(Bass drum beaten loudly.)
Booth led boldly with his big bass drum—
(Are you washed in the blood of the Lamb?)
The Saints smiled gravely and they said: 'He's Come.'
(Are you washed in the blood of the Lamb?)
Walking lepers followed, rank on rank,
Lurching bravos from the ditches dank,
Drabs from the alleyways and drug fiends pale—
Minds still passion-ridden, soul-powers frail:—
Vermin-eaten saints with moldy breath,
Unwashed legions with the ways of Death—
(Are you washed in the blood of the Lamb?)

(Banjos.)
Every slum had sent its half-a-score
The round world over. (Booth had groaned for more.)
Every banner that the wide world flies
Bloomed with glory and transcendent dyes.
Big-voiced lasses made their banjos bang,
Tranced, fanatical they shrieked and sang:—
'Are you washed in the blood of the Lamb?'
Hallelujah! It was queer to see
Bull-necked convicts with that land make free.
Loons with trumpets blowed a blare, blare, blare
On, on upward thro' the golden air!
(Are you washed in the blood of the Lamb?)

II

(Bass drum slower and softer.)
Booth died blind and still by faith he trod,
Eyes still dazzled by the ways of God.
Booth led boldly, and he looked the chief
Eagle countenance in sharp relief,
Beard a-flying, air of high command
Unabated in that holy land.

(Sweet flute music.)
Jesus came from out the court-house door,
Stretched his hands above the passing poor.
Booth saw not, but led his queer ones there
Round and round the mighty court-house square.
Then, in an instant all that blear review
Marched on spotless, clad in raiment new.
The lame were straightened, withered limbs uncurled
And blind eyes opened on a new, sweet world.

(Bass drum louder.)
Drabs and vixens in a flash made whole!
Gone was the weasel-head, the snout, the jowl!
Sages and sibyls now, and athletes clean,
Rulers of empires, and of forests green!

(Grand chorus of all instruments. Tambourines to the foreground.)
The hosts were sandalled, and their wings were fire!
(Are you washed in the blood of the Lamb?)
But their noise played havoc with the angel-choir.
(Are you washed in the blood of the Lamb?)
Oh, shout Salvation! It was good to see
Kings and Princes by the Lamb set free.
The banjos rattled and the tambourines
Jing-jing-jingled in the hands of Queens.

(Reverently sung, no instruments.)
And when Booth halted by the curb for prayer
He saw his Master thro' the flag-filled air.
Christ came gently with a robe and crown
For Booth the soldier, while the throng knelt down.

He saw King Jesus. They were face to face,
And he knelt a-weeping in that holy place.
Are you washed in the blood of the Lamb?

VACHEL LINDSAY

Abraham Lincoln Walks at Midnight

In Springfield, Illinois

It is portentous, and a thing of state
That here at midnight, in our little town
A mourning figure walks, and will not rest,
Near the old court-house pacing up and down,

Or by his homestead, or in shadowed yards
He lingers where his children used to play,
Or through the market, on the well-worn stones
He stalks until the dawn-stars burn away.

A bronzed, lank man! His suit of ancient black,
A famous high top-hat and plain worn shawl
Make him the quaint great figure that men love,
The prairie-lawyer, master of us all.

He cannot sleep upon his hillside now.
He is among us:—as in times before!
And we who toss and lie awake for long
Breathe deep, and start, to see him pass the door.

His head is bowed. He thinks on men and kings.
Yea, when the sick world cries, how can he sleep?
Too many peasants fight, they know not why,
Too many homesteads in black terror weep.

The sins of all the war-lords burn his heart.
He sees the dreadnaughts scouring every main.
He carries on his shawl-wrapped shoulders now
The bitterness, the folly and the pain.

He cannot rest until a spirit-dawn
Shall come;—the shining hope of Europe free:

The league of sober folk, the Workers' Earth,
Bringing long peace to Cornland, Alp and Sea.

It breaks his heart that kings must murder still,
That all his hours of travail here for men
Seem yet in vain. And who will bring white peace
That he may sleep upon his hill again?

Vachel Lindsay

Ploughing on Sunday

The white cock's tail
Tosses in the wind.
The turkey-cock's tail
Glitters in the sun.

Water in the fields.
The wind pours down.
The feathers flare
And bluster in the wind.

Remus, blow your horn!
I'm ploughing on Sunday,
Ploughing North America.
Blow your horn!

Tum-ti-tum,
Ti-tum-tum-tum!
The turkey-cock's tail
Spreads to the sun.

The white cock's tail
Streams to the moon.
Water in the fields.
The wind pours down.

Wallace Stevens

Life Is Motion

In Oklahoma,
Bonnie and Josie,
Dressed in calico,
Danced around a stump.
They cried,
"Ohoyaho,
Ohoo" . . .
Celebrating the marriage
Of flesh and air.

WALLACE STEVENS

Sunday Morning

Complacencies of the peignoir, and late
Coffee and oranges in a sunny chair,
And the green freedom of a cockatoo
Upon a rug mingle to dissipate
The holy hush of ancient sacrifice.
She dreams a little, and she feels the dark
Encroachment of that old catastrophe,
As a calm darkens among water-lights.
The pungent oranges and bright, green wings
Seem things in some procession of the dead,
Winding across wide water, without sound.
The day is like wide water, without sound,
Stilled for the passing of her dreaming feet
Over the seas, to silent Palestine,
Dominion of the blood and sepulchre.

Why should she give her bounty to the dead?
What is divinity if it can come
Only in silent shadows and in dreams?
Shall she not find in comforts of the sun,
In pungent fruit and bright, green wings, or else
In any balm or beauty of the earth,
Things to be cherished like the thought of heaven?
Divinity must live within herself:

Passions of rain, or moods in falling snow;
Grievings in loneliness, or unsubdued
Elations when the forest blooms; gusty
Emotions on wet roads on autumn nights;
All pleasures and all pains, remembering
The bough of summer and the winter branch.
These are the measures destined for her soul.

Jove in the clouds had his inhuman birth.
No mother suckled him, no sweet land gave
Large-mannered motions to his mythy mind.
He moved among us, as a muttering king,
Magnificent, would move among his hinds,
Until our blood, commingling, virginal,
With heaven, brought such requital to desire
The very hinds discerned it, in a star.
Shall our blood fail? Or shall it come to be
The blood of paradise? And shall the earth
Seem all of paradise that we shall know?
The sky will be much friendlier then than now,
A part of labor and a part of pain,
And next in glory to enduring love,
Not this dividing and indifferent blue.

She says, "I am content when wakened birds,
Before they fly, test the reality
Of misty fields, by their sweet questionings;
But when the birds are gone, and their warm fields
Return no more, where, then, is paradise?"
There is not any haunt of prophecy,
Nor any old chimera of the grave,
Neither the golden underground, nor isle
Melodious, where spirits gat them home,
Nor visionary south, nor cloudy palm
Remote on heaven's hill, that has endured
As April's green endures; or will endure
Like her remembrance of awakened birds,
Or her desire for June and evening, tipped
By the consummation of the swallow's wings.

She says, "But in contentment I still feel
The need of some imperishable bliss."

Death is the mother of beauty; hence from her,
Alone, shall come fulfilment of our dreams
And our desires. Although she strews the leaves
Of sure obliteration on our paths,
The path sick sorrow took, the many paths
Where triumph rang its brassy phrase, or love
Whispered a little out of tenderness,
She makes the willow shiver in the sun
For maidens who were wont to sit and gaze
Upon the grass, relinquished to their feet.
She causes boys to pile new plums and pears
On disregarded plate. The maidens taste
And stray impassioned in the littering leaves.

Is there no change of death in paradise?
Does ripe fruit never fall? Or do the boughs
Hang always heavy in that perfect sky,
Unchanging, yet so like our perishing earth,
With rivers like our own that seek for seas
They never find, the same receding shores
That never touch with inarticulate pang?
Why set the pear upon those river-banks
Or spice the shores with odors of the plum?
Alas, that they should wear our colors there,
The silken weavings of our afternoons,
And pick the strings of our insipid lutes!
Death is the mother of beauty, mystical,
Within whose burning bosom we devise
Our earthly mothers waiting, sleeplessly.

Supple and turbulent, a ring of men
Shall chant in orgy on a summer morn
Their boisterous devotion to the sun,
Not as a god, but as a god might be,
Naked among them, like a savage source.
Their chant shall be a chant of paradise,
Out of their blood, returning to the sky;
And in their chant shall enter, voice by voice,
The windy lake wherein their lord delights,
The trees, like serafin, and echoing hills,
That choir among themselves long afterward.
They shall know well the heavenly fellowship

Of men that perish and of summer morn.
And whence they came and whither they shall go
The dew upon their feet shall manifest.

She hears, upon that water without sound,
A voice that cries, "The tomb in Palestine
Is not the porch of spirits lingering.
It is the grave of Jesus, where He lay."
We live in an old chaos of the sun,
Or old dependency of day and night,
Or island solitude, unsponsored, free,
Of that wide water, inescapable.
Deer walk upon our mountains, and the quail
Whistle about us their spontaneous cries;
Sweet berries ripen in the wilderness;
And, in the isolation of the sky,
At evening, casual flocks of pigeons make
Ambiguous undulations as they sink,
Downward to darkness, on extended wings.

WALLACE STEVENS

The Idea of Order at Key West

She sang beyond the genius of the sea.
The water never formed to mind or voice,
Like a body wholly body, fluttering
Its empty sleeves; and yet its mimic motion
Made constant cry, caused constantly a cry,
That was not ours although we understood,
Inhuman, of the veritable ocean.

The sea was not a mask. No more was she.
The song and water were not medleyed sound
Even if what she sang was what she heard,
Since what she sang was uttered word by word.
It may be that in all her phrases stirred
The grinding water and the gasping wind;
But it was she and not the sea we heard.
For she was the maker of the song she sang,
The ever-hooded, tragic-gestured sea
Was merely a place by which she walked to sing.

Whose spirit is this? we said, because we knew
It was the spirit that we sought and knew
That we should ask this often as she sang.

If it was only the dark voice of the sea
That rose, or even colored by many waves;
If it was only the outer voice of sky
And cloud, of the sunken coral water-walled,
However clear, it would have been deep air,
The heaving speech of air, a summer sound
Repeated in a summer without end
And sound alone. But it was more than that,
More even than her voice, and ours, among
The meaningless plungings of water and the wind,
Theatrical distances, bronze shadows heaped
On high horizons, mountainous atmospheres
Of sky and sea.

               It was her voice that made
The sky acutest at its vanishing.
She measured to the hour its solitude.
She was the single artificer of the world
In which she sang. And when she sang, the sea,
Whatever self it had, became the self
That was her song, for she was the maker. Then we,
As we beheld her striding there alone,
Knew that there never was a world for her
Except the one she sang and, singing, made.

Ramon Fernandez, tell me, if you know,
Why, when the singing ended and we turned
Toward the town, tell why the glassy lights,
The lights in the fishing boats at anchor there,
As the night descended, tilting in the air,
Mastered the night and portioned out the sea,
Fixing emblazoned zones and fiery poles,
Arranging, deepening, enchanting night.

Oh! Blessed rage for order, pale Ramon,
The maker's rage to order words of the sea,
Words of the fragrant portals, dimly-starred,
And of ourselves and of our origins,
In ghostlier demarcations, keener sounds.

                            WALLACE STEVENS

The Emperor of Ice-Cream

Call the roller of big cigars,
The muscular one, and bid him whip
In kitchen cups concupiscent curds.
Let the wenches dawdle in such dress
As they are used to wear, and let the boys
Bring flowers in last month's newspapers.
Let be be finale of seem.
The only emperor is the emperor of ice-cream.

Take from the dresser of deal,
Lacking the three glass knobs, that sheet
On which she embroidered fantails once
And spread it so as to cover her face.
If her horny feet protrude, they come
To show how cold she is, and dumb.
Let the lamp affix its beam.
The only emperor is the emperor of ice-cream.

WALLACE STEVENS

The Red Wheelbarrow

so much depends
upon

a red wheel
barrow

glazed with rain
water

beside the white
chickens

WILLIAM CARLOS WILLIAMS

Flowers by the Sea

When over the flowery, sharp pasture's
edge, unseen, the salt ocean

lifts its form—chicory and daisies
tide, released, seem hardly flowers alone

but color and the movement—or the shape
perhaps—of restlessness, whereas

the sea is circled and sways
peacefully upon its plantlike stem

WILLIAM CARLOS WILLIAMS

Wisdom

It was a night of early spring,
    The winter-sleep was scarcely broken;
Around us shadows and the wind
    Listened for what was never spoken.

Though half a score of years are gone,
    Spring comes as sharply now as then—
But if we had it all to do
    It would be done the same again.

It was a spring that never came;
    But we have lived enough to know
That what we never have, remains;
    It is the things we have that go.

SARA TEASDALE

Address to My Soul

My soul, be not disturbed
By planetary war;

Remain securely orbed
In this contracted star.

Fear not, pathetic flame;
Your sustenance is doubt:
Glassed in translucent dream
They cannot snuff you out.

Wear water, or a mask
Of unapparent cloud;
Be brave and never ask
A more defunctive shroud.

The universal points
Are shrunk into a flower;
Between its delicate joints
Chaos keeps no power.

The pure integral form,
Austere and silver-dark,
Is balanced on the storm
In its predestined arc.

Small as a sphere of rain
It slides along the groove
Whose path is furrowed plain
Among the suns that move.

The shapes of April buds
Outlive the phantom year:
Upon the void at odds
The dewdrop falls severe.

Five-petalled flame, be cold:
Be firm, dissolving star:
Accept the stricter mould
That makes you singular.

ELINOR WYLIE

Lament for Glasgerion

The lovely body of the dead,
Wherein he laid him down to rest,
Is shrunken to corruption's thread;
The blood which delicately dressed
The flying bone, the sighing breast,
One with nothingness is made.

The darling garment is outworn;
Its fabric nourishes the moth;
The silk wherein his soul was born,
Woven of flesh and spirit both,
Is crumbled to a pitiful cloth:
His soul lies naked and forlorn.

So one that walks within the air,
Who loves the ghost below the ground,
Rejoices fervently to wear
A body shaken and unsound;
A brow divided by a wound;
A throat encircled by a care.

Shall I go warm above the cold
Wherein he sleeps without a shroud
Or shred of beauty left to fold
About the poor heart's solitude?
The vanishing dust of my heart is proud
To watch me wither and grow old.

ELINOR WYLIE

Hymn to Earth

Farewell, incomparable element,
Whence man arose, where he shall not return;
And hail, imperfect urn
Of his last ashes, and his firstborn fruit;
Farewell, the long pursuit,
And all the adventures of his discontent;

The voyages which sent
His heart averse from home:
Metal of clay, permit him that he come
To thy slow-burning fire as to a hearth;
Accept him as a particle of earth.

Fire, being divided from the other three,
It lives removed, or secret at the core;
Most subtle of the four,
When air flies not, nor water flows,
It disembodied goes,
Being light, elixir of the first degree,
More volatile than he;
With strength and power to pass
Through space, where never his least atom was:
He has no part in it, save as his eyes
Have drawn its emanation from the skies.

A wingless creature heavier than air,
He is rejected of its quintessence;
Coming and going hence,
In the twin minutes of his birth and death,
He may inhale as breath,
As breath relinquish heaven's atmosphere,
Yet in it have no share,
Nor can survive therein
Where its outer edge is filtered pure and thin:
It doth but lend its crystal to his lungs
For his early crying, and his final songs.

The element of water has denied
Its child; it is no more his element;
It never will relent;
Its silver harvests are more sparsely given
Than the rewards of heaven,
And he shall drink cold comfort at its side:
The water is too wide:
The seamew and the gull
Feather a nest made soft and pitiful
Upon its foam; he has not any part
In the long swell of sorrow at its heart.

Hail and farewell, beloved element,
Whence he departed, and his parent once;
See where thy spirit runs
Which for so long hath had the moon to wife;
Shall this support his life
Until the arches of the waves be bent
And grow shallow and spent?
Wisely it cast him forth
With his dead weight of burdens nothing worth,
Leaving him, for the universal years,
A little seawater to make his tears.

Hail, element of earth, receive thy own,
And cherish, at thy charitable breast,
This man, this mongrel beast:
He ploughs the sand, and, at his hardest need,
He sows himself for seed;
He ploughs the furrow, and in this lies down
Before the corn is grown;
Between the apple bloom
And the ripe apple is sufficient room
In time, and matter, to consume his love
And make him parcel of a cypress grove.

Receive him as thy lover for an hour
Who will not weary, by a longer stay,
The kind embrace of clay;
Even within thine arms he is dispersed
To nothing, as at first;
The air flings downward from its four-quartered tower
Him whom the flames devour;
At the full tide, at the flood,
The sea is mingled with his salty blood:
The traveller dust, although the dust be vile,
Sleeps as thy lover for a little while.

                                      ELINOR WYLIE

Fair Annet's Song

One thing comes and another thing goes:
Frosts in November drive away the rose;
Like a blowing ember the windflower blows
And drives away the snows.

It is sad to remember and sorrowful to pray;
Let us laugh and be merry, who have seen today
The last of the cherry and the first of the may;
And neither one will stay.

ELINOR WYLIE

Lethe

Nor skin nor hide nor fleece
    Shall cover you,
Nor curtain of crimson nor fine
Shelter of cedar-wood be over you,
    Nor the fir-tree
    Nor the pine.

Nor sight of whin nor gorse
    Nor river-yew,
    Nor fragrance of flowering bush,
Nor wailing of reed-bird to waken you.
    Nor of linnet
    Nor of thrush.

Nor word nor touch nor sight
    Of lover, you
Shall long through the night but for this:
The roll of the full tide to cover you
    Without question,
    Without kiss.

H. D.

The Steeple-Jack

Dürer would have seen a reason for living
    in a town like this, with eight stranded whales
to look at; with the sweet sea air coming into your house
on a fine day, from water etched
    with waves as formal as the scales
on a fish.

One by one, in two's, in three's, the seagulls keep
    flying back and forth over the town clock,
or sailing around the lighthouse without moving their
    wings—
rising steadily with a slight
    quiver of the body—or flock
mewing where

a sea the purple of the peacock's neck is
    paled to greenish azure as Dürer changed
the pine green of the Tyrol to peacock blue and guinea
grey. You can see a twenty-five-
    pound lobster and fish-nets arranged
to dry. The

whirlwind fife-and-drum of the storm bends the salt
    marsh grass, disturbs stars in the sky and the
star on the steeple; it is a privilege to see so
much confusion.

            A steeple-jack in red, has let
    a rope down as a spider spins a thread;
he might be part of a novel, but on the sidewalk a
sign says C.J. Poole, Steeple-Jack,
    in black and white; and one in red
and white says

Danger. The church portico has four fluted
    columns, each a single piece of stone, made
modester by white-wash. This would be a fit haven for
waifs, children, animals, prisoners,
    and presidents who have repaid
sin-driven

senators by not thinking about them. One
    sees a school-house, a post-office in a
store, fish-houses, hen-houses, a three-masted schooner on
the stocks. The hero, the student,
    the steeple-jack, each in his way,
is at home.

It scarcely could be dangerous to be living
    in a town like this, of simple people
who have a steeple-jack placing danger-signs by the church
when he is gilding the solid-
    pointed star, which on a steeple
stands for hope.

MARIANNE MOORE

No Swan So Fine

'No water so still as the
    dead fountains of Versailles.' No swan,
with swart blind look askance
and gondoliering legs, so fine
    as the chintz china one with fawn-
brown eyes and toothed gold
collar on to show whose bird it was.

Lodged in the Louis Fifteenth
    candelabrum-tree of cockscomb-
tinted buttons, dahlias,
sea-urchins, and everlastings,
    it perches on the branching foam
of polished sculptured
flowers—at ease and tall. The king is dead.

MARIANNE MOORE

Shine, Perishing Republic

While this America settles in the mold of its vulgarity, heavily
    thickening to empire,

And protest, only a bubble in the molten mass, pops and sighs
out, and the mass hardens,

I sadly smiling remember that the flower fades to make fruit,
the fruit rots to make earth.
Out of the mother; and through the spring exultances, ripe-
ness and decadence; and home to the mother.

You, making haste, haste on decay: not blameworthy; life is
good, be it stubbornly long or suddenly
A mortal splendor: meteors are not needed less than mountains: shine, perishing republic.

But for my children, I would have them keep their distance
from the thickening center; corruption
Never has been compulsory, when the cities lie at the monster's feet there are left the mountains.

And boys, be in nothing so moderate as in love of man, a
clever servant, insufferable master.
There is the trap that catches noblest spirits, that caught—
they say—God, when he walked on earth.

ROBINSON JEFFERS

The Eye

The Atlantic is a stormy moat, and the Mediterranean,
The blue pool in the old garden,
More than five thousand years has drunk sacrifice
Of ships and blood and shines in the sun; but here the Pacific:
The ships, planes, wars are perfectly irrelevant.
Neither our present blood-feud with the brave dwarfs
Nor any future world-quarrel of westering
And eastering man, the bloody migrations, greed of power,
battle-falcons,
Are a mote of dust in the great scale-pan.
Here from this mountain shore, headland beyond stormy head-
land plunging like dolphins through the gray sea-smoke
Into pale sea, look west at the hill of water: it is half the
planet: this dome, this half-globe, this bulging
Eyeball of water, arched over to Asia,

Australia and white Antarctica: those are the eyelids that never
    close; this is the staring unsleeping
Eye of the earth, and what it watches is not our wars.

ROBINSON JEFFERS

Bells for John Whiteside's Daughter

There was such speed in her little body,
And such lightness in her footfall,
It is no wonder that her brown study
Astonishes us all.

Her wars were bruited in our high window.
We looked among orchard trees and beyond,
Where she took arms against her shadow,
Or harried unto the pond

The lazy geese, like a snow cloud
Dripping their snow on the green grass,
Tricking and stopping, sleepy and proud,
Who cried in goose, Alas,

For the tireless heart within the little
Lady with rod that made them rise
From their noon apple-dreams, and scuttle
Goose-fashion under the skies!

But now go the bells, and we are ready;
In one house we are sternly stopped
To say we are vexed at her brown study,
Lying so primly propped.

JOHN CROWE RANSOM

Janet Waking

Beautifully Janet slept
Till it was deeply morning. She woke then
And thought about her dainty-feathered hen,
To see how it had kept.

One kiss she gave her mother,
Only a small one gave she to her daddy
Who would have kissed each curl of his shining baby;
No kiss at all for her brother.

"Old Chucky, Old Chucky!" she cried,
Running on little pink feet upon the grass
To Chucky's house, and listening. But alas,
Her Chucky had died.

It was a transmogrifying bee
Came droning down on Chucky's old bald head
And sat and put the poison. It scarcely bled,
But how exceedingly

And purply did the knot
Swell with the venom and communicate
Its rigor! Now the poor comb stood up straight
But Chucky did not.

So there was Janet
Kneeling on the wet grass, crying her brown hen
(Translated far beyond the daughters of men)
To rise and walk upon it.

And weeping fast as she had breath
Janet implored us, "Wake her from her sleep!"
And would not be instructed in how deep
Was the forgetful kingdom of death.

JOHN CROWE RANSOM

from

Priapus and the Pool

III

When trout swim down Great Ormond Street,
And sea-gulls cry above them lightly,
And hawthorns heave cold flagstones up
To blossom whitely,

Against old walls of houses there,
Gustily shaking out in moonlight
Their country sweetness on sweet air;
And in the sunlight,

By the green margin of that water,
Children dip white feet and shout,
Casting nets in the braided water
To catch the trout:

Then I shall hold my breath and die,
Swearing I never loved you; no,
'You were not lovely!' I shall cry,
'I never loved you so.'

XVII

Fade, then,—die, depart, and come no more—
You, whose beauty I abhor—
Out of my brain
Take back your voice that lodges there in pain,
Tear out your thousand golden roots
That thrust their tentacles in my heart
But bear no fruits.

Now like an exquisite but sterile tree
Your beauty grows in me
And feeds on light
Its lifted arms of leaves and blossoms white.
Come birds, come bees,
And marry flower with flower that it may bear
Like other trees.

Or else let hatred like a lightning come,
And flash, and strike it numb,
And strew on rock
These singing leaves, that, singing, seem to mock.
Thus let my heart once more be naked stone,
Bare under wind and hard with grief,
And leave not in a single crevice
A single leaf.

CONRAD AIKEN

Goya

Goya drew a pig on a wall.
The five-year-old hairdresser's son
Saw, graved on a silver tray,
The lion; and sunsets were begun.

Goya smelt the bull-fight blood.
The pupil of the Carmelite
Gave his hands to a goldsmith, learned
To gild an aureole aright.

Goya saw the Puzzel's eyes:
Sang in the street (with a guitar)
And climbed the balcony; but Keats
(Under the halyards) wrote 'Bright star.'

Goya saw the Great Slut pick
The chirping human puppets up,
And laugh, with pendulous mountain lip,
And drown them in a coffee cup;

Or squeeze their little juices out
In arid hands, insensitive,
To make them gibber . . . Goya went
Among the catacombs to live.

He saw gross Ronyons of the air,
Harelipped and goitered, raped in flight
By hairless pimps, umbrella-winged:
Tumult above Madrid at night.

He heard the seconds in his clock
Crack like seeds, divulge, and pour
Abysmal filth of Nothingness
Between the pendulum and the floor:

Torrents of dead veins, rotted cells,
Tonsils decayed, and fingernails:
Dead hair, dead fur, dead claws, dead skin:
Nostrils and lids; and cauls and veils;

And eyes that still, in death, remained
(Unlidded and unlashed) aware
Of the foul core, and, fouler yet,
The region worm that ravins there.

Stench flowed out of the second's tick.
And Goya swam with it through Space,
Sweating the fetor from his limbs,
And stared upon the unfeatured face

That did not see, and sheltered naught,
But was, and is. The second gone,
Goya returned, and drew the face;
And scrawled beneath it, 'This I have known' . . .

And drew four slatterns, in an attic,
Heavy, with heads on arms, asleep:
And underscribed it, 'Let them slumber,
Who, if they woke, could only weep' . . .

CONRAD AIKEN

The Poet and His Book

Down, you mongrel, Death!
    Back to your kennel!
I have stolen breath
    In a stalk of fennel!
You shall scratch and you shall whine
    Many a night, and you shall worry
    Many a bone, before you bury
One sweet bone of mine!

When shall I be dead?
    When my flesh is withered,
And above my head
    Yellow pollen gathered
All the empty afternoon?
    When sweet lovers pause and wonder
    Who am I that lie thereunder,
Hidden from the moon?

This my personal death?—
    That my lungs be failing
To inhale the breath
    Others are exhaling?
This my subtle spirit's end?—
      Ah, when the thawed winter splashes
      Over these chance dust and ashes,
Weep not me, my friend!

Me, by no means dead
    In that hour, but surely
When this book, unread,
    Rots to earth obscurely,
And no more to any breast,
      Close against the clamorous swelling
      Of the thing there is no telling,
Are these pages pressed!

When this book is mold,
    And a book of many
Waiting to be sold
    For a casual penny,
In a little open case,
      In a street unclean and cluttered,
      Where a heavy mud is spattered
From the passing drays,

Stranger, pause and look;
    From the dust of ages
Lift this book,
    Turn the tattered pages,
Read me, do not let me die!
      Search the fading letters, finding
      Steadfast in the broken binding
All that once was I!

When these veins are weeds,
    When these hollowed sockets
Watch the rooty seeds
    Bursting down like rockets,

And surmise the spring again,
　　Or, remote in that black cupboard,
　　Watch the pink worms writhing upward
At the smell of rain,

Boys and girls that lie
　　Whispering in the hedges,
Do not let me die,
　　Mix me in your pledges;
Boys and girls that slowly walk
　　In the woods, and weep, and quarrel,
　　Staring past the pink wild laurel,
Mix me with your talk.

Do not let me die!
　　Farmers at your raking,
When the sun is high,
　　While the hay is making,
When, along the stubble strewn,
　　Withering on their stalks uneaten,
　　Strawberries turn dark and sweeten
In the lapse of noon;

Shepherds on the hills,
　　In the pastures, drowsing
To the tinkling bells
　　Of the brown sheep browsing;
Sailors crying through the storm;
　　Scholars at your study; hunters
　　Lost amid the whirling winter's
Whiteness uniform;

Men that long for sleep;
　　Men that wake and revel;—
If an old song leap
　　To your senses' level
At such moments, may it be
　　Sometimes, though a moment only,
　　Some forgotten, quaint and homely
Vehicle of me!

Women at your toil,
　　Women at your leisure

Till the kettle boil,
    Snatch of me your pleasure,
Where the broom-straw marks the leaf;
    Women quiet with your weeping
    Lest you wake a workman sleeping,
Mix me with your grief!

Boys and girls that steal
    From the shocking laughter
Of the old, to kneel
    By a dripping rafter
Under the discolored eaves,
    Out of trunks with hingeless covers
    Lifting tales of saints and lovers,
Travelers, goblins, thieves,

Suns that shine by night,
    Mountains made from valleys,—
Bear me to the light,
    Flat upon your bellies
By the webby window lie,
    Where the little flies are crawling,—
    Read me, margin me with scrawling,
Do not let me die!

Sexton, ply your trade!
    In a shower of gravel
Stamp upon your spade!
    Many a rose shall ravel,
Many a metal wreath shall rust
    In the rain, and I go singing
    Through the lots where you are flinging
Yellow clay on dust!

EDNA ST. VINCENT MILLAY

Elegy

Let them bury your big eyes
In the secret earth securely,
Your thin fingers, and your fair,

Soft, indefinite-colored hair,—
All of these in some way, surely,
From the secret earth shall rise.
Not for these I sit and stare,
Broken and bereft completely;
Your young flesh that sat so neatly
On your little bones will sweetly
Blossom in the air.

But your voice,—never the rushing
Of a river underground,
Not the rising of the wind
In the trees before the rain,
Not the woodcock's watery call,
Not the note the white-throat utters,
Not the feet of children pushing
Yellow leaves along the gutters
In the blue and bitter fall,
Shall content my musing mind
For the beauty of that sound
That in no new way at all
Ever will be heard again.

Sweetly through the sappy stalk
Of the vigorous weed,
Holding all it held before,
Cherished by the faithful sun,
On and on eternally
Shall your altered fluid run,
Bud and bloom and go to seed;
But your singing days are done;
But the music of your talk
Never shall the chemistry
Of the secret earth restore.
All your lovely words are spoken.
Once the ivory box is broken,
Beats the golden bird no more.

EDNA ST. VINCENT MILLAY

The Buck in the Snow

White sky, over the hemlocks bowed with snow,
Saw you not at the beginning of evening the antlered
    buck and his doe
Standing in the apple-orchard? I saw them. I saw
    them suddenly go,
Tails up, with long leaps lovely and slow,
Over the stone-wall into the wood of hemlocks
    bowed with snow.

Now lies he here, his wild blood scalding the snow.

How strange a thing is death, bringing to his knees,
    bringing to his antlers
The buck in the snow.
How strange a thing,—a mile away by now, it may be,
Under the heavy hemlocks that as the moments pass
Shift their loads a little, letting fall a feather of snow—
Life, looking out attentive from the eyes of the doe.

EDNA ST. VINCENT MILLAY

from

Fatal Interview

SONNET XXX

Love is not all: it is not meat nor drink
Nor slumber nor a roof against the rain;
Nor yet a floating spar to men that sink
And rise and sink and rise and sink again;
Love can not fill the thickened lung with breath,
Nor clean the blood, nor set the fractured bone;
Yet many a man is making friends with death
Even as I speak, for lack of love alone.
It well may be that in a difficult hour,
Pinned down by pain and moaning for release,
Or nagged by want past resolution's power,
I might be driven to sell your love for peace,

Or trade the memory of this night for food.
It well may be. I do not think I would.

EDNA ST. VINCENT MILLAY

You, Andrew Marvell

And here face down beneath the sun
And here upon earth's noonward height
To feel the always coming on
The always rising of the night

To feel creep up the curving east
The earthly chill of dusk and slow
Upon those under lands the vast
And ever-climbing shadow grow

And strange at Ecbatan the trees
Take leaf by leaf the evening strange
The flooding dark about their knees
The mountains over Persia change

And now at Kermanshah the gate
Dark empty and the withered grass
And through the twilight now the late
Few travelers in the westward pass

And Baghdad darken and the bridge
Across the silent river gone
And through Arabia the edge
Of evening widen and steal on

And deepen on Palmyra's street
The wheel rut in the ruined stone
And Lebanon fade out and Crete
High through the clouds and overblown

And over Sicily the air
Still flashing with the landward gulls
And loom and slowly disappear
The sails above the shadowy hulls

And Spain go under and the shore
Of Africa the gilded sand
And evening vanish and no more
The low pale light across that land

Nor now the long light on the sea—
And here face downward in the sun
To feel how swift how secretly
The shadow of the night comes on. . . .

ARCHIBALD MacLEISH

L'an Trentiesme de Mon Eage

And I have come upon this place
By lost ways, by a nod, by words,
By faces, by an old man's face
At Morlaix lifted to the birds,

By hands upon the tablecloth
At Aldebori's, by the thin
Child's hands that opened to the moth
And let the flutter of the moonlight in,

By hands, by voices, by the voice
Of Mrs. Whitman on the stair,
By Margaret's "If we had the choice
To choose or not—" through her thick hair,

By voices, by the creak and fall
Of footsteps on the upper floor,
By silence waiting in the hall
Between the doorbell and the door,

By words, by voices, a lost way—
And here above the chimney stack
The unknown constellations sway—
And by what way shall I go back?

ARCHIBALD MacLEISH

Chanson Innocente

in Just-
spring   when the world is mud-
luscious the little
lame balloonman

whistles   far   and wee

and eddieandbill come
running from marbles and
piracies and it's
spring

when the world is puddle-wonderful

the queer
old balloonman whistles
far   and   wee
and bettyandisbel come dancing

from hop-scotch and jump-rope and

it's
spring
and
    the

        goat-footed

balloonMan   whistles
far
and
wee

                    E. E. Cummings

"All in green went my love riding"

All in green went my love riding
on a great horse of gold
into the silver dawn.

four lean hounds crouched low and smiling
the merry deer ran before.

Fleeter be they than dappled dreams
the swift sweet deer
the red rare deer.

Four red roebuck at a white water
the cruel bugle sang before.

Horn at hip went my love riding
riding the echo down
into the silver dawn.

four lean hounds crouched low and smiling
the level meadows ran before.

Softer be they than slippered sleep
the lean lithe deer
the fleet flown deer.

Four fleet does at a gold valley
the famished arrow sang before.

Bow at belt went my love riding
riding the mountain down
into the silver dawn.

four lean hounds crouched low and smiling
the sheer peaks ran before.

Paler be they than daunting death
the sleek slim deer
the tall tense deer.

Four tall stags at a green mountain
the lucky hunter sang before.

All in green went my love riding
on a great horse of gold
into the silver dawn.

four lean hounds crouched low and smiling
my heart fell dead before.

E. E. CUMMINGS

Old Countryside

Beyond the hour we counted rain that fell
On the slant shutter, all has come to proof.
The summer thunder, like a wooden bell,
Rang in the storm above the mansard roof,

And mirrors cast the cloudy day along
The attic floor; wind made the clapboards creak.
You braced against the wall to make it strong,
A shell against your cheek.

Long since, we pulled brown oak-leaves to the ground
In a winter of dry trees; we heard the cock
Shout its unplaceable cry, the axe's sound
Delay a moment after the axe's stroke.

Far back, we saw, in the stillest of the year,
The scrawled vine shudder, and the rose-branch show
Red to the thorns, and, sharp as sight can bear,
The thin hound's body arched against the snow.

LOUISE BOGAN

Song for a Slight Voice

If ever I render back your heart
So long to me delight and plunder,
It will be bound with the firm strings
That men have built the viol under.

Your stubborn, piteous heart, that bent
To be the place where music stood,
Upon some shaken instrument
Stained with the dark of resinous blood,

Will find its place, beyond denial,
Will hear the dance, O be most sure,
Laid on the curved wood of the viol
Or on the struck tambour.

LOUISE BOGAN

Song for the Last Act

Now that I have your face by heart, I look
Less at its features than its darkening frame
Where quince and melon, yellow as young flame,
Lie with quilled dahlias and the shepherd's crook.
Beyond, a garden. There, in insolent ease
The lead and marble figures watch the show
Of yet another summer loath to go
Although the scythes hang in the apple trees.

Now that I have your face by heart, I look.

Now that I have your voice by heart, I read
In the black chords upon a dulling page
Music that is not meant for music's cage,
Whose emblems mix with words that shake and bleed.
The staves are shuttled over with a stark
Unprinted silence. In a double dream
I must spell out the storm, the running stream.
The beat's too swift. The notes shift in the dark.

Now that I have your voice by heart, I read.

Now that I have your heart by heart, I see
The wharves with their great ships and architraves;
The rigging and the cargo and the slaves
On a strange beach under a broken sky.
O not departure, but a voyage done!
The bales stand on the stone; the anchor weeps
Its red rust downward, and the long vine creeps
Beside the salt herb, in the lengthening sun.

Now that I have your heart by heart, I see.

LOUISE BOGAN

Winter Mask

To the Memory of W. B. Yeats

I

Towards nightfall when the wind
Tries the eaves and casements
(A winter wind of the mind
Long gathering its will)
I lay the mind's contents
Bare, as upon a table,
And ask, in a time of war,
Whether there is still
To a mind frivolously dull
Anything worth living for.

II

If I am meek and dull
And a poor sacrifice
Of perverse will to cull
The act from the attempt,
Just look into damned eyes
And give the returning glare;
For the damned like it, the more
Damnation is exempt
From what would save its heir
With a thing worth living for.

III

The poisoned rat in the wall
Cuts through the wall like a knife,
Then blind, drying, and small
And driven to cold water,
Dies of the water of life:
Both damned in eternal ice,
The traitor become the boor
Who had led his friend to slaughter,
Now bites his head—not nice,
The food that he lives for.

IV

I supposed two scenes of hell,
Two human bestiaries,
Might uncommonly well
Convey the doom I thought;
But lest the horror freeze
The gentler estimation
I go to the sylvan door
Where nature has been bought
In rational proration
As a thing worth living for.

V

Should the buyer have been beware?
It is an uneven trade
For man has wet his hair
Under the winter weather
With only fog for shade:
His mouth a bracketed hole
Picked by the crows that bore
Nature to their hanged brother,
Who rattles against the bole
The thing that he lived for.

VI

I asked the master Yeats
Whose great style could not tell
Why it is man hates
His own salvation,
Prefers the way to hell,
And finds his last safety
In the self-made curse that bore
Him towards damnation:
The drowned undrowned by the sea,
The sea worth living for.

ALLEN TATE

Voyages: II

—And yet this great wink of eternity,
Of rimless floods, unfettered leewardings,
Samite sheeted and processioned where
Her undinal vast belly moonward bends,
Laughing the wrapt inflections of our love;

Take this Sea, whose diapason knells
On scrolls of silver snowy sentences,
The sceptered terror of whose sessions rends
As her demeanors motion well or ill,
All but the pieties of lovers' hands.

And onward, as bells off San Salvador
Salute the crocus lusters of the stars,
In these poinsettia meadows of her tides,—
Adagios of islands, O my Prodigal,
Complete the dark confessions her veins spell.

Mark how her turning shoulders wind the hours,
And hasten while her penniless rich palms
Pass superscription of bent foam and wave,—
Hasten, while they are true,—sleep, death, desire,
Close round one instant in one floating flower.

Bind us in time, O seasons clear, and awe.
O minstrel galleons of Carib fire,
Bequeath us to no earthly shore until
Is answered in the vortex of our grave
The seal's wide spindrift gaze toward paradise.

HART CRANE

At Melville's Tomb

Often beneath the wave, wide from this ledge
The dice of drowned men's bones he saw bequeath
An embassy. Their numbers as he watched,
Beat on the dusty shore and were obscured.

And wrecks passed without sound of bells,
The calyx of death's bounty giving back
A scattered chapter, livid hieroglyph,
The portent wound in corridors of shells.

Then in the circuit calm of one vast coil,
Its lashings charmed and malice reconciled,
Frosted eyes there were that lifted altars;
And silent answers crept across the stars.

Compass, quadrant and sextant contrive
No farther tides . . . High in the azure steeps
Monody shall not wake the mariner.
This fabulous shadow only the sea keeps.

                                    HART CRANE

Atlantis

*Music is then the knowledge of that which relates to love
in harmony and system.*—PLATO

Through the bound cable strands, the arching path
Upward, veering with light, the flight of strings,—
Taut miles of shuttling moonlight syncopate
The whispered rush, telepathy of wires.
Up the index of night, granite and steel—
Transparent meshes—fleckless the gleaming staves—
Sibylline voices flicker, waveringly stream
As though a god were issue of the strings. . . .

And through that cordage, threading with its call
One arc synoptic of all tides below—
Their labyrinthine mouths of history
Pouring reply as though all ships at sea
Complighted in one vibrant breath made cry,—
"Make thy love sure—to weave whose song we ply!"
—From black embankments, moveless soundings hailed,
So seven oceans answer from their dream.

And on, obliquely up bright carrier bars
New octaves trestle the twin monoliths
Beyond whose frosted capes the moon bequeaths
Two worlds of sleep (O arching strands of song!)—
Onward and up the crystal-flooded aisle
White tempest nets file upward, upward ring
With silver terraces the humming spars,
The loft of vision, palladium helm of stars.

Sheerly the eyes, like seagulls stung with rime—
Slit and propelled by glistening fins of light—
Pick biting way up towering looms that press
Sidelong with flight of blade on tendon blade
—Tomorrows into yesteryear—and link
What cipher-script of time no traveller reads
But who, through smoking pyres of love and death,
Searches the timeless laugh of mythic spears.

Like hails, farewells—up planet-sequined heights
Some trillion whispering hammers glimmer Tyre:
Serenely, sharply up the long anvil cry
Of inchling aeons silence rivets Troy.
And you, aloft there—Jason! hesting Shout!
Still wrapping harness to the swarming air!
Silvery the rushing wake, surpassing call,
Beams yelling Æolus! splintered in the straits!

From gulfs unfolding, terrible of drums,
Tall Vision-of-the-Voyage, tensely spare—
Bridge, lifting night to cycloramic crest
Of deepest day—O Choir, translating time
Into what multitudinous Verb the suns
And synergy of waters ever fuse, recast
In myriad syllables,—Psalm of Cathay!
O Love, thy white, pervasive Paradigm . . . !

We left the haven hanging in the night—
Sheened harbor lanterns backward fled the keel.
Pacific here at time's end, bearing corn,—
Eyes stammer through the pangs of dust and steel.
And still the circular, indubitable frieze
Of heaven's meditation, yoking wave

To kneeling wave, one song devoutly binds—
The vernal strophe chimes from deathless strings!

O Thou steeled Cognizance whose leap commits
The agile precincts of the lark's return;
Within whose lariat sweep encinctured sing
In single chrysalis the many twain,—
Of stars Thou art the stitch and stallion glow
And like an organ, Thou, with sound of doom—
Sight, sound and flesh Thou leadest from time's realm
As love strikes clear direction for the helm.

Swift peal of secular light, intrinsic Myth
Whose fell unshadow is death's utter wound,—
O River-throated—iridescently upborne
Through the bright drench and fabric of our veins;
With white escarpments swinging into light,
Sustained in tears the cities are endowed
And justified conclamant with ripe fields
Revolving through their harvests in sweet torment.

Forever Deity's glittering Pledge, O Thou
Whose canticle fresh chemistry assigns
To rapt inception and beatitude,—
Always through blinding cables, to our joy,
Of thy white seizure springs the prophecy:
Always through spiring cordage, pyramids
Of silver sequel, Deity's young name
Kinetic of white choiring wings . . . ascends.

Migrations that must needs void memory,
Inventions that cobblestone the heart,—
Unspeakable Thou Bridge to Thee, O Love.
Thy pardon for this history, whitest Flower,
O Answerer of all,—Anemone,—
Now while thy petals spend the suns about us, hold—
(O Thou whose radiance doth inherit me)
Atlantis, hold thy floating singer late!

So to thine Everpresence, beyond time,
Like spears ensanguined of one tolling star
That bleeds infinity—the orphic strings,

Sidereal phalanxes, leap and converge:
—One Song, one Bridge of Fire! Is it Cathay,
Now pity steeps the grass and rainbows ring
The serpent with the eagle in the leaves . . . ?
Whispers antiphonal in azure swing.

HART CRANE

Sundown

This is the time lean woods shall spend
A steeped-up twilight, and the pale evening drink,
And the perilous roe, the leaper to the west brink,
Trembling and bright, to the caverned cloud descend.

Now shall you see pent oak gone gusty and frantic,
Stooped with dry weeping, ruinously unloosing
The sparse disheveled leaf, or reared and tossing
A dreary scarecrow bough in funeral antic.

Aye, tatter you and rend,
Oak heart, to your profession mourning, not obscure
The outcome, not crepuscular, on the deep floor,
Sable and gold match lusters and contend.

And rags of shrouding will not muffle the slain.
This is the immortal extinction, the priceless wound
Not to be staunched; the live gold leaks beyond,
And matter's sanctified, dipped in a gold stain.

LÉONIE ADAMS

Bell Tower

I have seen, O desolate one, the voice has its tower,
The voice also, builded at secret cost,
Its temple of precious tissue. Not silent then
Forever—casting silence in your hour.

There marble boys are leant from the light throat,
Thick locks that hang with dew and eyes dewlashed,
Dazzled with morning, angels of the wind,
With ear a-point to the enchanted note.

And these at length shall tip the hanging bell,
And first the sound must gather in deep bronze,
Till, rarer than ice, purer than a bubble of gold,
It fill the sky to beat on an airy shell.

LÉONIE ADAMS

Lullaby

Hush, lullay.
Your treasures all
Encrust with rust,
Your trinket pleasures fall
      To dust.

Beneath the sapphire arch,
Upon the grassy floor,
Is nothing more
      To hold,
And play is over-old.
Your eyes

      In sleepy fever gleam,
Your lids droop
      To their dream.
You wander late alone,
The flesh frets on the bone,
Your love fails in your breast,
Here is the pillow.
      Rest.

LÉONIE ADAMS

X Minus X

Even when your friend, the radio, is still; even when her
          dream, the magazine, is finished; even when his
          life, the ticker, is silent; even when their destiny,
          the boulevard, is bare,
     and after that paradise, the dancehall, is closed; after
          that theatre, the clinic, is dark,

Still there will be your desire, and her desire, and his de-
          sire, and their desire,
     your laughter, their laughter,
     your curse and his curse, her reward and their reward,
          their dismay and his dismay and her dismay and
          yours—

Even when your enemy, the collector, is dead; even when
          your counsellor, the salesman, is sleeping; even
          when your sweetheart, the movie queen, has
          spoken; even when your friend, the magnate, is
          gone.

                                        KENNETH FEARING

The Groundhog

     In June, amid the golden fields,
     I saw a groundhog lying dead.
     Dead lay he, my senses shook,
     And mind outshot our naked frailty.
     There lowly in the vigorous summer
     His form began its senseless change,
     And made my senses waver dim
     Seeing nature ferocious in him.
     Inspecting close his maggots' might
     And seething cauldron of his being,
     Half with loathing, half with a strange love,
     I poked him with an angry stick.
     The fever arose, became a flame
     And Vigor circumscribed the skies,
     Immense energy in the sun,

And through my frame a sunless trembling.
My stick had done nor good nor harm.
Then stood I silent in the day
Watching the object, as before;
And kept my reverence for knowledge
Trying for control, to be still,
To quell the passion of the blood;
Until I had bent down on my knees
Praying for joy in the sight of decay.
And so I left; and I returned
In Autumn strict of eye, to see
The sap gone out of the groundhog,
But the bony sodden hulk remained.
But the year had lost its meaning,
And in intellectual chains
I lost both love and loathing,
Mured up in the wall of wisdom.
Another summer took the fields again
Massive and burning, full of life,
But when I chanced upon the spot
There was only a little hair left,
And bones bleaching in the sunlight
Beautiful as architecture;
I watched them like a geometer,
And cut a walking stick from a birch.
It has been three years, now.
There is no sign of the groundhog.
I stood there in the whirling summer,
My hand capped a withered heart,
And thought of China and of Greece,
Of Alexander in his tent;
Of Montaigne in his tower,
Of Saint Theresa in her wild lament.

RICHARD EBERHART

End of Summer

An agitation of the air,
A perturbation of the light
Admonished me the unloved year
Would turn on its hinge that night.

I stood in the disenchanted field
Amid the stubble and the stones,
Amazed, while a small worm lisped to me
The song of my marrow-bones.

Blue poured into summer blue,
A hawk broke from his cloudless tower,
The roof of the silo blazed, and I knew
That part of my life was over.

Already the iron door of the north
Clangs open: birds, leaves, snows
Order their populations forth,
And a cruel wind blows.

STANLEY KUNITZ

"April's amazing meaning"

April's amazing meaning doubtless lies
    In tall, hoarse boys and slips
Of slender girls with suddenly wider eyes
    And parted lips;

For girls must wander pensive in the spring
    When the green rain is over,
Doing some slow inconsequential thing,
    Plucking clover;

And any boy alone upon a bench
    When his work's done will sit
And stare at the black ground and break a branch
    And whittle it

Slowly; and boys and girls, irresolute,
    Will curse the dreamy weather
Until they meet past the pale hedge and put
    Their lips together.

GEORGE DILLON

"The world goes turning"

The world goes turning,
Slowly lunging,
Wrapped in churning
Winds and plunging
Rains. The land
And the waters turn.
The mountains stand
Solid and stern.
But the rivers slide
Gently in valleys.
Lithe fishes glide
In their cold alleys.
And there are creatures
Of various forms
And various natures.
Rosy worms
Wallow at dawn
In pools of dew.
Cloud-white upon
Amazing blue
The silken billow
Bellies and fills,
A windy pillow
For the heads of hills.
Ships fling a flag
And a golden sail
Down seas whose shaggy
Waters pale
On a rock-sharp shore
Where cold weeds swim.
In circle and soar
At the water's rim
Disconsolate gulls
Ride the air.
Moons convulse
A pond's sleek stare
To wave and ripple
Minutely bright.
Stars stipple
The roof of night.

Under that roof
Where thunders are
I stand aloof,
Watching a star.
What am I
That stand and watch?—
Two yards high.
More than a patch
Of blood and bones?
For a certain space
More than a stone's
Smooth sightless face?
For a little time
A little more
Than the waves that climb
On a timeless shore?
More than water
And dust, and all,
While pulses flutter
Their mystic small
Miraculous hour?
More than a bird
That has no power
Of weeping word?
More than creeping,
Leaping, winging
Creatures, weeping
Not, nor singing?
More than trees
That root in clay? . . .
More than these
For a little day?
In littleness
Proud and lonely
I am less
Than God, only.
Two yards high,
Under a star
In a windy sky
Where thunders are,
I watch and sing!
And the long-swaying

Wind-bells ring,
And the churning, braying
Waters lash,
And a star floats burning,
And clouds crash,
And the world goes turning.

GEORGE DILLON

No Question

Seeing at last how each thing here beneath
The glimmering stars is lawful: having found
By a wide watch how scrupulously Death
To keep his tacit promises is bound,
How from their vagrance the disbanded dusts
Resume integrity in blood or bloom,
How punctually the sun-struck red rose thrusts
Its rigid flame into the golden gloom;

Knowing that ultimate prospect where appears
The accurate ebb and flood of furious water,
The undirected wind's clean course, the sphere's
Deliberate strong spinning, I would utter
No question now, nor prosecute in words
Why birds must fly, seeing the flight of birds.

GEORGE DILLON

The Constant One

When love was false and I was full of care,
And friendship cold and I was sick with fear,
Music, the beautiful disturber of the air,
Drew near,

Saying: Come with me into my country of air
Out of the querulous and uncivil clay;
Fling down its aching members into a chair,
And come away,

And enter the wide kingdom beyond despair
Where beauty dwells unaltering, even such
As my invisible body made of air
Time cannot touch.

Take back your dreams, or take oblivion there,
Or an old madness setting memories free—
Or if all else has vanished into air,
Take me.

GEORGE DILLON

The Beast

I came to a great door,
Its lintel overhung
With burr, bramble, and thorn;
And when it swung, I saw
A meadow, lush and green.

And there a great beast played,
A sportive, aimless one,
A shred of bone its horn,
And colloped round with fern.
It looked at me; it stared.

Swaying, I took its gaze;
Faltered; rose up again;
Rose but to lurch and fall,
Hard, on the gritty sill,
I lay; I languished there.

When I raised myself once more,
The great round eyes had gone.
The long lush grass lay still;
And I wept there, alone.

THEODORE ROETHKE

The Voice

One feather Is a bird,
I claim; one tree, a wood;
In her low voice I heard
More than a mortal should;
And so I stood apart,
Hidden in my own heart.

And yet I roamed   out where
Those notes went, like the bird,
Whose thin song hung in air,
Diminished, yet still heard:
I lived with open sound,
Aloft, and on the ground.

That ghost was my own choice,
The shy cerulean bird;
It sang with her true voice,
And it was I who heard
A slight voice reply;
I heard; and only I.

Desire exults the ear:
Bird, girl, and ghostly tree,
The earth, the solid air—
Their slow song sang in me;
The long noon pulsed away,
Like any summer day.

THEODORE ROETHKE

Roosters

At four o'clock
in the gun-metal blue dark
we hear the first crow of the first cock

just below
the gun-metal blue window
and immediately there is an echo

off in the distance,
then one from the back-yard fence,
then one, with horrible insistence,

grates like a wet match
from the broccoli patch,
flares, and all over town begins to catch.

Cries galore
come from the water-closet door,
from the dropping-plastered henhouse floor,

where in the blue blur
their rustling wives admire,
the roosters brace their cruel feet and glare

with stupid eyes
while from their beaks there rise
the uncontrolled, traditional cries.

Deep from protruding chests
in green-gold medals dressed,
planned to command and terrorize the rest,

the many wives
who lead hens' lives
of being courted and despised;

deep from raw throats
a senseless order floats
all over town. A rooster gloats

over our beds
from rusty iron sheds
and fences made from old bedsteads,

over our churches
where the tin rooster perches,
over our little wooden northern houses,

making sallies
from all the muddy alleys,
marking out maps like Rand McNally's:

glass-headed pins,
oil-golds and copper-greens,
anthracite blues, alizarins,

each one an active
displacement in perspective;
each screaming, "This is where I live!"

Each screaming,
"Get up! Stop dreaming!"
Roosters, what are you projecting?

You, whom the Greeks elected
to shoot at on a post, who struggled
when sacrificed, you whom they labelled

"Very combative . . ."
what right have you to give
commands, and tell us how to live,

cry, "Here!" and "Here!"
and wake us here where are
unwanted love, conceit, and war?

The crown of red
set on your little head
is charged with all your fighting-blood.

Yes, that excrescence
makes a most virile presence,
plus all that vulgar beauty of iridescence.

Now in mid-air
by twos they fight each other.
Down comes a first flame-feather,

and one is flying,
with raging heroism defying
even the sensation of dying.

And one has fallen,
but still above the town
his torn-out, bloodied feathers drift down;

and what he sung
no matter. He is flung
on the gray ash-heap, lies in dung

with his dead wives
with open, bloody eyes,
while those metallic feathers oxidize.

· · · · ·

St. Peter's sin
was worse than that of Magdalen
whose sin was of the flesh alone;

of spirit, Peter's,
falling, beneath the flares,
among the "servants and officers."

Old holy sculpture
could set it all together
in one small scene, past and future:

Christ stands amazed,
Peter, two fingers raised
to surprised lips, both as if dazed.

But in between
a little cock is seen
carved on a dim column in the travertine,

explained by *gallus canit;*
flet Petrus underneath it.
There is inescapable hope, the pivot;

yes, and there Peter's tears
run down our chanticleer's
sides and gem his spurs.

Tear-encrusted thick
as a medieval relic
he waits. Poor Peter, heart-sick,

still cannot guess
those cock-a-doodles yet might bless,
his dreadful rooster come to mean forgiveness,

a new weathervane
on basilica and barn,
and that outside the Lateran

there would always be
a bronze cock on a porphyry
pillar so the people and the Pope might see

that even the Prince
of the Apostles long since
had been forgiven, and to convince

all the assembly
that "Deny deny deny,"
is not all the roosters cry.

In the morning
a low light is floating
in the backyard, and gilding

from underneath
the broccoli, leaf by leaf;
how could the night have come to grief?

gilding the tiny
floating swallow's belly
and lines of pink cloud in the sky,

the day's preamble
like wandering lines in marble.
The cocks are now almost inaudible.

The sun climbs in,
following "to see the end,"
faithful as enemy, or friend.

ELIZABETH BISHOP

"The heavy bear who goes with me"

"the withness of the body"—WHITEHEAD

The heavy bear who goes with me,
A manifold honey to smear his face,
Clumsy and lumbering here and there,
The central ton of every place,
The hungry beating brutish one
In love with candy, anger, and sleep,
Crazy factotum, dishevelling all,
Climbs the building, kicks the football,
Boxes his brother in the hate-ridden city.

Breathing at my side, that heavy animal,
That heavy bear who sleeps with me,
Howls in his sleep for a world of sugar,
A sweetness intimate as the water's clasp,
Howls in his sleep because the tight-rope
Trembles and shows the darkness beneath.
—The strutting show-off is terrified,
Dressed in his dress-suit, bulging his pants,
Trembles to think that his quivering meat
Must finally wince to nothing at all.

That inescapable animal walks with me,
Has followed me since the black womb held,
Moves where I move, distorting my gesture,
A caricature, a swollen shadow,
A stupid clown of the spirit's motive,
Perplexes and affronts with his own darkness,
The secret life of belly and bone,
Opaque, too near, my private, yet unknown,
Stretches to embrace the very dear
With whom I would walk without him near,
Touches her grossly, although a word
Would bare my heart and make me clear,
Stumbles, flounders, and strives to be fed
Dragging me with him in his mouthing care,
Amid the hundred million of his kind,
The scrimmage of appetite everywhere.

DELMORE SCHWARTZ

Auto Wreck

Its quick soft silver bell beating, beating,
And down the dark one ruby flare
Pulsing out red light like an artery,
The ambulance at top speed floating down
Past beacons and illuminated clocks
Wings in a heavy curve, dips down,
And brakes speed, entering the crowd.
The doors leap open, emptying light;
Stretchers are laid out, the mangled lifted
And stowed into the little hospital.
Then the bell, breaking the hush, tolls once,
And the ambulance with its terrible cargo
Rocking, slightly rocking, moves away,
As the doors, an afterthought, are closed.

We are deranged, walking among the cops
Who sweep glass and are large and composed.
One is still making notes under the light.
One with a bucket douches ponds of blood
Into the street and gutter.
One hangs lanterns on the wrecks that cling,
Empty husks of locusts, to iron poles.

Our throats were tight as tourniquets,
Our feet were bound with splints, but now
Like convalescents intimate and gauche,
We speak through sickly smiles and warn
With the stubborn saw of common sense,
The grim joke and the banal resolution.
The traffic moves around with care,
But we remain, touching a wound
That opens to our richest horror.

Already old, the question Who shall die?
Becomes unspoken Who is innocent?
For death in war is done by hands;
Suicide has cause and stillbirth, logic.
But this invites the occult mind,
Cancels our physics with a sneer,

And spatters all we knew of dénouement
Across the expedient and wicked stones.

KARL SHAPIRO

Terminal

Over us stands the broad electric face
With semaphores that flick into the gaps,
Notching the time on sixtieths of space,
Springing the traveler through the folded traps
Downstairs with luggage anywhere to go
While others happily toil upward too;
Well-dressed or stricken, banished or restored,
Hundreds step down and thousands get aboard.

In neat confusion, tickets in our brain,
We press the hard plush to our backs and sigh;
The brakeman thumbs his watch; the children strain
The windows to their smeary sight—Goodbye—
The great car creaks, the stone wall turns away
And lights flear past like fishes undersea;
Heads rolling heavily and all as one
With languid screams we charge into the sun.

Now through the maelstrom of the town we ride
Clicking with speed like skates on solid ice;
Streets drop and buildings silently collide,
Rails spread apart, converge, and neatly splice.
Through gasping blanks of air we pound and ford
Bulking our courage forward like a road,
Climbing the world on long dead-level stairs
With catwalk stilts and trestles hung by hairs.

Out where the oaks on wide turn-tables grow
And constellation hamlets gyre and glow,
The straight-up bridges dive and from below
The river's sweet eccentric borders flow;
Into the culverts sliced like lands of meat,
Armies of cornstalks on their ragged feet,
And upward-outward toward the blue-back hill
Where clouds of thunder graze and drink their fill.

And always at our side, swifter than we,
The racing rabbits of the wire lope,
And in their blood the words at liberty
Outspeed themselves; but on our rail we grope,
Drinking from one white trolley overhead
Hot drinks of action and hell's fiery feed.
Lightly the finger-shaped antennae feel
And lightly cheer the madness of our wheel.

We turn, we turn, thrumming the harp of sounds
And all is pleasure's move, motion of joy;
Now we imagine that we go like hounds
And now like sleds and now like many a toy
Coming alive on Christmas day to crawl
Between the great world of the floor and wall,
But on the peak of speed we flag and fall—
Fixed on the air we do not move at all.

Arrived at space we settle in our car
And stare like souls admitted to the sky;
Nothing at length is close at hand or far;
All feats of image vanish from the eye;
Upon our brow is set the bursting star;
Upon the void the wheel and axle-bar;
The planetary fragments broken lie;
Distance is dead and light can only die.

KARL SHAPIRO

The Quaker Graveyard in Nantucket

(For Warren Winslow, Dead at Sea)

*Let man have dominion over the fishes of the sea and the fowls
of the air and the beasts and the whole earth, and every creeping
creature that moveth upon the earth.*

I

A brackish reach of shoal off Madaket,—
The sea was still breaking violently and night
Had steamed into our North Atlantic Fleet,
When the drowned sailor clutched the drag-net. Light
Flashed from his matted head and marble feet,

He grappled at the net
With the coiled, hurdling muscles of his thighs:
The corpse was bloodless, a botch of reds and whites,
Its open, staring eyes
Were lustreless dead-lights
Or cabin-windows on a stranded hulk
Heavy with sand. We weight the body, close
Its eyes and heave it seaward whence it came,
Where the heel-headed dogfish barks its nose
On Ahab's void and forehead; and the name
Is blocked in yellow chalk.
Sailors, who pitch this portent at the sea
Where dreadnaughts shall confess
Its hell-bent deity,
When you are powerless
To sand-bag this Atlantic bulwark, faced
By the earth-shaker, green, unwearied, chaste
In his steel scales: ask for no Orphean lute
To pluck life back. The guns of the steeled fleet
Recoil and then repeat
The hoarse salute.

II

Whenever winds are moving and their breath
Heaves at the roped-in bulwarks of this pier,
The terns and sea-gulls tremble at your death
In these home waters. Sailor, can you hear
The Pequod's sea wings, beating landward, fall
Headlong and break on our Atlantic wall
Off 'Sconset, where the yawing S-boats splash
The bellbuoy, with ballooning spinnakers,
As the entangled, screeching mainsheet clears
The blocks: off Madaket, where lubbers lash
The heavy surf and throw their long lead squids
For blue-fish? Sea-gulls blink their heavy lids
Seaward. The winds' wings beat upon the stones,
Cousin, and scream for you and the claws rush
At the sea's throat and wring it in the slush
Of this old Quaker graveyard where the bones
Cry out in the long night for the hurt beast
Bobbing by Ahab's whaleboats in the East.

III

All you recovered from Poseidon died
With you, my cousin, and the harrowed brine
Is fruitless on the blue beard of the god,
Stretching beyond us to the castles in Spain,
Nantucket's westward haven. To Cape Cod
Guns, cradled on the tide,
Blast the eelgrass about a waterclock
Of bilge and backwash, roil the salt and sand
Lashing earth's scaffold, rock
Our warships in the hand
Of the great God, where time's contrition blues
Whatever it was these Quaker sailors lost
In the mad scramble of their lives. They died
When time was open-eyed,
Wooden and childish; only bones abide
There, in the nowhere, where their boats were tossed
Sky-high, where mariners had fabled news
Of IS, the whited monster. What it cost
Them is their secret. In the monster's slick
I see the Quakers drown and hear their cry:
'If God himself had not been on our side,
If God himself had not been on our side,
When the Atlantic rose against us, why,
Then it had swallowed us up quick.'

IV

This is the end of the whaleroad and the whale
Who spewed Nantucket bones on the thrashed swell
And stirred the troubled waters to whirlpools
To send the Pequod packing off to hell:
This is the end of them, three-quarters fools,
Snatching at straws to sail
Seaward and seaward on the turntail whale,
Spouting out blood and water as it rolls,
Sick as a dog to these Atlantic shoals:
Clamavimus, O depths. Let the sea-gulls wail

For water, for the deep where the high tide
Mutters to its hurt self, mutters and ebbs.
Waves wallow in their wash, go out and out,

Leave only the death-rattle of the crabs,
The beach increasing, its enormous snout
Sucking the ocean's side.
This is the end of running on the waves;
We are poured out like water. Who will dance
The mast-lashed master of Leviathans
Up from this field of Quakers in their unstoned graves?

V

When the whale's viscera go and the roll
Of its corruption overruns this world
Beyond tree-swept Nantucket and Wood's Hole
And Martha's Vineyard, Sailor, will your sword
Whistle and fall and sink into the fat?
In the great ash-pit of Jehoshaphat
The bones cry for the blood of the white whale,
The fat flukes arch and whack about its ears,
The death-lance churns into the sanctuary, tears
The gun-blue swingle, heaving like a flail,
And hacks the coiling life out: it works and drags
And rips the sperm-whale's midriff into rags,
Gobbets of blubber spill to wind and weather,
Sailor, and gulls go round the stoven timbers
Where the morning stars sing out together
And thunder shakes the white surf and dismembers
The red flag hammered in the mast-head. Hide,
Our steel, Jonas Messias, in Thy side.

VI

Our Lady of Walsingham

There once the penitents took off their shoes
And then walked barefoot the remaining mile;
And the small trees, a stream and hedgerows file
Slowly along the munching English lane,
Like cows to the old shrine, until you lose
Track of your dragging pain.
The stream flows down under the druid tree,
Shiloah's whirlpools gurgle and make glad
The castle of God. Sailor, you were glad
And whistled Sion by that stream. But see:

Our Lady, too small for her canopy,
Sits near the altar. There's no comeliness
At all or charm in that expressionless
Face with its heavy eyelids. As before,
This face, for centuries a memory,
Non est species, neque decor,
Expressionless, expresses God: it goes
Past castled Sion. She knows what God knows,
Not Calvary's Cross nor crib at Bethlehem
Now, and the world shall come to Walsingham.

VII

The empty winds are creaking and the oak
Splatters and splatters on the cenotaph,
The boughs are trembling and a gaff
Bobs on the untimely stroke
Of the greased wash exploding on a shoal-bell
In the old mouth of the Atlantic. It's well;
Atlantic, you are fouled with the blue sailors,
Sea-monsters, upward angel, downward fish:
Unmarried and corroding, spare of flesh
Mart once of supercilious, wing'd clippers,
Atlantic, where your bell-trap guts its spoil
You could cut the brackish winds with a knife
Here in Nantucket, and cast up the time
When the Lord God formed man from the sea's slime
And breathed into his face the breath of life,
And blue-lung'd combers lumbered to the kill.
The Lord survives the rainbow of His will.

ROBERT LOWELL

A Black November Turkey

Nine white chickens come
With haunchy walk and heads
Jabbing among the chips, the chaff, the stones
And the cornhusk-shreds,

And bit by bit infringe
A pond of dusty light,

Spectral in shadow until they bobbingly one
  By one ignite.

    Neither pale nor bright,
    The turkey-cock parades
Through radiant squalors, darkly auspicious as
    The ace of spades,

    Himself his own cortège
    And puffed with the pomp of death,
Rehearsing over and over with strangled râle
    His latest breath.

    The vast black body floats
    Above the crossing knees
As a cloud over thrashed branches, a calm ship
    Over choppy seas,

    Shuddering its fan and feathers
    In fine soft clashes
With the cold sound that the wind makes, fondling
    Paper-ashes.

    The pale-blue bony head
    Set on its shepherd's-crook
Like a saint's death-mask, turns a vague, superb
    And timeless look

    Upon these clocking hens
    And the cocks that one by one,
Dawn after mortal dawn, with vulgar joy
    Acclaim the sun.

                              RICHARD WILBUR

Upon the Death of George Santayana

Down every passage of the cloister hung
A dark wood cross on a white plaster wall;
But in the court were roses, not as tongue
Might have them, something of Christ's blood grown small,

But just as roses, and at three o'clock
Their essences, inseparably bouqueted,
Seemed more than Christ's last breath, and rose to mock
An elderly man for whom the Sisters prayed.

What heart can know itself? The Sibyl speaks
Mirthless and unbedizened things, but who
Can fathom her intent? Loving the Greeks,
He whispered to a nun who strove to woo
His spirit unto God by prayer and fast,
'Pray that I go to Limbo, if it please
Heaven to let my soul regard at last
Democritus, Plato and Socrates.'

And so it was. The river, as foretold,
Ran darkly by; under his tongue he found
Coin for the passage; the ferry tossed and rolled;
The sages stood on their appointed ground,
Sighing, all as foretold. The mind was tasked;
He had not dreamed that so many had died.
'But where is Alcibiades,' he asked,
'The golden roisterer, the animal pride?'

Those sages who had spoken of the love
And enmity of things, how all things flow,
Stood in a light no life is witness of,
And Socrates, whose wisdom was to know
He did not know, spoke with a solemn mien,
And all his wonderful ugliness was lit,
'He whom I loved for what he might have been
Freezes with traitors in the ultimate pit.'

ANTHONY HECHT

INDEX OF AUTHORS, TITLES, AND FIRST LINES